THE COMMONWEALTH AND INTERNATIONAL LIBRARY
Joint Chairmen of the Honorary Editorial Advisory Board
SIR ROBERT ROBINSON, O.M., F.R.S., LONDON
DEAN ATHELSTAN SPILHAUS, MINNESOTA
Publisher: ROBERT MAXWELL, M.C., M.P.

LIBERAL STUDIES DIVISION
General Editors: D. F. BRATCHELL AND E. F. CANDLIN

Background to Eastern Europe

Background to Eastern Europe

by

F. B. SINGLETON, M.A.

Lecturer, Social Sciences Department
Bradford Institute of Technology

PERGAMON PRESS

OXFORD · LONDON · EDINBURGH · NEW YORK
PARIS · FRANKFURT

Pergamon Press Ltd., Headington Hill Hall, Oxford
4 & 5 Fitzroy Square, London W.1

Pergamon Press (Scotland) Ltd., 2 & 3 Teviot Place, Edinburgh 1

Pergamon Press Inc., 122 East 55th Street., New York 10022

Pergamon Press GmbH, Kaiserstrasse 75, Frankfurt-am-Main

Set in 10 on 12 pt Times
and printed in Great Britain by
Billing & Sons Ltd., Guildford and London

DR
10
S55

85090

(2265/65)

CONTENTS

PREFACE

THIS book, like most of its kind, is the result of a co-operative effort. Although the responsibility for its accuracy and readability rests entirely with the author, he is conscious of his debt to the many scholars who have worked before him in the same field. No British student of Eastern Europe can ignore the writings of such distinguished scholars as R. W. and Hugh Seton-Watson, C. A. Macartney, especially on Hungary, and A. J. P. Taylor on the Habsburg Monarchy. A special debt of gratitude is owed to Professor Macartney for his generosity in reading through a large part of the original typescript and for making a number of helpful suggestions and corrections. Many valuable comments have also been made by my colleagues in the Department of Social Sciences, Bradford Institute of Technology, Prof. Paul Coles and Mr. J. Reynolds, and by Mr. G. F. Sedgwick of the Workers' Educational Association, Mr. A. McPherson of Queen's College, Oxford, and Mr. A. J. Topham of Hull University. Useful statistical information has been supplied by Mr. D. Warburton of Coleg Harlech, Dr. Laszlo Pintér of the Hungarian Legation in London and Mr. S. Mladenović of the Yugoslav Embassy.

Criticisms and suggestions from several friends in Eastern Europe have also been much appreciated, especially from a number of old friends in Yugoslavia. If what appears is not entirely to their liking, they will know that this implies no disrespect to their sincerely held views. In a field as controversial as this, it is impossible not to cause offence to some. One can only strive to achieve factual accuracy, and hope that in selecting what is significant one has not distorted the truth, and that, as far as possible, one's judgments are fair minded and grounded in evidence rather than prejudice. If the reader feels that this has not been achieved, the fault lies entirely with the author.

The preparation of a manuscript for the press is a labour which often threatens to deprive an author of any pleasure which he may have had in writing the book. I have been fortunate in having the services of a most helpful and patient team of typists — Mrs. D. Whiteley, Miss C. Roper and Miss C. Seed. Mr. David Newlove drew the excellent maps. Others whose help has made the book possible include Mr. and Mrs. J. Miller and Mrs. D. Ashman.

By no means least among the acknowledgments I should make in this connection is the encouragement and help of my wife, who has given up many hours of her leisure to the drudgery of checking the typescript and reading proofs.

Pudsey, April 1964.   F. B. SINGLETON

CHAPTER I

INTRODUCTION

AFTER the Second World War eight European countries[1] adopted a form of government known as People's Democracy. These eight countries form a continuous block stretching across the land bridge which joins Western Europe to the continental mass of Eurasia. To the west lie the Federal German Republic, Austria and Italy; to the east, the Soviet Union. Two of the eight countries — Czechoslovakia and Hungary — have no direct access to the sea, and the coasts of the other six all lie along the shores of enclosed seas — the Baltic, the Adriatic and the Black Seas. The outlets from these seas are controlled by nations outside eastern Europe, most of whom are linked politically and militarily with the Atlantic community.

The justification for treating these eight countries as a coherent unit is primarily political, for the one feature which they all share is that their forms of government and ways of life have been moulded during the last two decades under the influence of Soviet Communism. As we shall see later, however, there are other unifying features, the most significant of which derive from their geographical location. The area is a zone of transition, in both human and physical geography. Throughout history it has been a battleground in the struggle between rival national, political and cultural influences.

The political geography of Eastern Europe has been in a state

---

[1] The eight countries are Poland, Czechoslovakia, Hungary, Rumania, Yugoslavia, Bulgaria, Albania and the German Democratic Republic (East Germany). The G.D.R. is not internationally recognised as a separate country, but for almost twenty years it has been governed as such.

of continual change throughout modern times. If one were to draw a series of maps showing the political geography in each generation from the present day back to the eighteenth century, the changes which would have to be recorded west of a line from Trieste to the mouth of the Oder would be small in comparison with those between that line and the present borders of the Soviet Union. The maps would show the steady retreat of the Turks from the Balkan peninsula; the disintegration of the great multinational Empire of the Habsburgs; and the dismemberment and reconstitution of the state of Poland. They would show the stages by which the small nations struggled towards independence. They would also show the results of the efforts of the great powers to use these struggles to further their own ambitions. In the Balkans, for example, these moves produced the successive crises in the affair known to historians of the nineteenth century as "The Eastern Question". As the life of the Turkish Empire, the "sick man of Europe", drew to its close, each power aspiring to the role of its residuary legatee became embroiled in the nationalist struggles of the peoples who had for centuries lain under Turkish domination. The dawn which ended the long Turkish night also heralded a day of bitter nationalist wars, culminating in the world war of 1914–1918. The occasion which precipitated the war was the assassination of an Austrian archduke by a Serbian nationalist in the Bosnian town of Sarajevo — a town which a generation earlier had been a Turkish provincial capital. A quarter of a century later German penetration into Eastern Europe prompted the start of the Second World War. In more recent times, a number of major crises in the cold war have had their origins in Eastern Europe. The Czech crisis of 1948, the expulsion of Yugoslavia from the Cominform, the Berlin Blockade, the Hungarian revolt of 1956 are but a few of the seismic shocks which have disturbed the delicate balance of international relations during the last twenty years. It may be that the underlying causes of these crises lay outside the area, but the fact that so many manifestations of the tension between the great powers have erupted in the shatter belt of Eastern Europe, underlines its importance as a zone of political instability. We cannot regard developments in this part of Europe as the petty concerns of small, faraway countries in which we have no interest. It is the aim of this book to make a modest contribution towards the dissipation of the dangerous ignorance which exists about the affairs of the hundred million of our fellow Europeans who inhabit the eastern marchlands of our continent. It is hoped to provide a frame of reference which will help the reader to understand the sweeping changes which have taken place during the last generation, and to place current developments in the wider context of the geographical, historical and social forces which underlie them.

The Geographical Background

Eastern Europe is not a well-defined geographical region in the same sense as are, for example the Scandinavian peninsula or the Maritime Provinces of Canada. There is a great diversity in the pattern of physical features, climate, vegetation, and natural resources. The ethnic pattern is no less diverse. There are representatives of at least five of the major linguistic groups of mankind — Slav, Finno-Ugrian, German, Romance, and Illyrian. The cultural and religious pattern varies greatly from country to country, and even from province to province. This diversity should constantly be borne in mind when any attempts are made to generalise about Eastern Europe. No simple geographical definition can contain the truth about an area which includes the sandy plains of Pomerania and the Alpine peaks of Slovenia; the rice fields of Hortobagy and the arid karstlands of the Dinaric ranges; the marshy lagoons of the Danube delta and the crumpled massif of Macedonia. What generalisations can we make about human activity which would include the Moslem shepherds of Bosnia, the skilled artisans of Bohemia, the rose growers of Bulgaria and the coal miners of Silesia? The element which gives unity to the concept of Eastern Europe arises from its position between two powerful societies whose interests have so often, as at present, appeared to be mutually irreconcilable. This conflict of interests has expressed itself in different forms at different times. At present the clash of political ideology seems to predominate, whereas formerly the conflict expressed itself in nationalist terms, or, still earlier, it assumed the form of a religious struggle. Whatever the nature of the forces grappling for supremacy in Europe their battleground has frequently lain in Eastern Europe. Control of this area has been seen as the key to the control of the whole continent. Sir Halford Mackinder, the father of political geography in Britain, even claimed that the control of Eastern Europe was the key to world domination. His warning dictum

> Who rules East Europe commands the Heartland
> Who rules the Heartland commands the World-Island
> Who rules the World-Island commands the World

may have lost some of its validity in the half-century since he first enunciated it, but it still enshrines an important truth. The people of Eastern Europe know to their sorrow that the rulers of the nations in the twentieth century have acted on the assumption that Mackinder's thesis is correct, and the common historical experiences which they have endured in consequence of this gives point to the attempt to treat Eastern Europe as a unit in terms of political geography.

The Physical Basis

Looked at in its wider setting, Europe consists of a series of peninsulas attached to the land mass of Eurasia. The whole continent is itself a peninsula of the World-Island, and Eastern Europe as we have defined it is the neck of this European peninsula. The lines of human contact across this wide connecting link are largely determined by the configuration of the land. In the north the great plains of Poland and North Germany offer a zone of easy movement from the heart of Russia to the shores of the Narrow Seas. From Moscow to the Zuider Zee, by way of Warsaw and Berlin, the land seldom rises above 600 ft. Eastward across this featureless plain the armies of Napoleon and Hitler

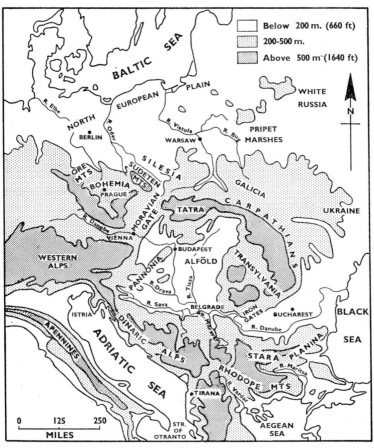

FIG. 1. Eastern Europe — physical.

rolled to their doom in their forlorn attempts to crush the power of Russia. It was at Tannenburg on the Polish plain that Von Hindenburg halted the Russian steamroller in 1914. Thirty years later, the Red Army's route to Berlin led through Warsaw and across the Polish plain. Ever since the first Slav speaking inhabitants appeared in Poland, the peoples of this area have been helpless victims of their geographical position.

South of the great plain lies a plateau region, the core of which consists of resistant, crystalline rocks which are rich in mineral deposits. The area includes the so-called "Bohemian Diamond", the mountain rim of the Prague basin, one of whose ranges is called the Ore Mountains because of its mineral wealth. The river Elbe emerges from the Prague basin in a deep gorge between the Ore Mountains and the Sudeten Mountains, and flows across the North German plain to enter the North Sea near the port of Hamburg. The valley of the Elbe provides land-locked Czechoslovakia with one of her vital outlets to the sea. To the east of the Bohemian Diamond, along the frontier region between the Czech province of Moravia and the southern part of Poland, the plateaux are lower, and the old, crystalline rocks are overlain by newer deposits which include coal-bearing strata. This region includes the Silesian coalfield, the Teschen industrial area, the oilfield of Jaslo and the rich agricultural land of Galicia. An important line of communications crosses this region, linking the Polish plain and the Baltic coasts to the north with the basin of the Danube in the south by way of the Moravian Gate.

The loess-covered uplands of Galicia rise southward to the foothills of the western Carpathians. The Carpathians are a great arc of Alpine fold mountains, many of whose peaks rise to heights of over 8000 ft. They curve south-eastward from the Polish – Slovak frontier to enclose the Transylvanian basin of Rumania, then swing westward to meet the Danube near the Yugoslav – Rumanian frontier, at the Iron Gates. Here the Danube has cut deep gorges through the mountains as it finds its way out of the Pannonian plains and breaks through into the plain of Wallachia, across which it flows to its mouth on the Black Sea coast. South of the Iron Gates the fold mountain system continues in the Balkan Ranges of Yugoslavia and the Stara Planina of Bulgaria. Together the Carpathian and Balkan ranges, known locally by many different names, form a huge reversed letter "S" across the map of Eastern Europe. Within the northern loop of the "S" lie the plains of Hungary, drained by the middle Danube and its tributaries, the Tisza and the Mures. The southern loop enfolds the Balkan plateau of northern Bulgaria and the plains of Wallachia, the heartland of historic Rumania.

The 100,000 square miles of the middle Danube basin which lie within the embrace of the Carpathians contain some of the richest and most densely populated[1] agricultural land in Europe. The modern state of Hungary lies wholly within this region, as do the plains of Vojvodina and Banat, now in Yugoslavia, but once part of the Greater Hungary of Habsburg days. Hungary has also reached out in the past to control the provinces of Transylvania in the east and Croatia – Slavonia in the southwest, thus extending her authority over the whole of the Pannonian[2] plain.

The Balkan peninsula which forms the southern part of Eastern Europe is bounded by the Danubian plains on the north, and by the waters of the Adriatic, the Aegean and the Black Seas on its other three sides. Yugoslavia, Albania and Bulgaria are the three Balkan nations which are included within the present study. Greece, with its Mediterranean environment and its Western political orientation, is excluded. In its original Turkish meaning, the word "Balkan" suggests a land of mountains, and this is certainly an appropriate description. From Slovenia, in the north-west of Yugoslavia, to the Greek–Albanian border 600 miles away to the south-east, the predominant feature is a series of high mountain

---

[1] The density of population for the whole of Hungary was 280 to the square mile in 1962, compared with the European average of 227. In Eastern Europe only East Germany, which is more industrialised, records a higher figure.

[2] The name Pannonia is derived from the Roman province of that name which covered the area between the Sava and the Danube. The Hungarian name is Dunántúl. The eastern half of the Middle Danube plain (covering the valleys of the Tisza and the Mures) is known as the Alföld.

ranges and intermontane plateaux which runs in a belt over 100 miles wide behind the island-studded Adriatic coast. These Dinaric ranges are composed chiefly of limestone. Few rivers cross them, the thin soils which cover them are parched for lack of the water which drains quickly underground through the cracks and joints of the soluble limestone rock. As the grain of the land runs parallel to the coast, communications between the Adriatic and the interior of the Balkan peninsula are difficult, so that the excellent natural harbours of the Dalmatian coast are of limited commercial value. Trieste and Rijeka at the head of the Adriatic are the most important ports of this coast, because they have access via the Postojna Gate into the Pannonian plain.

Between the Dinaric and the Balkan ranges lie the dissected plateaux of Macedonia and southern Serbia, composed of old crystalline rocks. These are trenched by the valleys of the Morava and its tributaries, which flow northward to the Danube near Belgrade, and by those of the Vardar system, which lead south to the Aegean near the Greek port of Salonika. The Vardar – Morava corridor is of particular importance in the history of the Balkans because it provides a line of movement between the middle Danube and the Mediterranean. In ancient times this was the southern end of one of the trade routes which led through Eastern Europe from the Baltic to the Aegean. From the Baltic coast the way lay through the Moravian Gate and along the Danube and the Morava to Greek Macedonia. The troubled history of Macedonia arises from its position astride this important routeway. The battlefield of Kossovo Polje, which lies near the watershed between the Vardar and Morava rivers, has twice witnessed the loss of Serbian independence. Once, in 1389, when the Turks were the victors, the invader came from the direction of the Aegean. On the second occasion, in 1915, the threat came from Austria–Hungary to the north.

Climate and Natural Vegetation

The diversity of relief which has been described above has an important influence on the climatic pattern of Eastern Europe.

Across the great northern plain there is a gradual merging of mild, oceanic influences from the west and the continental features of European Russia and eastern Poland. The continental type is characterised by severe winters, with temperatures averaging 20 to 30°F (−6·7 to −1·1°C) for the two or three coldest months of the year, and hot summers, with July temperatures of over 70°F (21·1°C) The pattern of precipitation follows that of the temperature curve, with most rain during the hottest months of the year, and low precipitation, mostly in the form of snow, during the winter. Much of the summer rainfall comes during thunderstorms of short duration but of great intensity, which usually occur during the later part of the afternoon. The figures for Moscow, given overleaf in the form of a graph, illustrate this type of climate. The oceanic type of Western Europe has a much smaller temperature range between summer and winter. (About 20°F (11·1°C) compared with Moscow's 50°F (27·8°C)) and the peak of rainfall is in the autumn or winter.

Table 1 and the accompanying graphs (Fig. 2) show the gradual transition from oceanic to continental climate across the north European plain from Holland via Berlin to Warsaw. Thus, Berlin has a temperature range of 34°F (18·9°C) between the July and December monthly averages, whilst Warsaw, 300 miles further east in the same latitude, has a range of 40°F (22·2°C). The total rainfall in Berlin is 23·1 in. (586·6 mm) per year, of which 32 per cent falls in the three summer months. Warsaw has a rainfall of 22 in. (558·8 mm) of which 38 per cent falls in the summer quarter. Another indication of the same phenomenon is apparent from a study of the pattern of natural vegetation, which is, of course, closely related to that of the climate. This relationship has been studied in Eastern Europe as a whole by the distinguished Hungarian geographer Count Teleki. He has shown that the maximum eastward extension of the oceanic influence corresponds with the furthest advance of German settlement into the Polish plain. Similarly, in the south, botanical evidence shows a great tongue of continental influence which extends westward from southern Russia into Wallachia and the Pannonian plain. This

TABLE 1

TEMPERATURE (°F)

	Jan.	Feb.	Mar.	Apr.	May	June	July	Aug.	Sept.	Oct.	Nov.	Dec.	Total
Amsterdam	36	36	41	46	53	59	62	62	57	50	42	37	26
Berlin	30	32	39	46	55	60	64	63	57	48	38	33	34
Warsaw	25	27	34	45	57	62	65	64	56	47	36	28	40

RAINFALL (in.)

	Jan.	Feb.	Mar.	Apr.	May	June	July	Aug.	Sept.	Oct.	Nov.	Dec.	Total
Amsterdam	2·0	1·5	2·0	1·5	1·8	2·2	2·8	3·0	2·6	3·1	2·3	2·8	27·6
Berlin	1·9	1·3	1·5	1·7	1·9	2·3	3·1	2·2	1·9	1·7	1·7	1·9	23·1
Warsaw	1·2	1·1	1·3	1·5	1·9	2·6	3·0	3·0	1·9	1·7	1·4	1·4	22·0

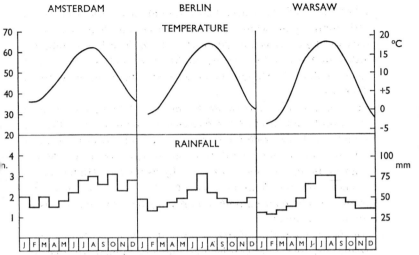

Fig. 2. Transition of oceanic to continental climate across the north European plain.

coincides with the routes of migration and settlement of the Asiatic nomads — the Huns, Avars and Magyars — who finally came to rest in the enclosed basin of the middle Danube, in what is now Hungary. Although the relationship can be overstressed, there is no doubt that the human pattern has been influenced by environmental factors such as these.

In the Balkan peninsula and the Carpathians the effects of high altitude modify the normal climatic pattern, producing a variety of local mountain climates. In general, the higher areas are cooler and wetter than the neighbouring lowlands. For example, the Dalmatian coastal strip lies within the Mediterranean climatic region, but places a few miles inland in the Dinaric Alps experience totally different conditions. Kotor, on the south coast of Yugoslavia, has an annual rainfall of 30 in. (762 mm) most of which falls in the winter months. There is a virtual drought in the summer. Crkvice, less than ten miles away, but 3600 ft above the Bay of Kotor, has over 180 in. (4·572 mm) in a year. In the higher parts of the Carpathians rainfall averages over 80 in. (2·032 mm) a year, whilst on the Hungarian and Rumanian lowlands the figure is nearer 20 in. (508 mm). The lowest falls recorded in Eastern Europe are in Masovia and the Black Sea coasts south of the Danube delta, where the figure is below 16 in. (406 mm).

The steeply rising mountains behind the Dalmatian coast also have a profound effect on the local wind systems of the Adriatic. In winter, cold air from the high-pressure centre over the central Balkans is drawn into the depressions which form in the Mediterranean basin. A wind known locally as the *bura* (Italian *bora*) descends from the mountains with great ferocity, bringing temperatures below freezing-point and playing havoc with the coastal shipping of Dalmatia.

Inland, beyond the Dinaric ranges, the plains of Serbia and Croatia experience a continental climate, similar to that of Hungary. Monthly averages of temperature are well above 70°F in summer, and fall below freezing-point in January. Skopje, for example, has a July average of 74°F (23·3°C) and a January figure of 29°F ($-1·7$°C). Most rain falls in the spring and summer. Thus Belgrade, with a rainfall of 24·6 in.(624·2 mm), receives 40 per cent of its total in May, June and July. During this period thunderstorms average two per week.

The Peoples of Eastern Europe

At first glance, the ethnic map of Eastern Europe presents a confused patchwork of linguistic and cultural groups, but on closer examination certain general themes emerge. The broad picture is of two Slav-speaking groups, the western and the southern Slavs, occupying respectively the northern and southern parts of the area, and separated by a wedge of non-Slav peoples across the centre. The western Slavs include the Poles, the Czechs and the Slovaks, and are the largest group, comprising over forty million people. The twenty-five million south Slavs of the Balkans are made up of the Bulgarians and the Yugoslavs. Between these two groups of Slavs are the ten million Magyars of

Hungary, and the eighteen million Rumanians. The non-Slav belt continues westward with the seven million German-speaking inhabitants of Austria. The Magyars, who occupy the plains of the middle Danube, derive their Finno-Ugrian speech from the nomadic horsemen who settled the area in the tenth century. The Rumanians speak a language which is derived from the Latin of their Roman conquerors, and which they have preserved during the seventeen centuries since the collapse of the Roman province of Dacia. Two other linguistic groups form the basis of national units in Eastern Europe. In the south-west are the two-and-a-half million Albanians, who have preserved in their isolation the Thraco-Illyrian tongue of the pre-Slav inhabitants of the Balkans. One-and-a-half million of them live in the state of Albania, but the remainder live cut off from their compatriots by the boundaries of Yugoslavia and Greece. In the north-west are the eighteen million Germans of the German Democratic Republic, now separated from their fellow Germans in the west as a result of the post-war redrawing of the political frontiers of Europe.

The boundaries of states, especially in Eastern Europe, often fail to coincide with the linguistic grouping of the peoples concerned. There are so many minorities still left on the "wrong" sides of frontiers, but there are perhaps fewer to-day than there were during the inter-war period. The wholesale expulsion of Germans from Czechoslavakia, Poland, the Danubian lands and the Balkans at the end of the Second World War forcibly removed one important group of minorities. The redrawing of frontiers, often accompanied by large migrations, has further reduced other minorities. Czechoslovakia, for example, has lost her half-million Ruthenians to Russia. Rumania has been forced to cede southern Dobrudja to Bulgaria, and Bessarabia and northern Bukovina to the Soviet Union — all areas which contained substantial numbers of non-Rumanians. The Nazi genocide policy removed most of the five million Jews from Eastern Europe. If, as a result of these changes, the nation states of Eastern Europe are more culturally homogeneous than they were previously, this is not to suggest that there are now no minority problems. There are still, for example, one-and-a-half million Magyars living in Rumanian Transylvania, another half-million in Yugoslavia, and over 400,000 in Czechoslovakia.

It is important not to confuse linguistic with racial terminology. There is no such thing as a Slav race, and such affinities as exist between the different Slav groups are based on cultural and linguistic similarities. Ever since the first Slav-speaking peoples settled in Eastern Europe after the fifth century A.D. they have interbred with the earlier inhabitants. Even within the confines of one nation, many physical types can be identified. Alpine, Nordic and Mediterranean traits are as inextricably mixed amongst the Slavs, the Magyars and the Rumanians as they are amongst the people of Western Europe. The Rumanians may cling to their Romance speech, which is a reminder of their brief Roman episode, but they are not distinguished racially from their Slav and Magyar speaking neighbours. The Bulgarians arrived in their present homeland as a Finno-Ugrian speaking people, but later adopted their present Slavonic tongue. Whatever divides the inhabitants of Eastern Europe, it is certainly not race. Language, religion, and historical experience are far more potent than any real or imaginary racial differences.

Religion. The Slavs, the Magyars, the Bulgars and other invaders from the east, contributed to and took advantage of the collapse of the Roman Empire, but something of the Roman heritage remained as a consequence of the conversion of the barbarians to Christianity. The line which divides the Roman Catholic from the Orthodox Church in south-east Europe to-day corresponds roughly with the frontier between the Eastern (Byzantine) and Western Empires. Serbia, Bulgaria, Bosnia, Macedonia and Rumania came under the influence of Byzantium, and to-day the Orthodox Churches claim the allegiance of most of their inhabitants. All but the Rumanians use the Cyrillic script which was developed during the tenth century, and which is named after the "Apostle of the Slavs", the monk Constantine-Cyril. Moravia was for a time also under the influence of the Eastern Church, but was later won by the Roman Catholics. Under German influence the Slovenes, the Croats, the Hungarians, the Czechs, the Slovaks and the Poles became Roman Catholics also. Since this religious pattern became established in the early Middle Ages there have been some important modifications, but the basic picture remains to-day what it was in the twelfth century. One important change resulted from the fall of Byzantium to the Moslem Turks, who eventually extended their authority throughout the Balkans and the Danube valley below Budapest. By 1914 the Turks had been expelled from all but a tiny corner of the Balkans, but there still remain to-day large communities of Moslems in Albania, Bosnia, South Serbia, Macedonia and Bulgaria. In some areas these people are known as Turks, although many are Slavs whose ancestors were converted to Islam.[1] The Protestant Reformation which completely changed the religious life of Western Europe had less impact in the East. To-day, even in the western Czech lands, the homeland of John Hus, Protestants are outnumbered by Roman Catholics. The only other large Protestant communities are in the German Democratic Republic, and to a lesser extent in Hungary. In the other countries of Eastern Europe the Protestants constitute only a tiny fraction of the population.

Eastern Europe's Economic Possibilities

The countries of Eastern Europe have always been dependent primarily on agriculture as a means of livelihood. There are large areas of level ground covered by fertile soils, in which the climate is well suited to cereal production. In the middle Danube basin, covering much of Hungary and the northern parts of Yugoslavia, wheat and maize are the chief crops, in Czechoslovakia barley is the most important cereal, and in Poland and the German Democratic Republic climatic conditions are best suited to the production of oats. On the great northern plain of Poland and Germany, and south of the Carpathians in Czechoslovakia, conditions

[1] In Bulgaria there was until recently a Turkish community of half a million, but in 1950 half of these were expelled to Turkey.

favour the production of potatoes, sugar beet and vegetables. Poland has the highest output of potatoes of any country in the world and both Czechoslovakia and the German Democratic Republic have a place in the first ten producers of this crop. The output of sugar beet from these three countries is greater than that of the U.S.A. and Britain combined. In the Balkans and the middle Danube basin the range of crops includes vines, tobacco and rice. This great variety reflects the diversity of climate, soils and relief which has been described above. In only two of the eight countries — Yugoslavia and Albania — does the percentage of arable land fall below 40 per cent of the total area. In both cases this is because of the mountainous nature of large parts of the terrain. Animal husbandry is particularly important in the areas where physical conditions make arable farming impossible. Thus the rearing of cattle, sheep, goats and pigs occupies two-thirds of the population of Albania, and is the major occupation of large parts of the mountain areas of Yugoslavia. In the arable areas also, stock raising is an important part of the rural economy. In Poland, Hungary and East Germany large numbers of pigs are reared. In Bohemia, Moravia and southern Poland dairy farming is combined with arable farming, but in Hungary and the Balkans cattle are kept primarily for meat production. In an area where agricultural methods are still primitive, and mechanisation has as yet made little headway, the horse is of vital importance. Poland, Yugoslavia and Hungary are the three countries where horse raising is of particular importance, and together they account for more than half the horses in the whole of Europe outside the U.S.S.R. Finally, in this brief survey of stock raising in Eastern Europe, mention should be made of the millions of poultry, especially geese, turkeys and ducks, which are reared by the peasants on farms throughout the area, but particularly in Hungary and Poland.

Despite the great potentiality for food production which these facts suggest, Eastern Europe is not without its problems of food supply. Although taken as a whole the area can provide itself with the basic foods and also an export surplus, this does not hold true for all areas at all times. Czechoslovakia, with the highest level of urbanisation, must always import some of its essential foods, and much of its raw cotton and wool. Partial failures of the harvest, which since the Second World War have afflicted Yugoslavia in at least six of the eighteen years, have forced her to spend much-needed foreign exchange on the import of basic foodstuffs. The real reasons why Eastern Europe has failed to realise its agricultural possibilities lie in the technical backwardness of the peasantry, the lack of capital investment in agriculture, and the resistance of the peasants to attempts by the authorities to change the basis of land ownership.

If the East Europeans have not as yet realised the full potentialities of their agricultural resources, they have made a start in exploiting their industrial wealth. Until the Second World War the only substantial industrial development was in the central belt which included the Silesian coalfield of East Germany, with its eastward extension into Poland, and in the western Czech lands of Bohemia and Moravia. Outside this area, the other important industrial developments were in scattered centres, such as the Budapest and Miskolc regions of Hungary, Łódz and Warsaw in Poland, the oilfields north of Bucharest in Rumania, and around Berlin. In most cases the emphasis was on the extraction of minerals, and the companies engaged in this work were usually of West European origin. Yet Eastern Europe is not deficient in the basic resources for industrial development. Perhaps the greatest weakness in the past was the inadequacy of hard coal reserves in most areas outside Silesia and Czechoslovakia. This deficiency has partly been made up by the development of lignite and brown coal resources. The hydro-electric potential of many countries was virtually untapped. Yugoslavia has shown what can be achieved in this field by her spectacular tenfold increase in output of hydro-electricity between 1947 and 1961. Given the power resources to smelt the ores and turn the wheels of industry, most East European countries have the mineral ores necessary for industrialisation. Albania and Bulgaria are the two which are notably deficient in this respect. If their economies are integrated, and the wasteful struggle for autarchy which characterised the economic plans of most of them until recently are forgotten, then there is a possibility that they may eventually achieve material standards comparable with the nations of Western Europe.

Table 2 opposite shows some of the chief industrial raw materials produced in Eastern Europe.

TABLE 2. INDUSTRIAL RESOURCES OF EASTERN EUROPE

Country and Population:	Albania 1·4 m	Bulgaria 7·6 m	Czecho-slovakia 13·6 m	German† Dem. Rep. 17·2 m	Hungary 10 m	Poland 30 m	Rumania 18·5 m	Yugo-slavia 18·5 m	U.S.A. 180 m	U.S.S.R. 218 m	U.K. 52·9 m
Basic Industrial Raw Materials	1·75*	(1961) 5·4									
Electricity (thou m. kW)	1·75*	5·4	27	43	8·4	32	8·6	10	879	326	128
Hard coal (m. tons)	0·2*	0·5	26·3	2·7	3·1	107	4·9	1·3	376	377	194
Brown coal & lignite (m. tons)	0·3	18	65	238	25	10	3·8	23	2·6	138*	—
Coke (m. tons)			8·5	1·0	0·5	7·5	1·0	1·0	47	59	18
Crude Petroleum (m. tons)	0·65	0·2	0·15		1·5	0·2	11·5	1·4	348	148	0·15
Iron ore (Fe content) (m. tons)	0·1	0·2	1·0	0·5	0·16	0·7	0·8	0·8	39	68	4·5
Crude steel (m. tons)		0·3	7·0	3·4	2·0	7·2	2·1	1·5	89	70	22
Copper ore (Cu con.) (thou tons)		15·2		25		12·1		38	1000		
Lead ore (Pb con.) (thou tons)		90				38	12	97	237		
Zinc ore (Zn con.) (thou tons)		73				140		60	421		
Bauxite (m. tons)					1·4			1·2	1·5	4	
Manganese (Mn con.) (thou tons)		10·4			33		47·5	4·4	19·3	2700	
Chrome (Cr₂O₃ con.) (thou tons)	20							28·1	28·6		

TABLE 2 (*continued*)

Crop Production 1961 (million metric tons)

Wheat	0·1	2·0	1·6	1·0	1·9	2·8	4·0	3·1	33·6	66	2·6
Rye	—	0·6	1·0	1·5	0·3	8·3	0·1	0·2	0·7	16·3§	—
Barley	0·15	—	1·6	0·95	—	1·3	0·5	0·6	8·5	16§	5·0
Maize	—	1·4	0·5	—	2·7	—	5·7	4·5	92	24	—
Potatoes	—	0·4	5·3	8·4	1·6	45·2	2·8	2·7	13·3	84·0	6·3
Sugar beet	—	1·6	7·8	6·8	2·4	11·6	3·4	1·7	—	58	6·2
Tobacco (thousand metric tons)	—	55·9	5·5	—	17·2	46·0	17·8	15·0	933	175	—
Wine (million hectolitres)	—	—	—	—	3·5	—	2·6	4·2	10·4	7·8	—

Livestock Numbers 1960/61 (million)

Cattle	0·4‡	1·4	4·3	4·6	1·9	9·1	4·5	5·7	97	76	12
Pigs	0·1‡	2·5	6·0	8·3	6·0	13·4	4·3	5·8	55	58	6
Sheep	1·6‡	9·3	0·6	2·0	2·6	3·5	11·5	10·8	33	133	29
Horses	0·05‡	0·3	0·3	0·4	0·5	2·7	1·0	1·2	3·0	11·0	0·1

* = 1959.   † E. Germany is also world's major producer of potash.   § = 1960.   ‡ = 1958.

CHAPTER II

HISTORICAL SURVEY

1. The Folk Migrations

To understand the present distribution of peoples in Eastern Europe one must go back to the period of the great folk migrations which accompanied and contributed to the fall of the Roman Empire. The pattern which emerged after centuries of turbulence remained unchanged in its broad outlines down to the twentieth century.

The frontiers of Roman power in Europe were fixed during the first century A.D. along the line of the Rhine and the Danube, although military expeditions occasionally probed beyond into the territory of the neighbouring Germanic tribes. In the lower Danube valley one such extension made during the reign of Trajan (A.D. 98–117) brought the province of Dacia within the Roman orbit for a century and a half. The present-day inhabitants of Dacia, the Rumanians, still speak a Latin-based language, and their historians have often laid great stress on the value of their distinct cultural heritage derived from ancient Rome. This has been a powerful prop to Rumanian national feeling, although it should be borne in mind that racially the Rumanians of to-day are not very different from their Slav and Magyar neighbours, for in the seventeen centuries since the expulsion of the Romans they have been subjected to a continuous process of intermixing, by reason of the innumerable invasions which have swept through their homeland.

The first groups to effect a major breach in the integrity of the Roman frontiers were Germanic speaking tribes — the Ostrogoths, the Visigoths, the Franks and the Lombards. By the fifth century they had established themselves in the Iberian peninsula, Italy and France. During the next three or four centuries they consolidated their position, absorbing much of the Roman culture of the peoples over whom they ruled and with whom they mixed. In this process the infant nations of France and Germany were born. The Germans of the Western Empire soon found themselves defending their heritage against new incursions from further east. Scholars have not reached agreement as to the causes of the successive waves of invasion which moved inexorably from east to west during the first millennium A.D. Climatic changes in the heartland of Eurasia may have diminished the grazing lands of the nomadic tribes in that area, forcing them to seek a new environment. They may have faced a crisis, due to a steady increase in population, which upset the balance of their adjustment to their original habitat. Another possibility is that they were impelled westward by the pressure of invaders from still further east. Whatever the causes may have been, it is the effects of these invasions on the human geography of Eastern Europe which concern us here.

One of the first groups of Asiatic nomads to burst into Eastern Europe was the Huns, who entered by way of the Ukraine and the lower Danube. By the middle of the fifth century they commanded almost the whole of the area bounded by the Rhine, the Danube and the Baltic. The Germanic inhabitants of this region were either subjugated or driven further west into the former Roman provinces. The Hunnish Empire did not survive the death of its great leader, Attila, although the modern name Hungary bears witness to its occupation of the middle Danubian plains before the arrival of the Magyars. After the death of Attila in A.D. 452 the combined efforts of the German and Roman inhabitants of Western and Southern Europe destroyed the power of the Huns.

Already before this time the Slavs had begun to emerge from their inhospitable homeland amongst the marshes and forests between the Vistula and the Dnieper. By the sixth century they had advanced across the great northern plain of Europe to reach the shores of the Baltic and the valley of the Elbe. Pockets of Slav-speaking people — the Sorbs, the Polabians and the Pomeranians — still survive amongst the Germans of Saxony and the lands between the Elbe and the Oder, as a reminder of this early westward expansion of the Slavs. Another group moved eastward from Poland, eventually merging with the Finnish-speaking[1] subjects of the Scandinavian warriors who controlled Novgorod and Kiev, thus laying the foundations of the Russian nation. Yet another Slav group filtered southward across the Carpathians and through the historic gateway of Moravia to occupy what is now Czechoslovakia, and even to penetrate as far as the Black Sea coast. This was the position in the middle of the sixth century when the next great wave swept in from the Eurasian steppes. The Slav advance was stopped by the Avars, a Turkish tribe of nomadic horsemen. The Avars smashed the Slav empire of the Antes, which stretched along the foothills of the Carpathians and over the plains between the Elbe and the Dnieper. In the Balkans they wrenched the provinces of Pannonia and Illyria from the Byzantines bringing with them, or driving before them, groups of Slavs who stood in the path of their advance. The Slovenes at this time reached their present habitat in the Alpine region near the head of the Adriatic Sea. A century later, the Byzantine Emperor Heraclius is thought to have invited the Serbs and Croats, survivors from the northern Slav kingdom of the Antes, to cross the Carpathians and join in the campaign against the Avars. The Avars were expelled from the Balkans and the Serbs and Croats remained to form the nucleus of the Yugoslav[2] nation.

After the defeat of the Avars, one group of Slavs, under the legendary Samo, established a kingdom which stretched from Bohemia and Moravia across the eastern Alps to Slovenia and Istria. After the death of Samo his kingdom collapsed, much of it falling under Frankish rule and eventually forming part of

[1] The name "Russia" probably derives from the Finnish word "Ruotsi" = Sweden. See Poszkiewicz, *The Making of the Russian Nation*, chapter III.

[2] Jug = south.

the empire of Charlemagne (crowned Emperor A.D. 800). It reappeared under Slav rule for a brief period during the ninth century as the Kingdom of Greater Moravia. On the disintegration of this short-lived kingdom the Magyar horsemen entered from the east and hammered home a lasting wedge between the two groups of Slavs. Nevertheless, the kingdom of Moravia was important in the development of Slav culture. For the few decades during which the western and southern Slavs joined hands across the Danube and the Alps a link was forged through the missionary activities of the Eastern (Byzantine) Church. The monks Constantine-Cyril and Methodius from the monastery of Hilander on Mount Athos were invited by Prince Rastislav to found a Slavonic Church in Moravia. The rituals of the church followed the Roman pattern, but the language was Slavonic. The glagolitic alphabet was devised, from which later developed the Cyrillic script which is used to-day in Serbia, Bulgaria and Russia. The Slavonic liturgy still survives in parts of Yugoslavia. The Moravian Church eventually submitted to Rome under pressure from the West.

On the heels of the Avars came the Bulgars, another group of Asiatic nomads. They appeared on the lower Danube in the seventh century and soon overran the eastern half of the Balkan peninsula. In time they lost their native Ural–Altaic language and adopted the language and cultures of the Slavs over whom they ruled.

In the ninth century yet another Ural–Altaic tribe, the Magyars, rode in from the steppes, to subjugate the peoples of the Danube basin. The Magyars eventually settled down in the rich plains within the Carpathian arc, once the home for a time of the Huns. To-day the Magyar-speaking Hungarians farm the plains of Pannonia and the Alföld, some still following a semi-nomadic way of life, but most of them tilling the rich soil of the most densely settled agricultural region of Europe.

The wedge of non-Slavs represented by the Rumanians and the Magyars was met by an eastward extension of German influence into what is now Austria (Österreich — the east land). Thus the separation between the western Slavs of Poland and Czecho-slovakia and the south Slavs of the Balkans was complete. The German State had been established by the Franks who, under the famous Charlemagne, became the leaders of the West. As Christians, they were the protectors of the Roman Church, which had, of course, survived the disintegration of the Empire.

Throughout all these movements the fate of the native inhabitants is lost in confusion. The Thraco-Illyrians of the Balkans, whose language survives to-day in Albania, and the Romanised Dacians of Rumania, either merged with the invaders, or retreated to the more inaccessible regions of their homeland, where they preserved their cultural identity.

By the end of the first millennium A.D. the foundations of modern Europe can be seen dimly emerging from the storms and stresses of the period of folk migrations. It should be remembered that the invaders were not usually small marauding bands. Whole tribes were on the move, and even when the counter-attack from the west drove them back, they left a permanent imprint on the face of Europe. By A.D. 1000 all that remained in Europe of the Roman Empire which once stretched from Hadrian's Wall to the Black Sea was a tiny eastern remnant, with a foothold in the Balkans and southern Italy.

The greater part of the Balkans was divided between the Bulgarians, the Serbs and the Croats. The middle and lower Danube was the centre of the Magyar Kingdom of Hungary. North of the Carpathians the Principality of Poland covered most of the present area of Poland. To the west, beyond the boundary which runs from the mouth of the Oder through Moravia to the head of the Adriatic, lay the great German Empire, the successor to the Roman Empire in the west. German influence extended from Rome to the North Sea, and westward beyond the Rhine into Flanders, Alsace and Lorraine. It was flanked on the north by the Kingdoms of Norway, Sweden, Denmark and England, and to the west by the Kingdoms of France and Burgundy and the Dukedom of Normandy. East of Poland and Hungary the "land of Rus" stretched from the Black Sea far north into the

B

Arctic twilight. The ethnic map of Europe was beginning to acquire a familiar shape.

2.   The Middle Ages

By the beginning of the second millennium another division of Europe was apparent, based not on linguistic and national differences — indeed transcending these barriers. This cleavage within Christendom was based on confessional differences between the Eastern and Western Churches. The Roman Empire had adopted the Christian faith as its official religion during the fourth century. Originally the Church had been organised into five Patriarchates, of which Rome was naturally the most important. With the advance of the Arabs into the Middle East during the seventh and eighth centuries the Patriarchates of Antioch, Alexandria and Jerusalem were eclipsed, leaving those of Rome and Constantinople to struggle for supremacy within the Church. The division of authority between these two branches of the Church followed that of the Empire, which had been divided during the fourth century, for reasons of military and administrative convenience. The collapse of Imperial power in the West did not destroy the Roman Church. The Franks absorbed Christianity as part of the cultural heritage which they took over when they settled within the confines of the Empire, and the Pope, freed from the control of the Emperor, was able to maintain his spiritual authority despite the decline of Rome's temporal power. Constantinople (or Byzantium), however, remained for another thousand years the centre of both temporal and spiritual power in the Eastern Empire. Doctrinal differences developed between the two halves of the once universal Church, and these eventually hardened into schism and enmity. As Eastern Europe settled down after the chaos of the Dark Ages, a struggle developed between Rome and Byzantium for the souls of the Slavs and the Magyars. The Germans, who adhered to the Roman Church, became the spearhead of its missionary activity in central and

Eastern Europe. Indeed, the idea of the Holy Roman Empire was that of an alliance between German temporal power and the spiritual authority of the Pope, to create throughout Europe a new and larger Roman Empire from the ashes of the one which had been destroyed by the barbarians. The idea of the unity of Christendom was supported both by Rome and Byzantium, and was accepted by rulers throughout Europe. Even when disputes developed between the German Emperors and the Pope, as they frequently did, the concept was not abandoned. For a time, too, there was co-operation between Rome and Byzantium, especially during the crusades against the Moslems.

The Byzantines had no difficulty in winning over the peoples of the southern Balkans — the Bulgarians, the Serbs and the Macedonians. We have seen how for a short time they even had successes in Moravia, and from there they began the conversion of the Magyars,[1] During the reign of the Emperor Otto I the Germans counter-attacked, and soon German bishops had been appointed in Bohemia, Moravia, Slovakia and Slovenia, bringing these lands within the embrace of Rome. On Christmas Day, A.D. 1000 Stephen of Hungary received his crown from the Pope, thus setting the seal on the work of his father, Geza, who had initiated the moves which drew Hungary into the Western orbit. As so often happened, German barons accompanied the German bishops into Hungary, thus ensuring that the change was not confined to matters of the spirit.

The attachment of Poland to the Roman world was accomplished by the conversion of its ruler, Mieszko, in the late tenth century. In Croatia, too, German influence succeeded in drawing this Slavonic land into the western world. The greatest success which the Eastern Church could set against these Roman victories was the conversion of Olga, ruler of Kiev, about A.D. 955. This led to the adherence of Russia to Byzantium.

By the end of the tenth century the confessional boundaries within Eastern Europe were established in a form which has

[1] It is possible that the Magyars may have been influenced by Byzantium as they moved into Hungary in the ninth century.

survived down to the present day. The Protestant Reformation won a temporary victory in Bohemia, Hungary and Poland, but the Catholic counter-attack was so successful in this area that even in Bohemia, the home of John Hus, Roman Catholics now outnumber Protestants. Poland, Hungary, Slovenia, Slovakia and Croatia are still predominantly Roman Catholic areas, whereas the churches of Serbia, Bulgaria, Rumania and Russia belong to the Eastern (Orthodox) community.

The first German ruler to attempt the creation of a Holy Roman Empire was Charlemagne, who became King of the Franks in 771. By a series of wars against the Avars and the Saxons on his eastern borders and against the Moslems in Spain, he created a Frankish Empire covering present-day France, the Netherlands, Austria, Slovenia, and a large part of what is now Italy, Czechoslovakia and Germany. The first attempt at a revival of the Roman Empire did not survive the ninth century. From its western provinces the Kingdoms of France, Germany and Italy emerged. The creation of the Kingdom of Greater Moravia absorbed most of its Slavonic provinces. Nevertheless, the German dream lived on and inspired ruler after ruler with the vision of a great Christian state under German leadership uniting both Eastern and Western Europe. Otto III almost succeeded in making the dream a reality, but his ambitious schemes were thwarted by his death in A.D. 1002. The Slavs, too, dreamt of an empire which, had it succeeded, would have formed a buffer from the Baltic southward to the Black Sea and the Adriatic between the rising power of Russia and the already firmly established German State. Echoes of this dream are to be found in the policies of Polish chauvinists in the 1920's and 30's. The nearest the Slavs came to achieving unification was under the Polish ruler Boleslas the Great, son of the Duke Mieszko whose conversion had brought the Roman Church to Poland. Boleslas built on the territorial acquisitions of his father — notably Cracow and Silesia — and extended Polish control over Bohemia, Moravia and Slovakia. By these extensions of his territory he brought Poland into direct contact with Hungary, then under the rule of its great King, St. Stephen. To the east, Polish power pressed hard against the lands of the Russian Duke Vladimir of Kiev. Boleslas' successes produced a reaction from his neighbours, especially that of his western neighbour, the German Emperor Henry II, and eventually the Polish–Czech State was broken up. Hungary seized Slovakia, and the western Czech lands reverted to German control during the early part of the eleventh century.

After the collapse of the Polish–Czech State, German penetration into Eastern Europe was intensified. The Slavs between the Elbe and the Oder were overwhelmed by a tide of German colonisation. The little Slav village of Bralin became the German town of Berlin. The crusading Order of Teutonic Knights was invited into Poland and began the conversion of the Prussians and the non-Christian Slavs and Balts of the lands later known as East Prussia, Latvia, Lithuania and Esthonia. Later in the Middle Ages, German merchants followed the crusading warriors, giving an early demonstration of the old maxim that trade follows the flag. The Hanseatic League of traders established those German cities along the shores of the Baltic whose names are familiar to students of Nazi penetration into the area, seven centuries later — Danzig and Memel for example.

During the fourteenth century a German King of Bohemia, Charles, made Prague the centre of the Holy Roman Empire, and established it as the cultural capital of Central Europe. He rebuilt the city, founding there the famous Charles University in 1348. At about the same time the Polish King Casimir founded the law school at Cracow, which eventually became the first university of Poland.

Although there was fierce rivalry between the various Christian rulers of Central Europe during the Middle Ages, the idea of Christendom could still inspire them to co-operate in the face of a common danger. This was demonstrated in 1364 when Cracow became the venue for a curious international conference. King Peter of Cyprus was endeavouring to raise a coalition against the Ottoman Turks, and journeyed to Europe to seek the help of his

Christian colleagues. The Emperor Charles IV joined Louis of Anjou, King of Hungary, Casimir of Poland and the King of Denmark in a meeting to discuss the launching of a crusade. Although in fact the only crusade that resulted was one led by Casimir against the Lithuanians, the Emperor did commend the project to his subordinate princes within the Empire. Far more important for the future of Poland was the arrangement made between Casimir and Louis which enabled the Hungarian King to inherit the throne of Poland when Casimir died in 1370.

The Kingdom of Hungary, even apart from the temporary union of crowns under Louis, was a much larger and more important state during the Middle Ages than it is to-day. It was a Roman Catholic country, as to-day, but then the lines of communication with the cultural community of Western Europe were fully open. After the extinction of its native royal line — that of the Arpads — it had a succession of foreign kings — Angevins, Luxemburgers and Jagellons — until the union with the Habsburg Crown was established in the sixteenth century. This union lasted for four hundred years, until the victorious allies after the First World War forced Charles of Habsburg to renounce his claims. At its greatest extent Hungarian control covered Transylvania, Croatia, Slovakia, part of Dalmatia and the province of Vojvodina.[1]

In the Balkans, between the power of Byzantium and that of Hungary lay two Slav principalities, Serbia and Bulgaria.

The first Serbian State seems to have been formed during the ninth century, and from its earliest days it was in conflict with both Byzantium and the rapidly expanding Bulgarian Kingdom. Between the eighth and the twelfth centuries a number of Serbian states were formed, and eventually disappeared. Usually they were unable to survive the death of their rulers. Their location changed, the centres being at different times in Montenegro and in the Morava and the Sava valleys. With the reign of Stephen Nemanja (1167–1196) a new phase began. For a time it seemed

[1] Now an autonomous region of Yugoslavia, lying between the Danube and the present Hungarian–Yugoslav frontier.

as if the Serbs would replace the Byzantines as the defenders of Christendom against the Turks. During the two centuries after the accession of Stephen, Serbia extended her control over the whole of Macedonia, Epirus, Thessaly and Albania. The record of medieval Serbia's cultural and religious vitality can still be seen in the famous monasteries of Dečani, Hilendar, Žiča and many others which were founded by the pious kings of the Nemanja dynasty. Signs of weakness and disintegration were already apparent, however, before the Turkish invasion which culminated in the loss of Serbian independence after the battle of Kosovo Polje (1389).

The Bulgarians during the period between the ninth and the fourteenth centuries had two periods of independence from Byzantine rule before they, like the Serbs, were overwhelmed by the Turks. In the middle of the ninth century the Byzantines recognised Bulgarian independence, in the hope that by so doing they would secure the adherence of the Bulgarian Church to the Patriarch of Constantinople, rather than to the Pope of Rome. At its greatest extent the first Bulgarian Empire controlled most of Macedonia and even reached as far as Zara (modern Zadar) on the Dalmatian coast. In 1014 the Byzantine Emperor, Basil II, inflicted a crushing defeat on the army of the Bulgarian, Samuel. Thousands of Bulgarian prisoners were blinded, one out of every hundred being left with one eye to guide their unfortunate comrades back to their King, who had fled to the Macedonian town of Prilep. By this savage act, Basil earned himself the title of "Bulgar slayer" (Bulgaroktonos). In the thirteenth century a second Bulgarian Empire emerged, but after a century of independence it fell to the Turks.

3. The Growth of Multi-national Empires

The Ottoman Turks, whose influence on the Balkans lasted until the first decade of the twentieth century, were Asiatic warriors who had embraced the faith of Islam during their migrations into Asia Minor from the lands beyond the Aral Sea. They eventually extended their rule over all the Arab lands of the Middle East, and through North Africa as far as the borders of the Arab sultanate of Morocco. Although their memory is associated with oppression and cruelty, largely because of their behaviour in the long period of decline during the eighteenth and nineteenth centuries, they were not everywhere regarded with fear or disapproval by the peoples they first conquered during the Middle Ages.

By the middle of the fourteenth century they had advanced through Asia Minor and over the Bosphorus into south-eastern Europe. The city of Byzantium resisted them until 1453, but by that time Ottoman power already extended throughout the Balkans. The Bulgars were subdued in 1371, and in 1389 the Serbs were defeated at the battle of Kosovo Polje (the field of the blackbirds). Kosovo Polje lies on the route between the Aegean and the Danube, close to the historic routeway of the Vardar–Morava Corridor. Once this area was in the possession of the Turks the way lay open to the rich plains of the Danube, and soon the Christian kingdom of Hungary felt the fury of the invader. At the battle of Mohács in 1526 the Hungarian army was defeated, their young king, Louis II, perished, and there began two centuries of partition and unrest during which the heart of the land was reduced to a wilderness. A thin strip of territory, from Slovakia across Pannonia (the Dunántúl) and Croatia to the Adriatic near modern Rijeka, remained outside the grip of the Moslems. But the fate of the Hungarians in this area was scarcely better than that of their brothers who bore the Turkish yoke. On the death of Louis, the Habsburg ruler, Ferdinand, who later became Holy Roman Emperor, claimed the succession to the Hungarian throne. Royal Hungary became little more than a military frontier march of the Empire, ruled over by unruly barons. Later, a third division of the country, Transylvania, was established under a Hungarian prince who owed allegiance to the Turkish Sultan. Suleiman the Magnificent (1520–1550) could describe himself in a grandiloquent string of titles as "Sultan of the

Sultans of East and West, fortunate Lord of the domains of the Romans, Persians and Arabs, Hero of Creation . . . Padishah and Sultan of the Mediterranean and the Black Sea . . . of Wallachia and Moldavia and Hungary and many kingdoms and lands besides.

The high-water mark of the Turkish advance into Europe was reached in the seventeenth century. Much of the history of the Balkans during the next three centuries is the story of the gradual replacement of Turkish rule first by that of the Habsburgs, and later of a number of independent national states. By the time of the First World War, Turkey had lost virtually all her European possessions, but the centuries of Turkish overlordship had bitten deeply into the cultural and religious life of the Balkans and its marks are still apparent. Many of the Balkan peoples were converted to the Islamic faith, and there are still to-day in Yugoslavia and Albania large groups of Moslems. In Macedonia and Bulgaria there are also Turkish minorities. That of Bulgaria numbered almost half a million until the expulsion to Turkey of a quarter of a million of them in 1950.

The House of Habsburg

With the extinction of the Serbian and Bulgarian principalities in the Balkans, followed by the fall of Constantinople, the leadership of the Eastern Church fell to the Russian principality of Moscow. In the West, the defence of Christendom was centred on the House of Habsburg. After 1438 the Imperial title became virtually hereditary in the Austrian House of Habsburg, a German family who, by war, marriage and diplomacy, had gradually amassed huge territories in Central Europe and even in the Netherlands and Spain. The divisions within Christendom which were associated with the Reformation gave rise to national churches. By giving spiritual sanction to national princes they undermined the concept of the Holy Roman Empire. Thus, although the name lingered on into the nineteenth century, what emerged was the Habsburg Empire which, as Voltaire remarked was neither holy, Roman nor an Empire.

The most remarkable thing about the Habsburgs was their staying power. For nearly six hundred years they ruled over a huge area of Central and Eastern Europe, until eventually their writ ran from Polish Galicia through the whole of present-day Czechoslovakia, Austria and Hungary, and a large part of Italy, Rumania and Yugoslavia. The only cement which bound this huge edifice together was the dynasty. No great idea united the lands of the House of Habsburg except that of historical continuity. Perhaps the desire to maintain some geographical continuity between the Crown lands in Central Europe and the peripheral kingdoms of Spain and the Low Countries explains the Habsburg interest in Germany, Italy and Bohemia. During the sixteenth and early seventeenth centuries, the Imperial lines of communication ran from Austria overland through Germany to the Netherlands, then by sea to Spain, and from Spain across the Mediterranean to Italy. This was the route which the Emperors took when they toured their domains.[1]

Whatever the forces which shaped their actions, the Habsburgs had a great influence on the destinies of Europe from the fifteenth to the nineteenth centuries, until the Empire finally broke asunder under the pressure of its subject nationalities. They were responsible for crushing the nascent Protestant nationalism of the Czechs during the counter-reformation in the early seventeenth century, but when they temporarily succeeded in uniting an exhausted Germany during the first phase of the Thirty Years War they incurred the wrath of both the Protestant Swedes and the Catholic French. The outcome of the Thirty Years War was not only the permanent exclusion of the Habsburgs from real power in Germany, but also the confirmation of their position in Austria, Hungary and Bohemia. They were later to expand their Empire over the territories abandoned by the Turks, as the flood which had once lapped to the gates of Vienna began slowly to ebb, uncovering one by one the Danubian lands and the Balkans. The Habsburgs profited by the waning of Turkish power, but they

[1] It was also of vital importance to the economy of the Empire to maintain the trade routes from Bohemia across Germany to the North Sea.

did little actively to accelerate the process. It was a Polish king, Jan Sobieski, who came to the rescue of Christendom when Kara Mustapha besieged Vienna in 1683. Fourteen years later Prince Eugene of Savoy, the Imperial Commander, followed up this advantage with his victory at Zenta. The Habsburgs were the chief beneficiaries of the Treaty of Karlovci (Karlowitz) in 1699 which restored Hungary, Transylvania and Croatia to the Empire.

Poland in the Eighteenth Century

Sobieski's great victories against the Turks might suggest that the Polish state was one of the major powers of Europe, but behind the dazzling achievements of its leader the Polish nation was fatally weak. Although some kind of Polish State had existed from the ninth century, and had often played an important role in European affairs, its geographical position laid it open to constant attack from both east and west. We have already mentioned the activities of the Teutonic knights and the German Emperors in the Middle Ages. During the sixteenth and seventeenth centuries the rise of Prussia on the west, Russia on the east and the Habsburg monarchy on the south hemmed Poland in on three sides. During the Thirty Years War Swedish armies marched across the Polish plain en route for Russia, and although they were eventually compelled to withdraw, the effects of their occupation on the cultural and economic life of Poland were disastrous. Finally, in the eighteenth century, Austria, Prussia and Russia moved in to partition a weak and divided Poland.

During the century before the partitions, Poland had fallen far from the glorious days of Casimir the Great. Internal quarrels amongst the Polish nobles, assisted by interested interference from her powerful neighbours, and by the exhaustion which followed the Swedish occupation and the wars of the seventeenth century, all contributed to the undermining of Polish independence. After the death of Sobieski, who had brought fame to the name of Poland by his defence of Vienna against the Turks, the election of his successor was manipulated by Prussia and Russia. The apparent democracy by which the nobles elected the ruler of their "royal republic", and the anarchic method of conducting the affairs of the Diet, made foreign intervention easy. In the Diet, for example, the principle of "*liberum veto*", which required that all decisions should be unanimous, meant that a single nobleman under the influence of a foreign power could exercise a veto over its decisions. Polish independence died in fact with Sobieski in 1696. A shadow of its former glory lived on for another century, but Polish history during the eighteenth century was really a chapter in the history of Prussia and Russia, with minor contributions by the Habsburgs and the Swedes. The ambitions and rivalries of rulers like Peter the Great and Catherine of Russia, Maria Theresa of Austria, Frederick the Great of Prussia and Charles XII of Sweden determined the course of events in Poland. A movement of national regeneration began under the reign of Stanislas Poniatowski who was elected King in 1764 with the support of Frederick II of Prussia and Catherine of Russia.[1] Despite the unsavoury circumstances of his election, Poniatowski made great contributions to the cause of Polish national revival by his encouragement of the arts, commerce and industry, and by the reform of political life. His very success in this respect was his undoing, and incidentally that of his country. The opposition which his reforms inevitably generated gave an opportunity for intervention by Frederick and Catherine. After a short war, Poland was partitioned in 1772 between Prussia, Russia and Austria, each taking a large slice of the Polish territory adjacent to their own borders. The small land-locked Poland which was left was further whittled down by the second partition of 1793. Even this tiny fragment was eventually swallowed up in the third partition of 1795, which came after a Polish revolt against the Russians, led by the romantic national hero, Tadeusz Koskiuszko. Koskiuszko had earlier fought in the American War of Independence, where he distinguished himself at the battle of Yorktown, and was rewarded by the U.S. Congress with the rank of Brigadier-General and the grant of American citizenship. The

[1] Whilst serving as Polish representative in St. Petersburg, Poniatowski had been one of Catherine's many lovers.

liberal nationalist ideas which inspired both the American and French revolutions made their first impact in Eastern Europe through the activities of Koskiuszko and his followers. Although the Polish revolutionaries were defeated by the Russian army, they were soon to get their revenge. In 1807 Napoleon drove the Russians out of Poland and established a Grand Duchy of Warsaw. The Grand Duchy was a poor substitute for an independent state,[1] but its existence helped to keep alive the hopes of the Polish nationalists. In 1809 there was a small extension of its territory at the expense of Austria, when the historic city of Krákow was incorporated. The civil code of the Duchy was modelled on that of France, and so the juridical, political and cultural ideas of the liberal movement of western Europe first took root in the soil of Eastern Europe. Their influence remained long after the defeat of Napoleon and the "fourth partition of Poland" made by the Congress of Vienna. "Congress Poland" was the name given by historians to the Kingdom set up under Russian tutelage in 1815. It was even smaller than Napoleon's Duchy of Warsaw, as Krákow was set up as a "free city" separated from the Kingdom. Galicia remained in Austrian hands and the province of Posen (Poznan) continued to be under Prussian control. As the constitution of the Kingdom required that the throne should be occupied by the Russian Tsar, the Poles could expect little real say in the affairs of their government. Koskiuszko realised this, and refused to return from his exile in France.

4. The Nationalist Movements

Poland was not the only Eastern European country to be brought in contact with the ferment of political and cultural ideas which stemmed from the French Revolution. From Finland in the far north to Greece and the Balkans in the south, the liberal

[1] Its limits were set as a result of a compromise between Napoleon and the Russian Emperor, Alexander I, at the Peace of Tilsit (1807).

movement awoke the submerged nations to a realisation of their separate identities. Before any political manifestations brought the national question to the attention of the chancelleries of the big powers, the work of teachers, poets, folklorists and scholars began to arouse the consciousness of individual national personality in the minds of the educated classes of Eastern Europe. Sometimes the influence of France was directly traceable to a Napoleonic occupation — as in Poland and the Ijlyrian provinces of the Balkans. Thus the Croatian cultural revival owed much to the effects of the French occupation from 1809 to 1813. The Illyrian movement led by the philologist Ljudovit Gaj started its activities by a campaign to reduce Hungarian cultural influence and to elevate the status of the Croatian language. It soon developed into a political movement. In Slavonia, romantic poets, drawing inspiration from the folk culture of their people, led the national movement against Austrian rule. It is significant that even to-day the romantic poets Prešeren and Vodnik are looked upon as national heroes in Slovenia, and that Napoleon's Marshal Marmont is still remembered in the name of a street in the Dalmatian town of Split.

Elsewhere the French influence was less direct, but none the less significant. In the early nineteenth century Rumanian nobles were in the habit of sending their sons to Paris to be educated. They returned home with more than an ability to speak fluent French and to ape the manners of Western European society. They brought back also the ideas of liberalism which had not died in France with the defeat of Napoleon.

Thus Eastern Europe was never the same after the passage of Napoleon. Although the Russian and Austrian Empires emerged apparently unscathed, and seemed to have succeeded in putting the clock back by a quarter of a century in the settlement they reached at the Congress of Vienna, the cement which bound their system together had been permanently loosened by the activities of the "Corsican upstart".

It was from France that the inspiration came for the next great revolutionary shock which marked a further stage in the break-up of the old order in Europe. The revolution of February 1848 which overthrew Louis Philippe fired the imagination of the radicals in the submerged nations of Eastern Europe. In Prague, the demand was raised for the restoration of an independent Czech state comprising "the lands of St. Wenceslas" — i.e. Bohemia, Moravia and Silesia. At first it seemed as if the Czechs might succeed, for, unlike the Poles whose rising in Galicia was easily crushed two years earlier, they were not alone. In 1848 Vienna was also in revolt, and in Germany a liberal parliament had established itself at Frankfurt. Metternich, the symbol of the old autocratic system, was sent scurrying to exile in England, and the Habsburg Emperor, Ferdinand, was forced to accept a Constituent Assembly. In Prague, the Governor of Bohemia refused to recognise the new government in Vienna, and set up a separate administration which included Czechs as well as Germans. The moderate Czech leaders distrusted the pan-Slav enthusiasm of the young students who had started the revolution, and they were quite prepared to work with the Austrians if they could be given a greater share in the government of the country. They were also afraid of the nationalist ambitions of the German parliament in Frankfurt, which appeared to want to revive in democratic dress a new version of the old German dream of a Holy Roman Empire. Thus Count Palacki, one of the moderate leaders, had turned down an invitation to sit in Frankfurt, declaring "I am a Bohemian of Slav race". Palacki called a Slav Congress, hoping to confine its membership to representatives of the Slavs within the Monarchy, and to steer its thoughts in the direction of an Austro–Slav alliance against the Germans. Polish and Russian delegates came, however, including the anarchist Bakunin. The divisions between the Slavs eventually led to disorders, and this gave the Austrian commander, Prince Windischgratz, the opportunity to suppress the Czech revolt — to the great relief not only of the German inhabitants of Bohemia, but also of many moderate Czechs who were disturbed by the course of events. The moderates then sent representatives to the Constituent Assembly in Vienna to put the case for a greater degree of self-government for Bohemia within the framework of a reformed Monarchy.

In Croatia, a similar view was expressed by the newly elected Governor (Ban) Jellačić. He advocated a union of the south Slavs who would then form a third element in the Monarchy, sharing equal status with the Hungarians and the Austrians. The idea of turning Dual into a Triple Monarchy also appealed to the Slovenes, whose leaders had no wish to sever completely their historic ties with the Habsburgs. The Croats and their neighbours the Serbs of Slavonia and Vojvodina had to fight the Hungarians to achieve their ends, for these territories were ruled by Hungary.

The Hungarians were also in revolt in 1848, but although they demanded greater freedom for themselves, they had no intention of granting the same rights to their subject peoples — the Slavs of Croatia and the Rumanians and Germans of Transylvania. Thus the Magyars found themselves under attack not only by the forces of the Imperial Field Marshal, Windischgrätz, but also by those of Jellačić. A combined invasion in September 1848 was thrown back by the Hungarians under Lájos Kossuth. The Emperor Ferdinand abdicated in a panic, handing over power to his nephew Franz Josef. Shortly afterwards the campaign swung back against the Hungarians, and in the first flush of victory the new Emperor dissolved the Constituent Assembly in Vienna and declared that the Monarchy was "an indivisible and indissoluble constitutional Austrian Empire". Kossuth's reply was to declare the independence of Hungary, with himself as head of state, and to issue an appeal to all lovers of freedom to support him. This attempt to enlist the support of the liberals abroad frightened not only Franz Josef; Tsar Nicholas of Russia was also anxious to prevent the dangerous heresy of nationalism from spreading to Poland. He had already acted against the first stirrings of national sentiment in the nominally Turkish provinces of Moldavia and Wallachia, and he was not unaware that Polish nationalists had played a distinguished part in the Hungarian rising. He was therefore more than willing to oblige Franz Josef. In August 1849, and not for the last time, the Russian steamroller crushed the resistance of the

Hungarians. Kossuth and his Polish general, Bem, fled abroad shortly before General Paškevic, the Russian governor of Poland, announced to the Emperor that "Hungary lies at the feet of your majesty". The complete subjugation of the country was left to an Austrian, General Haynau, who ruthlessly eradicated all traces of opposition. Haynau's misdeeds acquired world-wide notoriety, and so incensed public opinion in Britain that when he visited London in 1850 he was manhandled by an angry crowd.

By 1849 the old order had apparently recovered its balance, and reaction seemed everywhere to have triumphed. However, the memory of 1848 lived on in Eastern Europe, not only in the hearts of the defeated nationalists, but also in the fears of the victorious reactionaries who thereafter felt compelled to make concessions lest the events of the dreadful year of revolutions should be re-enacted.

Turkey and the Balkans

After their defeat at the hands of Sobieski in 1683 the Turks began slowly to retreat from their European possessions. In the fighting which followed the raising of the siege of Vienna, the Turkish army was driven out of Hungary, Croatia and Slavonia by the Austrian army of Prince Eugene of Savoy. The Treaty of Karlowitz in 1699 confirmed the possession of these territories to the Habsburgs. In the following half-century the Austrians pushed further south into Serbia and Bosnia, and were then forced back to the line of the Danube and the Sava. During this period a new element was injected into the struggle between Turk and Christian by the growth of Russian power. The Slav peoples of the Balkans began to look to Russia rather than to Austria as their deliverer from the Turkish yoke, and pan-Slav propaganda inspired by Russian agents was a potent force in the development of Balkan nationalism. Russia eventually won from the Turks recognition of her right to protect the Orthodox subjects of the Sultan. The Orthodox churches of Serbia and Bulgaria had for centuries been the upholders of Slav culture, and as national resistance developed it was natural for the people to turn to their church leaders.

The Russians and the Austrians had a common aim in wishing to see the decline of Turkish power in Europe, but they were rivals when it came to deciding who should succeed to the Turkish patrimony. Thus they sometimes acted together, especially during the earlier period of Turkish decline, but towards the end of the nineteenth century they were more frequently in opposition. The first of the Balkan nations to take advantage of Turkey's weakness after the Russo-Turkish wars of the late eighteenth century was Serbia. The Serbs particularly resented the behaviour of the Janissaries, originally a *corps d'élite* of the Sultan's army, but by 1800 an arrogant and self-seeking military clique who often acted independently of the Sultan. A tradition of patriotic banditry grew up amongst the Serbs, the outlaws being known by the Turkish name "haiduk". In 1804 the haiduks of the Šumadija area elected as their leader a farmer called George Petrović, later known as Karageorge. He approached the Turkish authorities with a list of complaints against the Janissaries, but was put off with vague promises. Realising that they were unlikely to achieve anything by talking, the Serbs passed over to open revolt. Russia, who was sympathetic to the Serbian demands, and incidentally had her own quarrels with Turkey, became involved in a war against the Sultan. Thus the Serbian independence movement became entangled with the wider aims of Russian foreign policy. In the long run this may have helped the Serbs to break the Turkish bonds, but there were many tortuous deviations which resulted from the association. For example, in 1812 the Tsar's ministers sensed that an invasion of their country by Napoleonic France was imminent, and in order to concentrate their efforts against it they were anxious to wind up the war with Turkey as quickly as possible. They abandoned their Serbian allies and the Turks soon re-established themselves in Belgrade. Karageorge fled to Austria, and the Second Serbian Rising, which took place in 1814, found a new leader, Miloš Obrenović. When Karageorge returned to his country, Miloš had him murdered. Much of the internal history of Serbia during the rest of the nineteenth century concerns the dynastic rivalries of the two houses of Karageorgević and Obrenović.

The Second Serbian Rising eventually succeeded. It was helped by the fact that other European subjects of the Turks — the Greeks and the Rumanians — chose the same period to make their bids for freedom. Russia also assisted by declaring war on Turkey, after first winning what concessions she could for both the Serbs and the Rumanians by negotiation. When the Sultan repudiated these concessions, which had been incorporated into a document known as the Convention of Ackerman (1826), Russia declared war and quickly occupied the Rumanian principalities of Moldavia and Wallachia. The Turks were defeated and signed a Treaty at Adrianople in 1829 which gave autonomy within the Turkish Empire to the Greeks and the Serbs, and gave Russia a virtual protectorate over the Rumanian principalities.

The painful process by which the modern states of Rumania, Bulgaria, Yugoslavia, Albania and Greece came to be born involved not only the Sultan and his subjects. Austria, Britain and France were as interested as Russia in the filling of the power vacuum left by the retreating Turks. Historians refer to the diplomatic and military activities which resulted from this interest of the big powers as "The Eastern Question". It involved a number of "summit conferences" and a few wars as well as innumerable diplomatic intrigues.

Russia had two important cards to play, especially where the Serbs and the Bulgarians were involved — the common linguistic traditions of the Slav peoples and the confessional links through the Orthodox Churches. She was able to use these cards with great effect to win points in her bid for control of the Straits. Her immediate rival in the Balkans was the Habsburg Monarchy. Britain and France were less directly concerned, and Germany hardly at all until the Bismarck era. After 1870 a re-united Germany under Prussian leadership resumed the ancient policy of "Drang nach Osten", the ultimate target being the Turkish provinces of the Levant. The symbol of this policy was the Berlin–

Baghdad railway the route of which lay through the heart of the Balkans. Because of all these outside interests, the struggle against the Turks could not be regarded simply as an affair between the emerging nations and their former masters. Every step which they took sent echoes through the chancelleries of the great powers, where statesmen watched every move to see whether it afforded them an opportunity to intervene in pursuit of their own interests.

The next nation to achieve independence after the Serbs was Rumania. Since 1714 the provinces of Moldavia and Wallachia had been ruled by Greek princelings under nominal subjection to Turkey. The Rumanian peasants paid a heavy burden of taxes to their alien masters. Their plight was described by the British Consul in 1820 in the following terms:

> There does not perhaps exist a people labouring under a greater degree of oppression from the effect of despotic power, and more heavily burdened with impositions and taxes than the peasants of Wallachia and Moldavia, nor any who would bear half their weight with the same patience and resignation.[1]

Despite Wilkinson's remarks on the patience of the Rumanian peasants, they did not always accept their yoke without protest. Just as the first protests of Karageorge were directed against the Janissaries and not against the Turks, so the Rumanian hero of the 1820's, Tudor Vladimirescu, thought in terms of an appeal to the Sultan over the heads of the Greek oppressors. Like Karageorge he did not live to see the independence of his country, for he was brutally murdered on the orders of the Greek leader Constantine Ypsilanti. The Principalities eventually achieved autonomy by the Treaty of Paris which ended the Crimean War in 1856. A futile attempt was made under this Treaty to separate the two provinces, but two years later Moldavia and Wallachia became united, and shortly afterwards the Rumanians invited the German Prince Karl (Rumanian Carol) of Hohenzollern to be their ruler. In 1877 they declared their complete independence

[1] W. Wilkinson, *An account of the principalities of Moldavia and Wallachia*, London 1820, p. 155.

from Turkey, and in 1881 Prince Carol took the title of King of Rumania.

The Bulgarians were the next people to shake off Turkish control. Their struggle for independence was at first directed to the removal of foreign Church leaders, for the Bulgarian Orthodox Church was under the control of Greeks from Constantinople. In 1870 they achieved the right to an autonomous Bulgarian Church, a right which the Turks conceded largely as a result of Russian pressure. In 1875 the Bulgarians revolted against the Turks, and Russia came again to their aid. At the same time the Bosnians had rebelled and were receiving support from Montenegro and Serbia. Rumania allowed Russian troops to cross her territory, and herself took part in the fighting. By the Treaty of San Stefano, which ended the war, Turkey was forced to recognise an independent Bulgaria whose boundaries extended well into Macedonia and Thrace. This "Big Bulgaria" was so obviously a Russian puppet that the powers intervened and compelled Russia to accept the mutilation of her protégé. Two Bulgarian provinces under nominal Turkish sovereignty were set up by the Congress of Berlin, which met under Bismarck's guidance in 1878. This artificial division of the Bulgarians, like that attempted a few years earlier in Rumania, was ended in 1885. A German prince, Alexander of Battenberg, was proclaimed Prince of Bulgaria, but after two years he was removed by the Russians, and Ferdinand of Coburg was put in his place.

The Congress of Berlin effected another important change in the Balkans. Austria–Hungary was allowed to occupy the Turkish provinces of Bosnia and Hercegovina and the Sanjak of Novi Pazar.[1] The Sanjak stood between Serbia and Montenegro, and its occupation by Austria denied the Serbs an outlet to the Adriatic through the territory of her friendly Slav neighbour. In compensation for this disappointment, the Serbs were encouraged to expand into Macedonia. The Serbian King Milan Obrenović

[1] In 1908, after the Young Turk Revolution, Bosnia and Hercegovina were formally annexed to the Monarchy, and the Sanjak was handed back to Turkey. During the Balkan Wars Serbia acquired the Sanjak.

FIG. 3. Eastern Europe in 1878.

eagerly fell into this trap, and when Bulgaria declared her independence in 1885 he demanded part of Macedonia as "compensation", backing his claim by an attempted invasion. The Bulgarians defeated him at the battle of Slivnica, and although they did not succeed in getting Macedonia for themselves, they made sure that their case was put to the Macedonian people as forcibly as possible by the agency of the notorious IMRO.[1]

The Balkan Wars

It was not in Russia's interest that the two South Slav nations should quarrel, and after Slivnica they directed their efforts to healing the breach between Serbia and Bulgaria. The aim was a Balkan League under Russian control which would, in the words of the Russian Foreign Minister, "bar the road for ever to German penetration, Austrian invasion". The obvious weakness of this scheme was that whilst the two Balkan nations might be willing to act together to remove Turkish influence, they would be likely to quarrel over the disposal of the territory taken from Turkey. Further complications were introduced by the accession of Greece to the Balkan League, for Greece and Bulgaria both laid claim to Thrace. In 1812 the League attacked Turkey, and much to their own and Russia's surprise they very quickly drove the Turks almost completely out of the Balkans. Russia was so nervous of the possible effects of a Bulgarian occupation of Constantinople that she mobilised her Black Sea fleet as a warning to her little Slav brother not to precipitate an international crisis.

The Bulgarians were dissatisfied with the settlement at the end of the First Balkan War, and, flushed with pride at their military prowess against the Turks, they rounded on their allies. They miscalculated badly, for they found ranged against them not only Serbia and Greece, but also Rumania and Turkey. Turkey re-occupied Adrianople, and Rumania held on to southern Dobrudja as a result of the Second Balkan War of 1913.

[1] Internal Macedonian Revolutionary Organisation.

The First World War

On the eve of the First World War there remained for the Slav nationalists only the problem of Austro-Hungarian rule in Bosnia–Hercegovina, Croatia–Slavonia and Slovenia. Serbia conceived it to be her mission to lead the struggle for the emancipation of the south Slavs of the Monarchy. The Yugoslav idea, which stemmed from the Illyrian Movement of the early nineteenth century, gradually developed from an assertion of the common cultural heritage of the various Slav peoples until it became a cry for political self-government. Within the Monarchy it was expressed in terms of an autonomous Slav unit linked to the Habsburg crown. It was generally conservative in its social aims and constitutional in its methods. The Slavs of the former Turkish lands had been schooled in a sterner tradition. They had developed a revolutionary ethos, and were far more militant and radical than the Slovenes and the Croats. The Monarchy might have held the movement in check within its own borders for at least another generation had it not been for the agitation led by the Serbs. The leaders of Vienna saw this, and came to the conclusion that Serbia must be crushed if the Monarchy was to survive. Similarly, the Serbs sensed that if the schemes of the heir to the throne, Archduke Franz Ferdinand, came to fruition, the Croats and Slovenes might be bought off by the creation of a semi-autonomous south Slav state within the Habsburg framework. On June 28th, 1914, Serbia's national day (Vidovdan), a young Serb, Gavrilo Princip, acting on instructions from one of the many secret societies inspired from Belgrade, assassinated the Archduke in the Bosnian capital, Sarajevo. The war party in Austria saw this as an opportunity to crush Serbia and remove the menace to the Monarchy. With German support they rejected Serbia's moderate reply to their ultimatum, and declared war. Within two weeks the First World War had started. Russia, France, Britain, Belgium, Montenegro, and later Rumania, were drawn in, in alliance with Serbia. Bulgaria and Turkey eventually joined the Central powers. The Serbs were soon overwhelmed, but part of their army, after terrible suffering, escaped via Albania and joined the Allied forces in Salonika. By their heroism the Serbs placed themselves in an unchallengeable position as the leaders of the movement for south Slav unity.

The war did not remove the threat of disintegration from the Monarchy. On the contrary, it brought about its complete collapse, along with that of Germany. The Bolshevik Revolution of 1917 caused a temporary withdrawal of Russian power in Eastern Europe. Thus the way was clear for the creation of a series of new national states all the way from the Baltic to the Adriatic. The national independence for which the peoples of Eastern Europe had so long striven was now within their grasp. We shall see in the next chapter how they faced the new challenge of independence, and how, partly through their own weakness and folly, and partly through the interference of others, they failed to keep their hard-won freedom.

CHAPTER III

EASTERN EUROPE BETWEEN THE WARS

The Versailles Settlement

When the allied leaders met at Versailles in 1919, Eastern Europe was in a state of chaos. The great multi-national Empire of the Habsburgs had already disintegrated, and the scattered fragments had already begun to regroup themselves around the nuclei of a number of new national states. The south Slavs within the Empire joined hands with their brothers in the Kingdoms of Serbia and Montenegro to form the new Kingdom of Serbs, Croats and Slovenes (later known as Yugoslavia). Bohemia, Moravia, Slovakia and part of Ruthenia made up the new state of Czechoslovakia, which Masaryk and Beneš had persuaded the Allies to recognise even before the war was over. An independent Poland was established within undefined frontiers, and laid claim to the former Habsburg province of Galicia. The rest of Poland was created out of the ruins of the other two great European empires which collapsed during the First World War — the German and the Russian. Under the former Socialist leader Piłsudski, Polish armies fought against Bolshevik Russia for the control of parts of White Russia and the Ukraine, against the new state of Lithuania for the Vilna region, and against the Czechs for the Teschen coalfield. Hungary, under its Communist leader Bela Kun, fought both the Rumanians and the Czechs. The Italians occupied part of Albania, and the Greeks fought the Bulgarians in Eastern Thrace. There was no shortage of candidates to fill the power vacuum left by the sudden disappearance from the European scene of the Habsburgs, the Hohenzollerns and the Romanovs.

Although the victorious Allies were officially the arbiters of the peace settlement, they were often powerless to impose their will on the warring nationalities, and frequently accepted the *faits accomplis* which were presented to them, rather than risk involvement in further hostilities. It was not until 1924 that some sort of agreement had been reached on all the outstanding frontier questions, but many of these agreements were never fully accepted by one or other of the parties involved. Often — as in the case of Transylvania and Teschen — both parties remained unsatisfied.

The Frontiers of Poland

One of the first frontiers to be settled by the Peace Conference was that which divided Germany from Poland. This was the subject of clauses in the Treaty of Versailles, which Germany and her conquerors signed in June 1919. Final demarcation was not possible, however, until plebiscites had been held in East Prussia and Upper Silesia to determine the wishes of the inhabitants. The new Poland was given an outlet to the Baltic through the former German province of Posen (Poznan), which was inhabited by a mixed Polish and German population. The old Hanseatic city of Danzig, on the Baltic, was so strongly German in character that it was not felt possible to hand it over to Poland. Instead a Free City under international control was established. The Poles were given a corridor about fifteen miles wide which gave them access to the Baltic between the borders of the Free Territory and Germany. East Prussia remained German, although cut off from the rest of Germany by the Polish Corridor. The coal-mining district of Upper Silesia was partitioned so that whilst Germany retained the larger share, Poland had three-quarters of the coal mines. South of the disputed Silesian coalfield, the Grand Duchy of Teschen, also rich in coal, was a bone of contention between Poland and Czechoslovakia. In this case the Allies dictated a settlement which gave most of the coalfield to the Czechs, but the Poles never accepted this arrangement, and took the whole area for themselves in 1938 when the Czechs were reeling under the impact of the Munich crisis.

On her eastern borders, Poland disputed control of large areas with the Bolsheviks. Lord Curzon, the British Foreign Secretary, proposed a line based on the ethnic boundary between Poles and White Russians which roughly corresponds to the present Russo-Polish frontier. The Poles thought they could do better by force of arms, and invaded White Russia and the Ukraine. The Ukraine was at this time the scene of a nationalist rebellion against the Bolsheviks, and Piłsudski used this revolt to Poland's advantage. In April 1920 he made an agreement with the Ukrainian leader, Petlura, under which the latter agreed to renounce his claims to eastern Galicia in return for Polish help in expelling the Bolsheviks. Piłsudski began to dream of a Polish sphere of influence from the Black Sea to the Baltic, but although he took Kiev and advanced well into the Ukraine, he was finally halted and driven back to the gates of Warsaw. After a further Polish advance, the two sides reached agreement at the Treaty of Riga (1921), which gave Poland a line well to the east of that suggested by Lord Curzon, and incidentally saddled her with nearly five million unwilling White Russian and Ruthenian (Ukrainian) subjects. Not content with this, Piłsudski also seized the Lithuanian city of Vilna. Both extensions of Polish territory were recognised by the Allies in 1923.

The new Poland was the largest of the "succession states" created out of the old empires. She had a population of twenty seven million, of whom about two-thirds were Poles. Apart from the large minorities along the eastern borderlands, there were over a million Germans in western Poland, and nearly three million Jews scattered throughout the country.

The New Nations of Central and South-east Europe

Czechoslovakia had less trouble than Poland in fixing her frontiers, largely because the three parties who might have objected — Hungary, Germany and Austria — lay prostrate before the victors, and had no power to back up their claims. Nearly a quarter of the fourteen million inhabitants of Czechoslovakia were Germans, mostly living in the western frontier region of Sudetenland. Ruthenians and Magyars in Slovakia numbered about three-quarters of a million each. Although forced to accept the new frontiers, their neighbours never forgave the Czechs, and twenty years later, with Hitler's assistance, they recovered the lands which had been taken from them in their hour of defeat.

Austria and Hungary were separated after an association under the Habsburg crown which had lasted for over 400 years. As ex-enemy countries they got short shrift from the peace-makers. Hungary lost all her non-Magyar areas, often by the direct intervention of the Czechs, the Rumanians and the Yugoslavs. The Treaty of Trianon (June 1920) confirmed these territorial losses and established a small Hungarian state, of ten million inhabitants, almost all of whom were Magyars. The only substantial minorities were half a million Germans and 75,000 Slovaks. On the other hand, one and a half million Magyars found themselves under Rumanian rule as a result of the annexation of Transylvania, and both Czechoslovakia and Yugoslavia acquired Magyar minorities of about half a million each.

Rumania fought on the Allied side during the war, and although knocked out in the fighting in 1916, she re-entered in 1918 on the eve of the collapse of the Central Powers. She was therefore able to press her claims against her neighbours, three of whom — Russia, Bulgaria, and Hungary — were in no position to appeal for help to the Allies. Only the newly created states on her borders — Czechoslovakia, Yugoslavia and Poland — were likely to receive any consideration in the event of a conflict between their interests and those of Rumania. Thus she was able to take Bessarabia from Russia, the Bukovina from Austria, southern Dobrudja from Bulgaria, and Transylvania and part of the Banat from Hungary. The Greater Rumania which resulted from these annexations was recognised by the Allies in complete contradiction to their professed belief in the rights of self-determination. The new state had an area equal to that of the British Isles, inhabited by a population of twelve million, of whom one and a half million were Magyar, half a million German, 300,000 Bulgarian and 600,000 Ruthenian. On the other hand, 70,000 Rumanians remained within the frontiers of Yugoslavia.

Yugoslavia, originally known as the Kingdom of Serbs, Croats and Slovenes, was built around the nucleus of independent Serbia, the state whose quarrel with Austria–Hungary had precipitated the war. Serbia had acquired most of Macedonia during the Balkan wars a few years earlier. She now joined with the former south Slav areas of the Habsburg Empire, gaining Slovenia from Austria, Croatia–Slavonia and the Vojvodina from Hungary, and Bosnia–Hercegovina which the Monarchy had annexed in 1908. In addition the little Kingdom of Montenegro voted to join Yugoslavia, and there were minor acquisitions at the expense of Bulgaria. The Allies recognised the Prince Regent, Alexander Karageorgević of Serbia, as King of the new state after his proclamation on December 1st, 1918. There were, however, certain frontier questions which remained to be settled by the Peace Conference. Yugoslav claims against Austria in the Klagenfurt region were settled by a plebiscite, although the Yugoslavs did not accept its results and had to be forced out of some areas which they had occupied. The delimitation of the frontier with Italy gave rise to an even greater difficulty. Italy entered the war as a result of the secret Treaty of London, by which the Allies promised amongst other things to support her claims to large territories in Dalmatia which were at that time ruled by the Habsburgs. The collapse of the Monarchy had not been envisaged in 1915, and when this occurred a new situation arose. In 1918 the Italians were pressing their claims not against a defeated enemy but against a nominal ally. This caused endless embarrassment to the Peace Conference, and a final settlement was only reached in 1924 by direct agreement between Italy and Yugoslavia. The Allies did manage to whittle down some of the Italian claims, but the matter was taken out of their hands by the activities of the adventurer, Gabriele D'Annunzio, who seized Fiume (Rijeka). This port at the head of the Adriatic was to have been a Free City, like Danzig. The Yugoslavs signed the Pact of Rome in 1924 because they knew they could get no better terms at that time, but they never accepted the loss to Italy of Istria, the Julian region and the ports of Fiume and Zara. They eventually succeeded in turning the tables on Italy after the Second World War. Italian ambitions were also directed towards Albania, the tiny Moslem state which lies along the eastern shore of the Strait of Otranto. The existence of Albania as an independent state arose from the desire of the big powers to deny Serbia an outlet to the Adriatic. Since the declaration of her independence in 1913 she has shared the fate of all politically undeveloped and economically weak countries which lie in positions of strategic importance. Her larger neighbours, and even powers geographically remote from her, constantly interfered in her affairs. During the inter-war period her independence was in pawn to Italy, who finally occupied her in 1939 after twenty years of infiltration. In 1919 Italy was given the port of Valona and the nearby island of Saseno in order to ensure Italian domination of the mouth of the Adriatic. From this bridgehead she was able to move in to the rest of the country. The authority of the Albanian State, such as it was, did not extend over more than half of the people of Shqiptar (Albanian) speech. Greece and Yugoslavia each had Albanian minorities of over half a million, whilst Albania had only one million inhabitants.

Bulgaria entered the war in 1916 on the side of the Central powers, wrongly calculating that this would be the winning side. As in the Balkan Wars a few years earlier and in the Second World War, a generation later, the Bulgarians backed the wrong horse, and suffered for their lack of judgment. The Treaty of Neuilly (November 1919) gave the coastal strip of Thrace to the Greeks, thus depriving Bulgaria of an outlet to the Adriatic. The Treaty also gave Allied blessing to the Rumanian seizure of South Dobrudja, and gave to Serbia a couple of strategically important salients in Bulgarian Macedonia. No attempt was made to square these territorial losses with the avowed principle of national self-determination. An older principle than that of Wilson was at work here — that of "the spoils to the victors". The Bulgaria of the Treaty of Neuilly contained only one important minority group, that of the half million Turks. Most of these were peasants whose forebears had settled in the Balkans during the early days of the Turkish advance into Europe. They were in no sense a dissatisfied irredenta, and raised no serious problem for the Bulgarians.[1] The Macedonian problem, however, created trouble for Bulgaria in her relations with Greece and Yugoslavia. All three countries claimed the allegiance of the Macedonians, a Slav-speaking people with historic links at different times with each of them. For a time, during the premiership of the Agrarian radical leader, Stambulisky, the Bulgarians made real efforts to solve this problem. One suggestion which he made, and which was later revived by the Communist Dimitrov in 1947, was for a south Slav Federation linking Yugoslavia and Bulgaria. After the murder of Stambulisky in 1923 nationalist elements came to the top, and Bulgaria became one of the main supporters of the terrorist organisation IMRO. Even after they agreed to the suppression of IMRO in 1934, the unsolved problem of Macedonia continued to bedevil Yugoslav–Bulgarian relations.

Minority Problems

From the above survey of the effects of the peace treaties on Eastern Europe it is clear that the various settlements were the result of compromises under the pressure of a number of conflicting interests. The lofty idealism of Woodrow Wilson's "Fourteen Points" was officially proclaimed by the European Allies, and accepted by Germany, as the basis for the ending of hostilities. The other Central Powers surrendered unconditionally, but the

---

[1] Nevertheless the Bulgarians expelled half of them back to Turkey in 1950, unceremoniously bundling them across the frontier without prior consultation with the Turkish authorities.

principle of self-determination was implied by the Allies as part of their general war aims. Opposing this principle was the desire for revenge, most apparent with the French, but present also in the hearts of all the victors. Another factor which militated against the idealists was the fact that many countries did not wait for the Peace treaties, but seized what they could in the confusion of the debacle of 1918, presenting the peacemakers with *faits accomplis*. Others, like Italy, presented for payment the IOU's which had been given to them during the war under cover of secret treaties. Even without these complications, the task of drawing frontiers which would give the expression to the principles of ethnic justice would have tried the patience of saints. Even if President Wilson aspired to a halo, "Tiger" Clemenceau, Lloyd George and the others were cast in a profaner mould. Where situations arose in which the populations of an area were an inextricable mixture of nationalities — as in Transylvania — they drew the lines in favour of their friends, and salved their consciences by writing into the treaties clauses designed to protect the rights of national minorities. These safeguards remained for the most part pious hopes, to which the governments of Eastern Europe, with the possible exception of Czechoslovakia, scarcely bothered to pay lip service.

There were two minority groups which were, for different reasons, in a special category — the Germans and the Jews. During the long centuries of German infiltration into Eastern Europe sizeable communities of German speaking people had established themselves in Eastern Europe. Only the Sudeten Germans in Bohemia and the Germans of western Poland lived anywhere near the frontiers of the homeland. The Germans of Transylvania, the Bukovina and northern Yugoslavia existed as island colonies within a Magyar, Rumanian or Slav sea. They retained their distinct cultural individuality, but were fully integrated into the commercial life of the communities in which they lived. They only became a danger to their hosts when Hitler began to use them as instruments to further his "Drang nach Osten".

C

The Jews often shared the commercial life of the towns with the Germans, especially in Poland, Hungary and Rumania. No minority clauses in the peace treaties protected their rights. As always their fate seemed to be to provide scapegoats for the economic and social distress of their Christian neighbours. The largest group of Jews in Eastern Europe were the two and three-quarter million who lived in Poland. They formed the professional and trading classes in many of the Polish towns of Galicia and the eastern provinces, the countryside around being farmed by the Ruthenian and White Russian peasants. During the Piłsudski dictatorship they were frequently persecuted although their sufferings were mild compared with the virtual extermination which was to follow during the Nazi occupation.

In Hungary the association of the Jews with Béla Kun's short-lived Communist régime (both Kun and his chief hatchet-man Szamuelly were Jews) did much to exacerbate the already bad relations which existed between them and the Magyars. Large-scale Jewish migration into Hungary began in the eighteenth century, after the Habsburg Emperor Joseph II had removed the restrictions on their movement from Galicia, following the incorporation of that province into the Empire. By 1900 there were over 800,000 Jews in Hungary — that is almost five per cent of the population. After 1918 the Rumanians estimated that there were well over half a million Jews in their country. The Jews of Hungary and Rumania were a vital element in the intellectual, political and commercial life of the community. A distinguished British writer on Hungarian affairs has stated that "Hungary owed to her Jews a considerable proportion of her most boasted achievements in the fields of science and the humanities".[1] This did not stop the Hungarian Government from passing laws restricting the right of Jews to take up certain appointments, and permitting a mild degree of anti-Semitism, although they did not behave as badly towards the Jews as did the Rumanians and Poles. In Czechoslovakia, however, the large Jewish community played a full part in national life without harassment by the authorities.

[1] C. A. Macartney, *Hungary*, p. 192.

Problems of the Inter-war Period

It is clear that the nationalities question alone would have been sufficient to tax all the resources of statesmanship at the command of the new nations of Eastern Europe. Statesmanship, alas, was one of the resources, but not the only one, which was in short supply. There were many other elements essential to the health and strength of nations which were lacking. One of the most important of these was social cohesion and a sense of national purpose, for these nations inherited many of the social problems of the multi-national empires which they replaced. One of the biggest of these was the "peasant problem".

The "Peasant Problem"

All except Czechoslovakia depended for their livelihood primarily on the produce of the land. From the Danube northward to the Baltic the rural scene was dominated by the existence of large estates owned either by titled magnates who were often absentees, by large corporations or by the Roman Catholic Church. The estates were worked by poor, landless peasants whose meagre cash wages were supplemented by payments in kind from the harvests which were gathered for their masters. The atmosphere of feudalism hung heavily over the land even if serfdom had been legally abolished. There were exceptions to this general rule, of course, in the rich farmlands of southern Hungary and the well-ordered countryside of Bohemia. South of the Danube, in the Balkans, small-holdings predominated, but the peasant proprietors were seldom able to enjoy more than the shadow of independent private ownership. They were saddled with debts to moneylenders and crippled by unjust taxes. Population density on the land was far too high in relation to the productivity of the farms, and in the absence of large-scale industry to attract the under-employed rural workers, many sought a solution to their difficulties in emigration across the Atlantic. This particular safety valve was closed by the American Immigration Acts of the 1920's, and the pressure of rural overpopulation built up to dangerous proportions. With this abundance of manpower, there was little incentive for the peasants to adopt more efficient agricultural methods. In most areas modern machinery, fertilisers, high-quality seed, scientifically bred livestock and adequate systems of crop rotation were unknown. Yields of the staple grain crops even on the best land were far below those of Western Europe. For example, the average yield of wheat in Yugoslavia was 11 quintals per hectare, compared with the Danish figure of 36·6. Yet the Yugoslav countryside supported a population of 157 inhabitants to the square kilometre, whilst Denmark had only 29.

The new régimes after the First World War made promises of land reform, and occasionally carried them out. Rumania, Yugoslavia and Czechoslavakia all redistributed land from the big estates to the peasants, but in the first two countries many of the new proprietors were forced to sell back their land to its former owners. The half-hearted attempts at reform in Poland and Hungary still left most of the best farmland in the hands of the big estates. Land redistribution, even if socially desirable, was not in itself an answer to the economic problems of the peasantry. The big estates were more efficient and better managed than the pocket-handkerchief plots of the smallholders, and agricultural production often suffered as a result of the change in ownership.

Before the changes resulting from land reform could be assimilated, the world economic crisis of the late twenties and early thirties undermined the already unstable economies of the East Europeans. Agricultural prices slumped on the world markets, and were slow to recover when the worst of the storm had passed. Industrial prices, however, were more quickly re-established. Nationally this meant that there was no possibility of earning adequate amounts of foreign currency by the export of agricultural produce. Individually it meant that the load of debt and taxation bore even more heavily than before on the peasant farmers, who were now reduced to even more desperate penury.

The political parties which acted in the name of the peasants were never able to formulate programmes which met the needs of their supporters. There were periods when they held power (as in Bulgaria before 1923) or when they shared power with the bourgeois parties, but they were seldom an effective voice for the real grievances of the depressed peasantry. For the most part they contented themselves with chauvinistic slogan shouting, proclaiming the superiority of the simple rural life over the clique-ridden corruption of the towns.[1] The Croat Peasant Party, for example, was far more concerned with the national question of Croatia's role in the new Yugoslavia than with the economic and social emancipation of the Croat farmers. One solution which they usually avoided was the creation of some form of co-operative farming. If state credits could have been provided to assist co-operative ventures in the purchase of machinery and seed, and if an adequate system of agricultural education at all levels could have been established, some progress might have been made towards overcoming the economic evils arising from the division of the land into tiny holdings. All attempts at radical solutions were branded with the hated label of Bolshevism, and Church, State and political parties combined to feed the innate conservatism of the peasants.

In Hungary, Poland and Czechoslovakia some progress towards industrialisation had already been made before 1918. Poland's industrial belt included the Upper Silesian coalfield the Łódź textile region and the Poznan area which had been developed under German control before the post-war frontier changes. Hungary and Czechoslovakia had begun to develop their industries during the period of Habsburg rule. The Czech lands of Bohemia and Moravia included — and still include — the most highly developed areas of manufacturing industry in East and Central Europe. Coal, iron and steel, glass, china, chemicals, furniture and a wide range of light industries were established on the basis of the rich variety of local resources, and before 1914

[1] E.g. Stambulisky on Sofia — "a Sodom and Gomorrah, the total disappearance of which I should see without regret".

benefited greatly by the availability of markets within the Habsburg lands. In Rumania and the Balkans, however, large-scale industrial development was restricted to the extraction of mineral ores for export to Western Europe. Rumanian oil, and Yugoslav copper and lead, were under the control of West European capital, and the exploitation of these resources was of little value to the inhabitants of the country in which they were found. Although efforts were made to establish manufacturing indus-

TABLE 3. ESTIMATED AGRICULTURAL POPULATION OF EASTERN AND CENTRAL EUROPE ABOUT 1930

Country	Est. total pop. (000's)	Males eng. in agric. (000's)	Persons dependent on agric. (000's)	Percentage dependent on agric.
Albania	1003	240	800	80
Turkey	14,700	3383	11,289	78
Yugoslavia	13,934	3219	10,629	76
Bulgaria	5479	1173	4088	75
Rumania	18,057	4064	13,069	72
Lithuania	2367	546	1657	70
Poland	32,107	5636	19,347	60
Finland	3562	635	2015	57
Estonia	1126	204	626	56
Latvia	1900	375	1036	55
Hungary	8688	1552	4472	51
Greece	6205	993	2829	46
Czechoslovakia	14,730	1484	4812	33
Austria	6760	627	1772	26
Total for Eastern and Central Europe	130,618	24,131	78,441	59·5
Total for all Europe (except USSR but with Turkey)	431,201	48,833	147,649	34·2

(This estimate is based upon data from W. E. Moore, *Economic Demography*, published by the League of Nations at Geneva in 1945, pp. 26 and 180–92.)

tries behind protective tariff walls (e.g. the Rumanian textile industry), little was done during the inter-war period to shift the basic economic pattern of Eastern Europe. After twenty years it was still predominantly an area of peasant farming, whose few big industries were controlled by foreign capital. Only Czechoslovakia was able to provide a living for more than half its population outside agriculture.

Politics

The establishment of a number of small nations in place of a few multinational empires was a triumph for the concepts of nineteenth-century liberalism. It was not surprising, therefore, that the new rulers of Eastern Europe, whose political ideas had been formulated in the struggle against legitimist autocracy, should base their new constitutions on the ideas of liberal parliamentary government. The monarchies, like Yugoslavia, Bulgaria and Rumania, were originally conceived as constitutional monarchies. The republics, like Poland and Czechoslovakia, controlled their presidents through the medium of elected parliaments. But professions of liberalism enshrined in constitutional documents cannot of themselves create a climate of democracy. A parliamentary system cannot function in a society at war with itself. When the basic premises of the society are questioned — either on national or social grounds — by powerful sections of the community who are prepared if necessary to use force to forward their claims, government by consent cannot survive. This situation is particularly acute in newly independent nations whose political and economic life has been stultified by the presence of alien rulers. Only Czechoslovakia, with its broadly based social structure, its strong native middle class, and its long tradition of political activity on a national basis, had a chance of survival as a Western democracy. Even here, the backwardness of Slovakia and Ruthenia and the pressures from abroad arising from the presence of national minorities put a severe strain on Czech democracy.

The Revisionists—Hungary and Bulgaria

In Hungary the bitterness of defeat and the shame of Trianon poisoned the political life of the country. An attempt was made by the first post-war government, led by Count Mihály Károlyi, to heal Hungary's wounds. Károlyi hoped to lead his country back into the community of nations by a policy of reconciliation abroad and liberal reform at home. In March 1919, after only a few months in powers, he was swept aside by a Communist-led revolution. Béla Kun, the leader of this revolution, might have survived if he had been less fanatical, for he had at first the support of many sections of the community. He promised Russian help to restore Hungarian control in Transylvania, and his militancy against the Rumanians was welcomed even by right wing elements. He quickly forfeited all support, however. The peasants were alienated by Kun's policy of land nationalisation, and the industrial workers by the reign of terror which his lieutenant Szamuelly conducted with such obvious relish. The nationalists withdrew their support as a result of his military failures against the Rumanians and Czechs. After less than five months in office he fled, first to Vienna and then to Russia,[1] leaving Budapest open to the Rumanian White Guards. After several months of utter chaos a government was found which was acceptable to the Allies. The new leader was Admiral Horthy, the last Commander-in-Chief of the Habsburg navy in the Adriatic. In 1920, an Admiral without a navy, he became the Regent of a Monarchy without a King. The Allies forbade a restoration of the Habsburgs, but there was a strong monarchist party in Hungary many of whom wanted Charles, the last Habsburg Emperor, as their King. (Charles in fact made two attempts to mount the

[1] Kun disappeared in Russia during the Stalin purges of the late 1930's. See account by "Poika" Tuominen in *The Bells of the Kremlin.*

throne in 1921, but the Allies intervened to prevent this.) Horthy's government submitted to the dictated Trianon Treaty in March 1920, but the Hungarian nation in its heart rejected it. For the next twenty years Hungarian political life was dominated by the struggle to tear up the Treaty of Trianon. Because of this obsession, which overshadowed all other questions, Horthy's Hungary never got down to the task of re-moulding the life of the nation to enable it to tackle the new economic and social problems which faced it. Hungarian society remained frozen in the rigid framework of a past age. For the first decade the autocratic Horthy ruled with the help of a group of aristocrats whose social philosophy was as out of date as his own. There was a new and dangerous radical element with which they had to contend, however. The disasters of 1918 and 1919 had effectively destroyed any hope of support for radical movements on the left, but they had also helped to create the conditions for a Right-wing radical movement. This movement drew its strength from the large class of ex-Imperial officers and civil servants whose function in society disappeared with the dissolution of the Habsburg monarchy. Fervently nationalist, bitterly anti-communist, angry at the loss of their former privileges, and in a desperate economic plight, they were perfect recruits for Fascism.[1] Their chance came when the economic blizzard of the 1930's hit Hungary and drove the old-fashioned conservative, Count Bethlen, from office.

Bethlen ruled as Horthy's chief minister for ten years. During this period some limited social progress was made. The currency was stabilised, there was a timid instalment of land reform and new industrial developments were begun. A kind of parliament functioned, and there was a limited amount of political freedom for social democrats, liberals and other opposition groups. Trade Unions were permitted in Budapest and the big industrial centres, although any suggestion of Communism was ruthlessly suppressed. In the countryside, however, the spirit of feudalism survived. The big estates were hardly touched by the land reform, and their

[1] "Fundamentally ruling class anarchists" is the phrase used by Professor Macartney to describe this group.

aristocratic owners, backed by the Church, clamped down on all
expression of liberal reform amongst the peasantry. Bethlen
revived the old system of open voting in the rural electoral
districts, although he allowed the secret ballot in the towns. Thus
Hungary existed in a state of social schizophrenia, with the towns
half in the modern world, and the countryside firmly buried in the
Middle Ages. In 1932 came the first hint of a break with the past.
Horthy summoned a Fascist army officer, Gyula Gömbös to form
a government. Gömbös led Hungary along the first stage of the
journey which ended in the disastrous alliance with Hitlerism.
Like Hitler, Gömbös was a strident nationalist whose chief aim
in foreign policy was to undo the work of the peace conference.
His whole political creed was dominated by the desire to restore
to Hungary the territory which had been taken away by the
Treaty of Trianon, and in this objective he had the full support of
most Hungarians. His method was at first to build an alliance
with Mussolini, but he later came to regard Hitler as a more
effective backer for his policy. Gömbös died in 1936 before his
work had been completed. After a period of uncertainty and
vacillation, Hungary eventually drifted closer to the German orbit
until in 1938 Horthy's Minister President, Imrédy, appointed the
young aristocrat, Csáky, as Foreign Minister. Csáky declared
that his policy was "quite simply, that of the Rome–Berlin Axis
all along the line".

Bulgaria, also a revisionist power, eventually found herself in
the company of Hungary and Germany, although for a few years
after 1918 it did seem possible that she might concentrate her
energies on her internal problems, rather than on quarrels with
her neighbours over the frontier questions. From 1919 until 1923
the ruling party was the Agrarian Union, led by the colourful
Stambulisky. Stambulisky was a strong-minded and blindly
prejudiced demagogue who made no secret of his contempt for
those members of the community who were unfortunate enough
not to be peasants. He made outrageous attacks on the professional classes, calling them "verminous parasites", and found
equally insulting epithets to express his detestation of the inhabi-

tants of Sofia, the commercial and trading classes and even the industrial workers. This wholesale denunciation was backed up by legislation which unashamedly favoured the peasants against the rest of the community. The severity of his repressive measures against his political opponents earned him many enemies, but he was sustained by the fervent support of the peasantry, who constituted over 80 per cent of the population. His measures to reform land ownership and to raise living standards in the countryside were of lasting benefit to his country, and his praise-worthy attempt at a reconciliation with Yugoslavia was sincerely conceived as a contribution to peace in the Balkans. Unfortu-nately for Stambulisky, the nationalists and militarists, secretly aided by King Boris, were able to unite the opposition against his policy of conciliation with Yugoslavia. In 1923 they seized power and had Stambulisky murdered in circumstances of appalling brutality. For the next twenty years political murder was a common occurrence in Bulgaria. In 1925, for example, the Communists attempted to murder King Boris, but only succeeded in killing one of his ministers. During the funeral service for the victim, a bomb exploded in the cathedral, killing over a hundred of the mourners. Eventually the Communist Party, which had up to this time held fifty seats in the Sobranje (Parliament), was outlawed. The military clique who ruled during the next decade subordinated everything to the struggle against the peace settle-ment. Yugoslavia was the chief target of attack, and the terrorist organisation IMRO was given every encouragement in its efforts to stir up trouble in Yugoslav Macedonia. Attempts were made to enlist the help of Mussolini, himself no friend of Yugoslavia, in the furtherance of this policy. At home the weapons of terror and assassination were used to keep down the opposition. Dis-content grew as a result of the economic depression of the early 1930's, and the authorities answered it with even more savage repression. As crisis followed crisis, King Boris gradually emerged from the wings to assume dictatorial powers. Under his guidance Bulgaria moved closer towards the Nazi sphere, until she eventually became involved in war as an ally of Germany.

The Beneficiaries of Versailles—Poland, Yugoslavia, Rumania, Czechoslovakia

Hitler, as the arch revisionist, had an obvious appeal for the Hungarians and Bulgarians because of the losses which they had sustained under the peace treaties. One might expect that France, as the champion of the sanctity of the Versailles settlement, would equally appeal to the remaining countries in Eastern Europe. Poland, Yugoslavia and Czechoslovakia owed their national existence to the support of the Allies, and Rumania had more than doubled its area and population for the same reason. Although there were complaints against some details of the post-war settlement — e.g. in Dalmatia, Istria and Teschen — the broad outlines were very much to their liking. Although they did sign a number of treaties linking them with France, and although Yugoslavia, Rumania and Czechoslovakia came together under French patronage in an alliance known as the Little Entente, only Czechoslovakia followed a consistently anti-revisionist policy. The vacillation and weakness of France in the thirties, the apparent indifference of Britain, and the attractive force of German economic and military power after the rise of Hitler, all helped to undermine the Little Entente. If the Soviet Union could have been brought in to the alliance, it might have stood a chance of withstanding Hitler, but the fear of Bolshevism was far stronger than the fear of Nazism, and only Czechoslovakia was prepared to consider seriously the possibility of a system of collective security which included the U.S.S.R. Rumania became an ally of the Germans on the eve of the Second World War, Yugoslavia's drift towards the Axis was only halted by a revolt of her people, and Poland did not awake to her perilous situation until it was too late.

Poland

Poland's tragedy lay in her geographical situation, which placed her between two potentially powerful and aggressive neighbours. Her resurrection in 1918 was only possible because the powers which had partitioned her a century and a half earlier were temporarily exhausted by war and revolution. She fought for her independence, and eventually had it recognised by international agreement, but she could never feel secure in the enjoyment of her new status as she watched Germany and Russia recover from the after effects of the war.

The man principally responsible for the re-emergence of Poland as a nation was the former socialist, Jozsef Piłsudski, who was Commander-in-Chief of the Polish forces during the independence struggle. After the establishment of peace, Piłsudski retired from public life because he objected to the new constitution which he felt gave too little power to the President and his executive, and too much to the Sejm (Parliament). Like General De Gaulle a generation later, Piłsudski did not cease to wield influence despite his withdrawal from office. When the time of crisis came he was waiting to answer the appeal for a strong man, and he stepped in to assume the dictatorial powers which he had been denied by the earlier constitution. In 1926, after a number of coalition governments had struggled ineffectually with the financial and economic problems of the post-war situation, Piłsudski staged a *coup d'état*. At first he won immense popularity by his economic measures. He stabilised the currency and reversed the flight of capital from Poland which had been undermining the economy during the previous five years. He had a lucky windfall accruing from the British General Strike of 1926. Polish coal exports had been unable up to this time to compete with Britain's, especially in the nearby market of Scandinavia. In 1926 the Poles captured the Scandinavian market and began to challenge Britain elsewhere. The economic improvements of the last half of the twenties enabled Poland to keep living standards from falling despite the rapid increase in population. Between the census of 1921 and that of 1931, the population rose from 27 million to 32 million, despite heavy emigration. The world crisis wiped out the economic gains of the previous years and, as in other East European countries, stimulated movements of protest from the workers and peasants. Piłsudski's reply was to attack what remained of Polish

democracy, and to strengthen his dictatorial powers. Shortly
before his death in 1936 he instituted a new constitution which
built in to the organic law of the state many of the practices by
which he had climbed to absolute power. The régime which
followed that of Piłsudski was known as government of the Col-
onels, because so many of its leading members were army officers.
This government followed an unreal policy based on the assumption that Polish independence could somehow be safeguarded by
the creation of a Polish sphere of influence extending from the
Baltic coast of Lithuania to the Black Sea coast of Rumania.
There was no hope of Poland's achieving this, but the attempt to
do so antagonised potential allies, and helped to drive nails into
the coffin of the Little Entente. It also involved Poland in parallel
actions, if not outright collusion, with Nazi Germany, which in
the long run helped no one but Hitler. Thus in 1936 Poland and
Germany collaborated in the removal of the international government of the Free City of Danzig, an action which made it easy for
the Nazis to take over completely in 1938. When Hitler began the
process of destroying Czechoslovakia, Poland's contribution was
to seize the Czech part of Teschen. The fear of Bolshevism which
Piłsudski and his successors shared with most East European
rulers meant that they would not consider seriously any proposal for associating Russia with the anti-revisionist Powers.
France and Czechoslovakia both signed pacts with Russia
in 1935, the latter providing for Russian assistance to the
Czechs only on condition that France also sent help. Poland
criticised these moves, and for a time drew closer to Germany.
Thus Poland's leaders, oblivious to the danger from Germany,
and imprisoned by their prejudices and unreal ambitions, were
easily lulled into a false sense of security. When they awoke to
the danger it was too late. The nation was morally and materially
unprepared for the attack which Hitler had long planned, and
which finally took place on September 1st, 1939.

Rumania

Despite the appearance of continuity with the pre-war era, the

Rumania of the twenties and thirties was in fact a new country. The enormous increase in territory and population after 1918 altered the political balance in the country, and put an end to the leisurely game of musical chairs which the Liberal and Conservative parties had played to an accompaniment provided by the King. The new King, Carol II, who replaced his pro-German father, Ferdinand, in 1918, found himself dealing with a parliament dominated by Transylvanians, amongst whom a strongly radical tendency was apparent. The government which came to power after the first post-war elections instituted a number of important reforms, but before they had time to carry them to fruition the right wing elements, led by the King, struck back and a reaction set in. In 1920 the King called on General Averescu to form a government. The new government ruled with a firm hand, suppressing opposition, especially that from the left, but it also carried out an important measure of land re-distribution at the expense of the foreign and absentee landlords of the newly acquired territories. As a result of this reform, Rumania became a land of small peasant proprietors.[1] Until 1928 Averescu's national coalition alternated with the Liberals in the enjoyment of royal favour and the sweets of office. Both groups manipulated elections to ensure their majorities when their turn for office came. The Liberals were responsible for the introduction of a new constitution which concentrated power in the hands of the King and the central government at the expense of parliament and the various agencies of local government. In 1928 another element forced its way into prominence — a Peasant movement led by the Transylvanian Iuliu Maniu. The opportunity for this group to win power was created by the death of King Ferdinand. As his son Carol was thought to be unfit to reign because of his scandalous private life, a Regency in the name of Carol's young son, Michael, was established. The Regents allowed free elections, and the Liberal clique was unseated.

Any hope that the Peasant leader could succeed in cleansing

[1] Figures for 1930 show that 60 per cent of the land was held in units of under 10 hectares.

Rumanian political life of the corruption of the previous decade, or that he could begin to lead the country towards a more stable and democratic way of life, was destroyed by the great depression. This theme constantly recurs throughout Eastern Europe. Many of the new nations might have offered their subjects the hope of social progress and national unity if they had not been stricken by the effects of the world depression at a time when they were only just emerging from their infant struggles to establish themselves in the community of nations. Economic collapse bred social discontent. Strikes, street battles, anti-Jewish riots, mass unemployment and poverty all accompanied the chaos of the depression. Governments reacted with severity to any signs of protest, and eventually semi-Fascist dictatorships emerged. In Rumania the disgraced King Carol seized the throne in 1930 and gradually introduced a royal dictatorship. The Liberals returned to office, but became increasingly the puppets of the King and the new class of Rumanian industrialists. A Fascist strong-arm movement, the Iron Guard, led by a rabid anti-Semite called Codreanu, began to agitate for an alliance with Nazi Germany. In 1933 a wave of strikes, in which the future Communist leader Gheorghiu-Dej won his spurs as a working-class leader, was severely put down by the government. For a time Carol and his friends played with the idea of the Little Entente, but at the same time they moved closer to Germany. After the new constitution of 1938 had given the King even more dictatorial power than before the move towards Hitler gathered momentum. Despite obvious similarities of aims and methods, Carol detested the Iron Guard and would brook no competitor for national leadership. He had Codreanu arrested in 1938 and later murdered. The Iron Guard was suppressed, along with all other political organisations, and Carol was left to bear the full burden of guilt for the destruction of Rumanian independence. For the two years which remained to him before he was compelled to abdicate, he made feeble efforts to break out of the prison which his own policy had created, but the keys were now held by Germany, whose economic and political stranglehold on Rumania was inexorably tightening.

Yugoslavia

The Kingdom of Serbs, Croats and Slovenes which the Serbian King proclaimed in December 1918 was in fact an enlarged Serbia. Its Constitution, announced on the Serbian National Day (Vidovdan) 1921, created a centralised monarchy governed from Belgrade, the Serbian capital. Its ruler, Alexander Karageorgević was a descendant of the man who had led the Serbian struggle for independence against the Turks in the early nineteenth century, and his first Prime Minister, Nikola Pašić, was the leader of the Serbian Radicals. The Serbs had their way in the voting in the Constituent Assembly, but their victory was an empty one. Although the constitution of Vidovdan provided for universal manhood suffrage, and for a parliament modelled on the liberal traditions of Western Europe, any hope of peaceful government by consent was undermined by the fact that substantial minorities of the population rejected the basis of the constitution. At first the Croats, the Slovenes and the extreme left boycotted the assembly. After a few months the fifty-eight Communist deputies were unseated after one of their supporters had been implicated in the murder of a minister. Henceforth the Party and its associated trade unions operated underground. Despite police repression and internal bickering, the Communists maintained their organisation and even recruited many of the dissatisfied intellectuals who rejected the squalid political chicanery of the ruling Serbian groups.

The removal of the Communists from the political arena, and the strict control exercised over other working-class organisations, pushed the social question into the background. The issue which dominated the political scene was the demand of the non-Serbs, and especially the Croats, for an equal share in the management of affairs. The Slovenes, skilfully led by Mgr. Korošec, and at some advantage by virtue of their greater level of economic and cultural development, managed to win a *de facto* autonomy for themselves. The much larger Croat minority were less fortunate. They had the disadvantage of being led by an unreliable and narrow-minded man, the Peasant leader, Stjepan Radić. A state of cold war existed between them and the Serbs, which occasionally erupted into violence. In 1924 Pašić outlawed the Croat Peasant Party on the grounds that it was part of a Communist conspiracy.[1] He later changed his tactics and invited Radić to join his government. This apparent reconciliation lasted for only a few months, and by 1925 relations between the two groups were as bad as they had ever been. In 1928 an incident occurred which demonstrated how thin the veneer of parliamentary democracy really was. A government supporter produced a pistol during a debate in the Skupština and shot Radić and five of his deputies. Radić and two of the others died from their wounds. Faced with a complete disintegration of his country, King Alexander assumed the direction of affairs, dismissing the Skupština and the government. He made some effort to bring about a reconciliation between the Serbs and Croats, but without success. The few Croats who joined his new government were disowned by their own people. Many of the Croat leaders fled abroad, including Ante Pavelić, the man who later became dictator of Croatia during the Nazi occupation. One of the first acts of the royalist dictatorship was to rename the country, abolishing the clumsy title by which it had been known since 1918, and substituting the shorter name of Yugoslavia. The old administrative provinces were recast to conform more closely with the historic units into which the south Slav peoples had been divided. In 1931 a new constitution was introduced, which left most power in the hands of the King. Elections to the weak Skupština were by universal suffrage, but as there was no secret ballot the manipulation of the votes by the authorities made a mockery of political freedom. The reality was still a Serbian dominated autocracy. Opposition from the national minorities, or from socially discontented groups, was put down with great severity. In 1931 the leaders of the three main opposition groups, the Croats, the Slovenes and the Moslems, were imprisoned for supporting the Zagreb Manifesto, which called for a return to democratic practices and the granting of freedom to the national minorities. Economic

[1] Radić had visited Moscow during a period of exile the previous year.

troubles consequent upon the world crisis added to the difficulties of the early thirties. Violence bred of despair led to serious
disorders. When men can find no constitutional outlet for the
redress of their grievances, they begin to organise illegal resistance. Already by 1934 Alexander was beginning to realise that
his attempt to compel the Yugoslavs to be one nation under
Serbian leadership had failed. He did not live to try new methods,
for in 1934, whilst on a state visit to France, he was shot by a
Croat terrorist. The murder seems to have been planned by Ante
Pavelić with the connivance of the Hungarian and Italian authorities.[1]

The death of the King did not change much in Yugoslavia,
although it led to a realignment in foreign policy. The Regent
who succeeded him, Prince Paul, made some gestures of reconciliation to the Croats and Slovenes, but these were insufficient
to persuade them to drop their opposition. The various Serb-
dominated governments continued to receive majorities in parliament, largely because the elections were rigged in their favour.

In foreign affairs the new régime began to draw away from the
policy of the Little Entente which had been the cornerstone of
Alexander's foreign policy. As Nazi power in Germany increased,
and German economic penetration made headway, Yugoslavia
was caught in the same current which drew Hungary, Rumania
and Bulgaria into the vortex. Pacts were signed with Italy,
Bulgaria and Hungary, the traditional enemies of the Yugoslavs.[2]
After the Anschluss of 1938, when the Nazis took power in Austria,
Yugoslavia acquired a common frontier with the German Reich.
The proximity of the Germans and their striking success at
Munich hypnotised the Yugoslav leaders.[3] They abandoned all

[1] The Yugoslavs were prevailed upon to name only the Hungarians when
they brought their case to the League of Nations.

[2] That with Bulgaria in 1937 was entitled "Treaty of Perpetual Friendship",
that with Hungary three years later "Pact of lasting Peace and Eternal
Friendship".

[3] An attempt at reconciliation between the Serbs and Croats, the
"*Sporazum*" of 1939 came too late to affect Yugoslavia's will to resist German
encroachments.

caution and began to make gestures of submission to the Nazi giant. In March 1941 they formally signed Yugoslavia's adherence to the Tripartite Pact and promised all help to the Germans in their projected invasion of Greece. The Yugoslav people, however, did not accept the acts of their leaders. A *coup d'état*, supported by popular demonstrations in several of the larger towns, deposed Paul in favour of the eighteen-year-old Peter, and a government of national resistance was formed. The new government had no time to organise for the expected German attack, and when it came on April 6th the army surrendered within a fortnight.

Czechoslovakia

We have seen how the East European nations all eventually succumbed to some form of authoritarian rule. By the 1930's the only democracy which remained was that of Czechoslovakia; for only Czechoslovakia possessed the social basis for a liberal parliamentary regime. It also had a parliamentary tradition which extended back even to the period before independence. Czech political parties had operated within the Habsburg Empire, although the parliament in which they participated was the Austrian Reichsrat, whose powers were subordinate to the Emperor. Nevertheless this experience was of value in providing the new state with a corps of politically experienced leaders. The Constituent Assembly which drew up the new constitution was composed of former Czech representatives in the old Reichsrat of 1911, with the addition of a group of co-opted Slovak delegates. The Assembly produced a republican constitution in which the three main elements were a chamber of deputies and a senate, both elected by universal suffrage, on a basis of proportional representation, and a President who was elected by both houses of parliament, to serve for a term of seven years. Safeguards were written into the document to secure the interests of the large national minorities. All the classic freedoms of liberal democracy were expressly guaranteed — freedom of political associations, freedom of the press and the independence of the judiciary. The first government was composed of M.P.s from the five political parties of the centre and moderate left which had functioned under the Habsburgs. The Communist Party, which originated from a split within the Social Democrats after the general strike of 1920, soon found a place within the ranks of the parliamentary opposition. It was never forced underground, as in the other East European countries, and its existence was never seen as a menace to the established order. As time passed the representatives of the national minorities began to share in the responsibility of government, and the coalitions, which were almost inevitable under the system of proportional representation, were widened to include Germans and Slovaks. After the Locarno Treaties of 1925, which paved the way for the readmission of Germany into the family of nations, the Sudeten Germans seemed to have turned away from their dreams of re-absorption in the Reich and there were hopes that in time they would become reconciled to their place in Czech society. In 1926 an Agrarian and a Christian Socialist from the Sudeten area joined the ministry in Prague led by the Agrarian Antonia Švehla. The problem of the Sudeten Germans at this time arose from the fact that under the Habsburg régime they had occupied a privileged position. It was difficult for them to accept the loss of their former privileges under the new dispensation.

The Slovak problem was of a different order. Under Magyar rule the Slovaks had been a depressed and under-privileged group. Their cultural level was well below that of the Czechs, and their country was economically underdeveloped. They resented the Czech administrators, teachers, lawyers and businessmen who came into their country from the remote capital of Prague. Their grievances arose partly from the circumstances under which the Allies had agreed to the union of the Czech and Slovak lands. During the war the Czech leader, Thomas Masaryk, had held a meeting with Slovak émigrés in America, and at Pittsburgh they had signed a declaration which promised Slovak support for the new state, but affirmed Slovakia's right to her own parliament. This promise was later evaded. Slovak nationalism was led by the Catholic hierarchy and encouraged for obvious reasons by the government of Hungary. Despite these difficulties, the Slovak clerical leader, Mgr. Tiso, was persuaded to join the Švehla government in 1927, and thereafter, until the loss of Czech independence in 1938, Slovaks took part in all subsequent administrations.

The various coalitions which governed Czechoslovakia during the twenty years after 1918 made serious efforts to promote the welfare of their people. They were more fortunate than many of their neighbours in having to deal with a politically mature people whose standard of living, based on a strong industrial foundation, was relatively high. One of the first acts of the new republic was to tackle the problem of the big landed estates, especially in Slovakia. Private land ownership was restricted to the possession of a maximum of 375 acres of arable land, and all holdings above the permitted limit were expropriated by the government, the former owners receiving compensation at pre-war prices. The land so acquired was sold to small-holders, the average size of the new plots being about seven acres of arable land.   Generous government loans were offered not only to private buyers but also to co-operatives. By 1937, four and a half million acres had been distributed in this way, and over a third of the farming population were participating in some form of co-operation. The existence of a class of independent and relatively prosperous farmers contrasted favourably with the position in other East European countries, where the effects of land reform were often nullified by the absence of government financial assistance to prevent the peasants from falling into debt, or even in some cases being compelled to sell their land back to its former owners.

The world depression hit Czechoslovakia along with all her neighbours, but its economy was better able to meet the challenge. Nevertheless, unemployment soared from under 90,000 in 1929 to over 900,000 in 1932. One of the areas most seriously affected was the Sudetenland, ironically because of the economic policies of the Germans. As a land-locked country, Czechoslovakia had to depend for its export outlets on the goodwill of her neighbours, and one of its chief access roads to the outside world lay along the Elbe valley to Hamburg. German tariffs against Czech textiles hit the Sudetenland particularly, and Hitler's abrogation of the Versailles clauses guaranteeing transit rights for Czech goods through Hamburg aimed a heavy blow at the whole of Czech industry. However, due to a severe currency devaluation in 1934, Czechoslovakia was able to hold her own in world markets, and her engineering products, glass, ceramics, textiles and chemicals found markets not only in the less industrialised lands of Eastern Europe, but also in France, Britain and even U.S.A.

Czechoslovakia and the "Little Entente"

Because of her geographical position and because of the circumstances of her creation, Czechoslovakia had a strong vested interest in the maintenance of the *status quo* as established by the Versailles Treaties. In her quest for security she looked first to the East and then to the West. In the East she saw the rising power of the Soviet Union, and although her leaders were not Communists, they had no pathological fear of Bolshevism. Their own Communist Party played the parliamentary game without seriously disturbing the stability and comfort of the middle-class society, and they never feared it sufficiently to want to ban it. In the past, Pan-Slav sympathies had influenced the Czech nationalist movement. In the period before independence, this tendency, had been strongly voiced by the Young Czech leader, Karel Kramař. The change of government in Russia weakened but did not wholly destroy pro-Russian feelings based on Pan-Slavism. Thomas Masaryk and Edward Beneš represented the pro-Western element, whose hopes were centred not on their immediate neighbour to the West, Germany, but on France, Britain and America. As Czech independence came as a result of the victory of the Western Allies it was natural that the pro-Western tendency should be in the ascendant in the period between the wars. Masaryk was President until his retirement in 1935. Beneš, who succeeded Masaryk as President, was the guiding spirit in the conduct of foreign policy throughout the period.

It is not surprising, therefore, that Beneš should have taken the initiative in forming the alliance of anti-revisionist powers known as the Little Entente, or that he should later have attempted to strengthen that body by drawing in both France and the Soviet Union. One of the first steps towards the formation of the Entente was a Treaty, signed in 1920, between Czechoslovakia and Yugoslavia. This was directed against "an unprovoked attack by Hungary", and came after an unsuccessful attempt to restore the Habsburgs to the Hungarian throne. The possibility of a union between Germany and Austria (the "Anschluss', which had been forbidden by the Versailles Treaty) was also feared by the Czechs. In 1921 Rumania, also suspicious of Hungary, aligned herself with the Yugoslavs and Czechs. In 1924 Beneš signed a treaty with France, and France later signed treaties with both Yugoslavia and Rumania. In 1933 the three members of the Little Entente signed a Pact of Organisation which it was hoped would turn the loose system of alliances into a closely knit international community. France was not directly concerned in this, but by her various treaty obligations was associated with all three of its members. In fact the Little Entente never became an international community, and when put to the test it crumbled.

The Little Entente was one of the creations for which Beneš was primarily responsible. Elsewhere his influence was felt in the work of the League of Nations, of which he was a devoted supporter. He was active in the moves which led to the Locarno Treaties of 1925. These attempted to lay the ghost of German revisionism which was haunting the capitals of Eastern Europe. He also worked for the admission of Germany to the League, which came in 1926, and after that for the admission of the U.S.S.R. which was achieved in 1934, shortly after Hitler had taken Germany out.

After Hitler's accession to power in 1933, Beneš saw much that he had striven for and much that he had helped to achieve in the establishment of a stable order in Eastern Europe wilfully destroyed. The history of Czechoslovakia after 1933 is really the history of her relations with Germany, for this issue over-shadowed all others. Hitlerism was one of the seeds which were sown by the men of Versailles. It required the world economic depression to bring the poisoned growth to its full maturity. Czecho-slovakia as a child of Versailles, was an obvious target for Nazi attack. The opportunity to strike came as a result of the econo-mic distress of the Sudeten Germans. Hitler, the great oppor-tunist, made the most of it.

The Munich Crisis

Although some Sudetans had apparently become reconciled to their place in the Czech republic, most refused to be integrated into the life of an alien Slav community. The fires of pan-German nationalism re-awoke when Hitler stirred the embers which the economic misery of the depression had caused to smoulder. A uniformed Nazi party, the *Sudetendeutsche Partei*, armed and equipped from across the frontier, made its appearance. In the elections of 1935 nearly two-thirds of the Germans voted for it. Beneš sensed the danger, and immediately began talks with both France and Russia. As a result, Czechoslovakia was promised military help by both, but the guarantee of Russian help was conditional upon that of France being put into effect. It was also dependent on either Rumanian or Polish goodwill in permitting the passage of troops, as Russia had no common frontier with Czechoslovakia at that time. Beneš summed up the position in a speech to the Czech parliament in November 1935:

> . . . our state is the key to the whole post-war structure of Central Europe. If it is touched either internally or internationally, the whole fabric of Central Europe is menaced, and the peace of Europe seriously infringed. It would not be long before all Europe would be grievously conscious of the fact.

It would appear that at this time there was at least one nation which was not conscious of the truth of Beneš's assertions. This was Great Britain. When the Sudeten Germans raised their demands, on orders from Hitler, and began to foment a crisis in order to give Germany an excuse for intervention, the British Government sent a mission, headed by Lord Runciman, to mediate between the Czech Government and the Sudeten leader, Henlein. Runciman and the British government under Neville Chamberlain accepted the reasonableness of the German case for incorporating into the Reich all those areas in which there was a German-speaking majority. The British appeasers in their belated conversion to the principle of self-determination — although without consultation with the people concerned — ignored the nature of Hitler's régime, and the plain fact that the Sudeten Germans were being used as instruments for the total destruction of Czechoslovakia. In May, two months before Runciman went to mediate, Hitler had issued a directive to his generals which read, "It is my unalterable decision to smash Czechoslovakia by military action in the near future. It is the business of the political leadership to await or bring about the suitable moment from a political or military point of view."

Aided by Mr. Chamberlain's gullibility, or perhaps by his fear of war, the situation turned to Germany's advantage in the autumn of 1938. After a bellicose speech by Hitler at Nuremberg on September 12th, Chamberlain flew to Berchtesgaden to see the Führer. He received the German demands and returned home to secure their acceptance by the French and the Czechs. Having received the required assurances he duly reported back to Hitler at Godesberg, only to discover that the German leader was now insisting that as well as the claim which he had pressed on behalf of the Sudeten Germans, he now wanted to see the satisfaction of the Polish claim to Teschen and the Hungarian claims in Slovakia. Meanwhile a reaction had set in against the concessions already promised. Litvinov, the Soviet Foreign Minister, was urging France to honour her obligations to the Czechs, and promising Russian support for a collective stand against the Germans. Rumania appeared willing to allow Soviet troops to cross her territory. Well into September the Czechs were still being assured by the French that the treaty obligations which they had entered into would be honoured. On September 27th, Mr. Chamberlain sent a personal message to Hitler telling him that he could "get all essentials without war and without delay". This is in fact what happened. Mussolini took the initiative in calling a conference at Munich which was attended by Chamberlain, Hitler and the French Premier, Daladier. The Czech delegates shared a hotel with the British, but were not called into the conference. They were conveniently on hand, however, to be told by Mr. Chamberlain of the settlement which had been reached. The Czechs felt that they had been "condemned without a hearing" by their so-called friends. Chamberlain and Daladier returned home to be acclaimed by cheering crowds as the saviours of peace.

In Prague a great cry of anguish went up from the heartbroken Czechs. Thousands wept openly in the streets, not only for the loss of territory, but also because the mutilation of their country had been engineered by those in whom they had put their trust. German troops soon moved in to the Sudetenland, re-uniting three million Germans with their brothers in the Reich, and incidentally taking over territory occupied by 800,000 Czechs. Poland delivered an ultimatum and immediately took the part of Teschen which she had claimed. Only the Hungarians had to wait a few months before they obtained part of what they wanted in Slovakia.

The Munich settlement was the beginning of a process of disintegration which was completed by March of the next year. The Czechs, stunned by what they regarded as the betrayal of Munich, made no effort to resist. During the few months left between Munich and the full occupation of the country they had turned in their bitterness to pro-German leaders. Beneš and many of his associates left the country and formed a government in exile. His successor in the Presidency, the aged Dr. Hacha, "placed the destiny of the Czech people and country with confidence under the protection of the German Reich". Who can blame him? No one else seemed able or willing to stand up for the independence of Czechoslovakia. It is doubtful if even Mr.

Chamberlain believed in the guarantee which he had given to the Czechs after Munich — backed up by a loan of £10 million as a consolation prize for the loss of national honour. At Munich, France had already shown herself incapable of standing by her obligations. Hardly anyone noticed that she repeated the performance when German troops marched into Prague six months later.

During the short interregnum between the occupation of Prague and the outbreak of war, Hitler secured another forward position in Eastern Europe. Memel was taken from Lithuania and added to East Prussia. Not to be outdone by his German friend, Mussolini drove the Italian puppet, King Zog, from Albania on Easter Day, 1939, and formally annexed what had in fact been an Italian colony for at least a decade. The other little nations of Eastern Europe were as demoralised as the Czechs by what had happened. Many of their leaders had already shown a willingness to put their heads into the tiger's mouth, especially if their judgment was affected by the obsession with revisionism as was the case with the Hungarians and Bulgarians. The Little Entente was incapable of achieving anything without the backing of an outside power — either France or Russia, or preferably both. The abdication of responsibility by the French and the apparent lack of interest of the British, combined with the general desire to keep Russia at arm's length, prevented the formation of a united front against Nazism. Hitler played skilfully on the jealousies and rivalries of the little powers, picking them off one by one as circumstances suited him. In this he was greatly helped by the policies of his economic experts, Schacht and Funk, who organised the successful German economic penetration of Eastern Europe.

A fitting summary to this period was given by Winston Churchill, when he said of the nations who fell into the German orbit:

> Each one hopes that if he feeds the crocodile enough, the crocodile will eat him last. All of them hope that the storm will pass before their turn comes to be devoured.[1]

[1] B.B.C. Broadcast, January 20th, 1940.

CHAPTER IV

EASTERN EUROPE DURING THE SECOND WORLD WAR

THE war which began in September 1939 was in some respects merely a continuation of the great European civil war which had erupted in 1914. There was a brief lull during the 1920's but after Hitler's rise to power in Germany hostilities were resumed. At first, diplomatic and economic weapons were used more often than armed force, but increasingly after 1935 military power was used to support the other techniques. The recurrent crises which marked the stages of Germany's expansion into Eastern Europe were manifestations of tensions which lay much deeper than the immediate problem presented by the temporary dictatorship of the Nazi opportunists. One key to the situation arises from a consideration of Germany's industrial needs.

Before 1871 the development of German industry had been retarded by the absence of a single administrative and political unit for the whole of Germany. When full nationhood was achieved, Germany was too late to be able to take a major part in the race for overseas colonies. Britain, her chief rival, had solved her major internal problems much earlier, and, assisted by her domestic stability, she had taken the lead both in industrialisation and in colonisation. German industry expanded rapidly after 1871. Her neighbour, France, although still powerful, was considerably weakened by the losses she sustained as a result of her defeat in the Franco-Prussian war. On the continent of Europe, France was no match for Germany in the struggle for

Fig. 4. Frontiers before and after the Second World War.

industrial supremacy. French influence in Eastern Europe could easily be undermined by a forceful German expansion. As an area producing food and raw materials, Eastern Europe offered Germany some of the advantages which Britain obtained from her overseas Empire. As long as Russia was preoccupied with her internal problems and at a primitive stage of industrial development, the field was open for German expansion eastwards. Germany suffered a temporary setback as a consequence of her defeat in 1918, but when she recovered the attack was resumed. France made feeble efforts to organise a constellation of small East European nations to resist the pressure, but she was too weak from the losses she incurred during the war, and her will was sapped by her own internal divisions. Her ally, Britain, also appeared to lack either the power or the will to stop the German advance.

Another important factor which worked to Germany's advantage was the morbid fear of Bolshevism which overshadowed European politics during the inter-war period. The Western democracies were intensely suspicious of Soviet intentions, and refused to take seriously Russian offers to join in collective security against the Nazis. The little nations of Eastern Europe were even more suspicious and afraid of Russia, and were also blinded by nationalist passions which prevented them from combining to preserve their independence.

We have seen in the last chapter how the democracies attempted to avoid war with Germany by acquiescing in Hitler's demands. They hoped that by showing themselves to be "reasonable" they would eventually appease Germany's appetite for expansion. In fact, they only whetted it. When at last they decided to make a stand the victim happened to be Poland, but it might well have been Czechoslovakia or Austria. Had they taken a stand earlier, they might have prevented the catastrophe, but in 1939 there seemed to be no alternative to war as a means of stopping Germany from achieving the domination of the whole of Europe.

On the eve of the invasion of Poland Stalin decided that he must make a bargain with Hitler in order to delay the attack on

Russia which the Führer clearly intended. Hitler also welcomed the opportunity for a breathing space. Germany has always dreaded a war on two fronts. If the invasion of Poland should finally stir the Western Powers to action Hitler intended to deal with them first before embarking upon the task of liquidating the Russian menace. His plans almost succeeded. By 1941 Germany controlled the whole of Europe from the Channel coast to the Soviet border, and from the Mediterranean and the Black Sea to the Baltic. Only Britain continued to resist, despite the apparent hopelessness of her situation. In June 1941 the Wehrmacht advanced into the Ukraine, thus bringing the Soviet Union into the anti-Nazi coalition.

We must now turn to examine the fate of the East European nations who were the victims of Germany's initial advance.

Czechoslovakia

Czechoslovakia had, of course, fallen victim to Nazi aggression before the outbreak of the war. The part played by France and Britain in the tragedy stunned and embittered the Czechs, many of whom felt that they had no alternative but to accept German domination. The Czech lands of Bohemia and Moravia became a German protectorate in March 1939, the Sudeten areas having already been incorporated in the Reich after the Munich Agreement of 1938. Although the Germans at first permitted a Czech Government within the Protectorate, this was merely an administrative device. The real aim of German policy was to destroy the Czechs as a nation, deporting or exterminating that part of the population which resisted Germanisation. The first group to feel the full fury of Nazi brutality were the intellectuals. In November 1939 all the Czech Universities and Colleges were closed, the students and teachers arrested *en masse*, and many tortured and executed. In 1941, the able sadist, Reinhard

Heydrich, was appointed to assist the Sudeten-German Gestapo leader, Hermann Frank, in pursuing a policy which aimed at the elimination of the Czechs as a nation. The reign of terror which Heydrich instituted did not end when he was assassinated in June 1942, after less than a year in office. In fact, one of the consequences of the killing was the massacre of all the male inhabitants of the Czech village of Lidice, and the mad attempt to erase the name of that settlement from the memory of man. Most countries in occupied Europe remember similar victims of the insane savagery of the Nazis, but the tragedy of Lidice caught the imagination of the world, perhaps because of the publicity which the Germans themselves gave to their crime. Until 1943 the resistance of the Czechs showed itself chiefly in isolated acts of sabotage or in the peculiarly Czech brand of dumb insolence and passive resistance which Hasek has immortalised in his stories of *The Good Soldier Švejk*. After the victory of the Red Army at Stalingrad the tide began to turn against the Germans, and hope of liberation became more than a far-off dream. Czechoslovak resistance began to grow, and the leadership of the movement sometimes fell to Communists. Meanwhile, in London, the Government in exile, led by President Beneš, gained full recognition by all the allies. Britain repudiated the Munich Agreement and pledged herself to work for the restoration of the pre-1938 frontiers of Czechoslovakia. Beneš signed a twenty-year Treaty of Friendship with the Soviet Union in 1943, and recognised that Czechoslovakia must in future rely heavily on the support of her eastern neighbour. In Moscow Gottwald and the Communists assisted in the recruitment of a Czechoslovak brigade which fought with the Red Army on the Eastern Front.[1] Early in 1944 Czechoslovak troops under General Svoboda entered Ruthenia, and began to move into Slovakia in company with their Soviet allies. By the end of the year most of Slovakia had been cleared of German troops, and in April 1945 Beneš and his ministers flew to Košice to join the Communists under Gottwald.

[1] There were, of course, Czechoslovak units in the armies of the Western Allies.

D

Together, they formulated the programme which the provisional government would implement on its return to Prague. This event did not occur until a week after the formal surrender of the German Army, as the local commander in Prague continued to fight on against the Czech Partisans in the capital until the arrival of the Red Army. Some controversy has been occasioned since that time by the action of the Anglo-American forces who were already in Bohemia, and could have advanced on Prague. Under the terms of the agreements between the Western Allies and the Soviet Union they stayed put until the Red Army was in a position to take the city. Thus Beneš arrived in his capital in the wake of Soviet tanks.

The situation in Slovakia was very different from that in the western Czech lands. As in Yugoslavia, the Germans pursued a policy of divide and rule, cleverly playing on the national differences between the different elements in the state. After the dismemberment of Czechoslovakia in 1939 an independent Slovakia was created. Hungary was allowed to occupy some of the southern Slovak districts, where there was a large Magyar-speaking population, and Ruthenia where the population was of Ukrainian origin. What remained of eastern Czechoslovakia was treated as a sovereign state.

Slovakia did in fact enjoy a greater degree of political and economic autonomy than almost any other of the puppet régimes in Nazi-occupied Europe. Monsignor Josef Tiso, the leader of the Catholic Slovak Peoples Party, seemed to enjoy special favour in the eyes of the Führer. As long as this enabled him to preserve the illusion of independence Tiso received the support of the majority of Slovaks for his one-party corporate state. At least until the end of 1943 Slovakia felt the misery and deprivation of the war less even than the Germans themselves. The Bratislava régime did not begin to crumble until the arrival of the Soviet and Czech forces on the borders of Ruthenia at the end of 1943. A Slovak Partisan Movement emerged in which Communists took an active part, and the Germans were eventually compelled to occupy the country in order to ensure their military position.

Tiso was finally swept from power during the winter of 1944 by the advance of the Red Army.

Poland

After Czechoslovakia, the next victim was Poland. The destruction of Czech independence was as much to the liking of the Polish government as it was to Hitler's. At the height of the Munich crisis they had marched into the Czech part of the partitioned Grand Duchy of Teschen, the ownership of which had been a bone of contention between the two countries since the end of the First World War. Colonel Beck, the Polish Foreign Minister, continued to dream of a Greater Poland whose influence would dominate the area between the Black Sea and the Baltic, oblivious to the fact that Hitler had other plans for his country. When the invasion of Poland began on September 1st, 1939, the Poles were unable to offer any effective resistance. Although she had been promised support by Britain and France — both of whom became involved in war with Germany as a result of the attack — her allies could do nothing to prevent her collapse. After less than two weeks of fighting, Warsaw was in German hands, and shortly afterwards, in accordance with the secret protocols of the Nazi–Soviet Pact, the Red Army moved into eastern Poland. A division of Polish territory was made, similar to that of the Second Partition of 1793. Western Poland was incorporated into the Reich, the lands east of the Bug were absorbed into the adjoining Soviet Republics of the Ukraine and Bielo-Russia, and the area in between, including Warsaw, Krakow, Lublin and Częstochowa, became a German colony under the title of the General Government of Poland. Many Poles and most Jews in the territories annexed to Germany were expelled to the area of the General Government, their places being taken by Germans. Field-Marshal Göring summed up the Nazi policy towards the incorporated area in the following terms:

> The reconstruction and expansion of their economy and the safeguarding
> of their production and supplies must be pushed forward with a view to
> complete absorption as soon as possible in the German economic system.

In contrast to this, in the General Government everything save
what was "absolutely essential for the maintenance at a low level
of the bare existence of the inhabitants must be transferred to
Germany". The General Government became a vast concentration camp in which millions of Poles and Jews were exterminated
during the five long years of Nazi occupation. In the one camp
at Oswięcim (Auschwitz) in the province of Katowice at least
three million Jews were murdered, according to the statement of
its German Commandant. Whilst awaiting "the final solution"
the Jews were herded into ghettoes in the larger cities, and
periodic raids were made on them when the Nazi commanders
required a fresh quota of victims. Occasionally, at the whim of
the occupiers, a trainload of Jews would be sent on a journey in
cattle trucks without food or water, being shunted aimlessly
around the country until all the passengers had died. In 1940
over 400,000 Jews were walled up in the Warsaw ghetto, the
number being gradually reduced by systematic deportation until
by the end of 1942 less than 100,000 remained. This last remnant
of Polish Jewry decided to make a hopeless stand against their
oppressors in the spring of 1943, and for over a month they held
out until only a handful survived. A few escaped to join the
Polish Underground Movement. Once in possession of the ghetto,
the Germans dynamited the remaining buildings and reduced the
whole area to rubble. The non-Jewish population of Poland,
although not perhaps treated with such appalling savagery,
nevertheless suffered terribly. Many were starved, beaten,
deported to forced labour camps, tortured and put to death in
gas-chambers. The educated classes were the main target of attack,
for as the Governor-General, Hans Frank, wrote in his diary:
"everything revealing itself as a Polish power of leadership must
be destroyed again and again with ruthless energy".

In the Soviet occupied area more than half the population were
not Poles, but Ruthenians and White Russians. Some Poles

were deported from the area and reappeared later in the war when they were released from Soviet internment camps to join the Polish forces then being formed on Russian soil. The nature of the Soviet administration in the former Polish territories and the condition of the people during the twenty months from the arrival of the Red Army in 1939 to the German attack on Russia in 1941 are matters about which the outside world still knows little. It would appear that active steps were taken in 1939 to register the formal incorporation of the territories into the appropriate Soviet republics. A "Western Ukrainian" and a "Western Byelorussian" assembly appeared in October 1939, and each voted for admission into the Soviet Union. Resolutions were passed by both assemblies calling for the nationalisation of banks and industries and the confiscation of big estates belonging to Polish landowners and to the Churches. Political and national opposition to Soviet rule was suppressed, and there were an unknown number of deportations. There was, however, nothing remotely comparable to the insane policy of genocide which was practised in the German occupied areas. The whole area fell into German hands after the invasion of Russia in June 1941 and was reoccupied by the Red Army in 1944.

When Polish resistance collapsed in 1939 the government fled to Rumania, later moving via France to settle in London. The first Premier of the exiled government was a famous soldier, General Władysław Sikorski. Its ministers were drawn from the non-Communist opposition parties who had opposed the totalitarian régimes of Piłsudski and Beck — the socialists, peasants, reformist Catholics and middle-class radicals. Its policy was to prosecute the war against both Soviet and Nazi occupying forces, refusing to accept the frontier changes which had been made in 1939. It dissociated itself from the old régime, and put forward a general political line which was liberal and democratic in the western sense, accepting the need for land reform, the management of industry in the interests of the people, and the restoration of the traditional political freedoms which had been trampled on by the Piłsudski régime. It also accepted the rights of the

Ruthenian and the Ukrainian minorities to national self-determination, and expressed a desire for reconciliation with the Jews. It did not attempt to draw up detailed programmes for the future, but contented itself with general statements which left many problems unsolved.

The London Government maintained close contact with its supporters in the homeland, and attempted to organise an underground Polish State with its own courts, civil administration and even its own army, known to the West as the Home Army (*Armija Krajowa*). By 1944 this army, under Generals Rowecki and Bór-Komarowski had enlisted 380,000 men, and had earned for itself a high reputation amongst the resistance forces in occupied Europe.

Meanwhile another resistance movement had grown up under Soviet guidance. Its nucleus had been formed of survivors from the Stalin purge of the Polish Communist Party who had moved into the Soviet occupied areas in 1939. The situation was completely transformed by the German invasion of Russia in 1941. Pockets of Soviet resistance remained behind the German lines and were joined by Polish partisans. After the battle of Stalingrad, when the tide of war turned against the Germans, Red Army paratroops were dropped in front of its advancing forces to strengthen the newly formed "Peoples' Army" in Eastern Poland. There were also Polish units with the Red Army whose existence had been made possible by an agreement signed in London in 1941 between Sikorski and the Soviet ambassador, Ivan Maisky.[1] Just as the Home Army accepted the political authority of the London Poles, so the Poles in Russia and Eastern Poland came under the orders of a rival government in embryo led by Communists. This body eventually became known as the Lublin Committee, after the merger of the National Council of the Homeland and the Moscow-based Union of Polish Patriots.

In January 1944 the first units of the Red Army crossed the

[1] Many Poles released from imprisonment in Russia as a result of this agreement chose to join General Anders in the Middle East, but others remained to fight under General Berling in association with the Red Army.

pre-war frontier of Poland, and very soon the question arose as to which of the two rival provisional governments would rule in liberated Poland. The issue was settled in favour of the Lublin Committee by the power of the Soviet Union. The Western allies could only register a vain protest, for in international power politics, possession is nine points of the law, and the Red Army was in possession of Poland by the end of 1944. The only body which might have disputed its authority was eliminated in the autumn of that year, when the Home Army was massacred by the Germans during the Warsaw rising.

During 1943 relations between the London Poles and the Soviet government had been broken off in an atmosphere of bitter recrimination, following the allegations that the Red Army had massacred captured Polish officers in the Katyn Forest. The allegations had first been made by the Germans, and the London Poles had accepted that there was a case for the Soviet Union to answer, as they knew that hundreds of Polish officers captured in 1939 had disappeared in Russia. Any hope that Sikorski's successor, the radical peasant leader Mikolajczyk, could effect a genuine reconciliation were shattered by the events of August 1944. In late July the Red Army reached the east bank of the Vistula at the Warsaw suburb of Praga, and even established a small bridgehead across the river near the capital. It seemed as if they were poised to make the final assault on the city within a few days, a supposition which was strengthened by the broadcasts from Moscow radio calling on the Poles to rise. "The hour of liberation is at hand. Poles, to arms! There is not a moment to lose." On August 1st the Home Army began the battle for Warsaw, but the Red Army did not move. Despite the entreaties of Mikolajczyk, and the request of the British to permit the use of Russian airfields by R.A.F. planes which were ready to drop supplies for the Poles, the Red Army commanders insisted that they were unable to help the Home Army. The Soviet Government accused the Poles of failing to consult them about their plans, and argued that until they had time to bring up more supplies and prepare for a further advance, an offensive on

Warsaw would be militarily impossible. For sixty-four days the Home Army fought on in the ruined streets of Warsaw. 200,000 Poles died in vain before the Home Army was crushed by the Germans. With the death of the Home Army went the hopes of the London Poles. In January 1945 the Red Army occupied the snow-covered heap of rubble which had once been Warsaw, and installed there the Lublin Committee as the Provisional Government of Poland. Whatever explanations may be given for the macabre episode of the Warsaw rising, there can be no doubt about its consequences; it removed from the scene the only important non-Communist resistance movement in Eastern Europe, and ensured that the future government of Poland would be one made in the image of its Soviet patrons.

Yugoslavia

At a ceremony in Vienna on March 25th, 1941, the Yugoslav Premier, Cvetković, and his Foreign Minister, Cincar-Marković, put their signatures to the Tripartite Pact, and acknowledged that their country would henceforward share in the construction of the "New Order" in Europe under German leadership. As Hungary, Rumania and Bulgaria were already members of the pact, Ribbentrop could boast that "practically the whole of the formerly neutral Balkans now find themselves in the camp of the New Order". The only Balkan nation outside the Axis orbit was Greece, which was at that time defending herself with British help against an Italian invasion from Albania. Hitler was anxious that the Greeks should be defeated before substantial British aid could reach them, and that Yugoslavia should also be brought under the *Pax Germanica* with as little delay as possible. He could not risk an Allied advance into the Balkans as this would endanger his lines of communication through the Danube valley, a danger which must be scotched before he gave the order to invade Russia. He preferred to gain the support of the Yugoslavs by diplomatic means if possible, and was willing to make some empty concessions in order to win them over. He promised to respect the integrity of Yugoslavia, and to allow her to take the port of Salonika when he had crushed the Greeks. He had no difficulty in persuading the Yugoslav Government to accept these terms, but the Yugoslav people were less amenable than their leaders. When the ministers returned to Belgrade after signing the pact, they found that the city was in a state of uproar. A wave of protest swept the country when the terms of the agreement became known. A bloodless *coup d'état* led by the head of the air force, General Simović, led to the abdication of the Regent, Prince Paul, and the arrest of his chief ministers. The young King Peter assumed the royal prerogatives and summoned Simović to form a government of national unity. Dr. Maček, the Croat leader, agreed to serve as Vice-Premier, and representatives of the other nationalities also entered the new cabinet.

This action by the Yugoslavs was interpreted by Hitler as a slap in the face which he could not ignore. It was the first major diplomatic setback which he had suffered since Mussolini in 1934 had forced him to delay the operation of his plan for the annexation of Austria. If he could not make the Yugoslavs see reason, he must crush them by force. On April 6th German troops operating from Bulgaria invaded both Yugoslavia and northern Greece. Belgrade, which had been declared an "open city", was heavily bombed. A few days later Hungarian troops marched into the Vojvodina, and Italians invaded Slovenia and Dalmatia. King Peter and his government fled to Egypt, and later set up their headquarters in London. In less than two weeks organised Yugoslav resistance had collapsed, although some guerilla bands continued to fight on in the woods and hills. The Germans and their allies then shared out the territory which they had occupied. Serbia was placed under German military control, but the civil administration was entrusted to General Nedić, the former Minister of War in the Cvetković Government. Nedić accepted the role of a puppet, and agreed to "assist the German troops to relinquish the tasks which are the concern of the Serbs themselves" and to "co-operate in reconstruction". Serbia was reduced to an area approximately the same as it had been in the nineteenth century. The Vojvodina was awarded to Hungary, Macedonia was taken by Bulgaria, and the Kosovo-Metohia region was attached to Mussolini's Albanian colony. Montenegro and Dalmatia were also placed under Italian occupation, and Slovenia was divided between Italy and Germany. The area which remained, Croatia and Bosnia, was organised into the "Independent State of Croatia" and was placed in the care of the Croat terrorist, Ante Pavelić.[1]

Pavelić ruled with the help of a Fascist militia known as the Ustaši. The atrocities committed by these thugs against Serbs, Jews and even fellow Croats bear comparison with those of the Gestapo in their savage inhumanity. Many of the inhabitants of the Croat State were members of the Serbian Orthodox Church, and in Bosnia there was a large Moslem community. Pavelić was a Roman Catholic, and had the support of many leading figures in the hierarchy. A particularly distasteful feature of his régime was the forcible conversion of Serbs to the Roman Church. The conviction that the Ustaši were performing God's work in persecuting the Serbs no doubt enabled them to overcome any scruples which they may have had regarding the limits to which men may go in the commission of bestial acts against their brothers. Ironically, the Ustaši were less brutal to the Moslems than they were towards their separated brethren of the Orthodox Church.

Thus, the Yugoslav State which had existed for little more than twenty years was torn asunder by foreign invaders. It was not the first time that the south Slav nation had been dismembered and occupied, but this last crucifixion was perhaps more terrible in its effects than any which preceded it. In less than four years nearly two million Yugoslavs died, and the greatest tragedy of all was that half of these were killed by brother Yugoslavs. All the pent-up hatreds of the Serb–Croat struggle which had been simmering during the previous generation burst forth to produce

[1] The Italian Duke of Spoleto took the title King Tomislav II of Croatia, but he never once visited his new kingdom.

acts of appalling ferocity. The social and political antagonisms which the old régime had failed to reconcile led to deep divisions even in the ranks of the resistance movement. Two groups emerged, one pledged to the maintenance of the old order, the other determined to make national liberation the first stage in a social revolution which would sweep away all traces of the old régime. The former group, led by a regular officer in the Royal Army, Colonel Draža Mihailović, was at first recognised by the Allies as the official resistance movement. The London Government of King Peter made Mihailović its Minister of War and regarded his "Četniks" as part of the King's Army. It later appeared that many of the successes which the London Government claimed for these forces were in fact the work of another group, the Communist-led Partisans. By 1943 it was generally accepted that the Četniks were less effective than the Partisans as an anti-Nazi force, and the Allied Powers withdrew recognition from Mihailović. There is evidence that the Četniks actually collaborated with the Germans and Italians against the Partisans. For example, in 1943 one of the Četnik commanders went to Rome to discuss with the Italians the plans for a major offensive against the "Communist bandits". Mihailović often organised "parallel actions" to coincide with German and Italian attacks on the Partisans, and he also worked with Nedić, the Serbian quisling, on plans for a common front against the Communists. These facts became known to the Allies after the military mission, led by Brigadier Maclean and Randolph Churchill, had reported on their meetings with Tito. In May 1944 Winston Churchill explained to the House of Commons why he had decided to back Tito against Mihailović.

"The reason why we have ceased to supply Mihailović with arms and support is a simple one. He has not been fighting the enemy, and, moreover, some of his subordinates have made accommodations with the enemy, from which have emerged armed conflicts with the forces of Marshal Tito. . . . We have proclaimed ourselves strong supporters of Marshal Tito because of his heroic and massive struggle against the German armies."

In 1941 Tito and Mihailović were both operating in the Šumadija region, an area of wooded hills in central Serbia. The two leaders were unable to agree on the terms by which they could co-operate, their differences being both military and political. At his trial in 1946 Mihailović excused his inaction on the grounds that sporadic attacks on isolated German units had little military value, but provoked terrible reprisals against the civil population. He claimed that it was better to play a waiting game until the resistance movement was strong enough to strike a decisive blow. One can perhaps understand his hesitations when one realises how savage were the German reprisals. For example, near Kragujevac in October 1941 the Partisans killed twenty-six German soldiers. The town was required to produce 2600 male hostages — a hundred Serbs for every dead German. When all the adult males had been rounded up there were still too few prisoners. The deficit was made up from the upper forms of the local schools. The hostages were then marched to a hill above the town where they were sprayed with machine gun bullets and then run over by tanks.

Atrocities of this kind occurred regularly throughout the war, and it is not surprising that Mihailović was unnerved by them. However, in total war, he who hesitates is lost. Mihailović may have started by holding his hand because of his fear of reprisals, but he soon moved to military action against the Partisans which involved him in co-operation first with Nedić and then with the Italians and Germans. Once he had embarked on "parallel actions" he was well down the slippery slope which led to outright collaboration.

The Partisan leader, Josip Broz, alias Comrade Walter, alias Tito, has been described by Winston Churchill as "an outstanding leader, glorious in the fight for freedom". He was a Croatian engineer who enlisted in the Austrian army during the First World War and was taken prisoner on the Russian front. During the Russian Revolution he was released from prison, and on his return home he joined the Yugoslav Communist Party. The Party was banned in 1921 but Tito continued to serve it illegally.

In 1937 he became the Party secretary and during the next four years he concentrated on the task of building up a highly disciplined and influential organisation whose contacts extended into all ranks of Yugoslav society. Until his assumption of leadership the Communist movement had been rent by internal dissension, but after 1937 Tito quickly restored the unity of the party. His colleagues included many intellectuals from all parts of the country — for example, the Montenegrin, Djilas, the Slovene, Kardelj and the Jew, Pijade — as well as trade unionists, peasants and even a millionaire's son. During the wartime struggle he drew to his banner many who were not Communists, but who saw in the Partisans the only effective force against Fascism. They were, moreover, the only important element which stood for equality between the different national groups within Yugoslavia. Again, to quote Winston Churchill:

> Around and within these heroic forces, a national and unifying movement has developed. The Communist element had the honour of being the beginners, but, as the movement increased in strength and numbers, a modifying and unifying process has taken place and national conceptions have supervened.[1]

Although Tito would accept into the ranks of his Partisans any Yugoslav, regardless of his opinions, who was prepared to fight the enemy, he never lost sight of the political objectives of his movement. To the Communists, national liberation would have little meaning if it were not also the prelude to social revolution. They were determined that a new Yugoslavia should emerge from the struggle, owing nothing to the old Serbian dominated kingdom of pre-war days. Wherever they found themselves in control of liberated territory they introduced Peoples' Committees, and began to educate the civilian population in the ABC of Communism. The Partisan units were training schools for the future leaders of the party and the country, political and military training going hand-in-hand. In all this work they received scant support from the Soviet Union, although they never ceased to

[1] Parliamentary Debates, *Hansard*, Vol. 397, pp. 692–4.

acknowledge their debt to Lenin and Stalin as the interpreters of Marxism.

Their immediate political objectives were set out in a manifesto which was published in 1942. Shortly afterwards they set up an embryo provisional government, the Anti-Fascist Council for National Liberation, whose figurehead was a respected pre-war liberal politician, Dr. Ivan Ribar. For most of the next year they were too hard pressed to proceed much further with their political plans, for the Germans launched an offensive against them which threatened their very existence. With great skill Tito extricated his men from the jaws of a pincer movement, and despite heavy losses brought them from Montenegro, where they had been driven by the weight of the German attack, back into Bosnia. The epic battle of this period was the forcing of the Sutjeska river in June 1943. The Italian collapse later in that year transformed the military situation, and by November most of Bosnia was in Partisan hands. On November 30th at Jajce the anti-Fascist Council formally announced the creation of a Provisional Government for the whole country. They gave notice to the Allies that they, and not the Royal Government in London, would direct the future course of events in Yugoslavia.

The Allied advance up the Italian peninsula gave an opportunity for direct contact with the Partisans across the Adriatic.[1] and the links which had been established by the military mission of Brigadier Maclean were strengthened by a direct meeting between Tito and Churchill. As a result of this meeting, Tito agreed to broaden his government to include representatives of the King, but he insisted that Peter himself should not be allowed to return until the will of the people was known.

Thus with Allied backing, and with his own undisputed mastery of the anti-Fascist forces in Yugoslavia, nothing could stop Tito from assuming the leadership of his country when the war ended.

---

[1] The Italian collapse also gave a great impetus to the Albanian Partisan movement under the leadership of a Communist ex-schoolmaster Enver Hoxha. Tito made contact with Hoxha and Albanian and Yugoslav Paritsans worked together in a number of operations.

In October 1944 the Red Army entered Belgrade in company with Bulgarian forces which it had recruited during its advance along the Danube. The Soviet soldiers did not bring with them any exiled Yugoslav Communists to place in the seats of power in Belgrade. No Yugoslav Rákosi was necessary. The Partisans were in control of most of the country, and their Communist leaders had fought and suffered with them throughout the war. The fact that Tito owed nothing to the Soviet Union helps to explain the greater independence of the Yugoslav Party when compared with those of Hungary, Rumania and the other Peoples' Democracies. It also explains why hardly any prominent party members sided with Russia and the Cominform in 1948 when an attempt was made by Stalin to discipline the Yugoslav Party.

Hungary

Of the three remaining countries, Bulgaria and Hungary were revisionist powers, who had great hopes that an alliance with the arch revisionist, Hitler, would enable them to regain the territories which they lost at Versailles. Hungary's policy during the period of Hitler's rise has been summed up by C. A. Macartney as a balancing act designed to enable her to "pluck for herself the fruits which Germany's growing power brought within her reach, while escaping the dangers".[1] Although it had some temporary successes, this policy eventually led to the loss of Hungarian independence. Obsession with the evils of the Trianon Treaty and fear of the "Red Menace" blinded the Hungarian leaders to the obvious fact that if the little nations of Eastern Europe did not hang together, they would certainly hang separately. When the Nazis tore Czechoslovakia asunder, Hungary was rewarded for her sympathy and understanding by the grant of parts of Slovakia and Ruthenia to which she had laid claim. In April 1941, when Yugoslav independence was destroyed, German troops were allowed to pass through Hungary, and as soon as Yugoslav resistance seemed at an end the Horthy Govern-

[1] C. A. Macartney, *Hungary: A Short History*, pp. 226–7.

ment announced that as Yugoslavia no longer existed, the "Pact of Eternal Friendship" between the two countries was a dead letter.[1] He therefore authorised the annexation of Vojvodina and Prekomurje, two areas of Yugoslavia which had a Magyar-speaking population. In June 1941 Hungary agreed to send a token force to join the German army in Russia, but still did not regard herself as fully committed to belligerency. The policy of the Regent, Admiral Horthy, was to continue the balancing act for as long as possible, in the hope that Hungary might emerge unscathed from the war. For almost three years Hungary did retain some control over her internal affairs, one of the most notable results of which was to delay the extermination of the large Hungarian Jewish community. This illusory independence was abruptly ended by Hitler in March 1944, and most of the Hungarian Jews joined their Polish brothers in the gas chambers of Auschwitz.[2] A last desperate bid by Horthy to make a separate peace led to his replacement by the paranoiac leader of the Fascist Arrow Cross movement, Ferencz Szálósi, and the Hungarians fought on throughout the bitter winter of 1944–5 in a desperate last stand against the remorseless advance of the Red Army. By the beginning of 1945 everything which "Trianon" Hungary had stood for had been swept into the dustbin of history. A Communist-led Provisional Government followed in the wake of the Red Army. Many of its members were Jewish. One of its first acts was to renounce all the territory which Hungary had acquired as a result of her association with the Nazis. The constitutional apparatus of the old régime was dismantled, and in its place a "Peoples' Democracy" began to grow in the image of the Soviet Union. Horthy's balancing act, which he had conducted with great agility, came to a sudden end when the Red Army cut the tightrope.

[1] "Eternity" in this case lasted for four months. The pact was signed in December 1940.

[2] Even so, Horthy did prevent the deportation of some Jews from Budapest during his last months in office, although whether the man who supplied some of the fuel which started the fire should be commended for plucking a few brands from the burning is a matter of opinion.

Bulgaria

Like the Hungarians, the Bulgarians also hoped to extract as much territory as possible from their neighbours without becoming too closely involved in the war. In this they had more success than the Hungarians. As a revisionist power (their badge of shame was the Treaty of Neuilly) they had a natural affinity for the Germans, reinforced by the predilections of their German King, Boris, and his Italian wife. Under the personal dictatorship of Boris, Bulgaria had entered into close economic and political ties with the dictatorships during the 1930's. Its army was trained and equipped by Germany, and by 1939 two-thirds of its foreign trade was with the Reich. With Hitler's assistance, Rumania was forced to hand over southern Dobrudja in 1940. In 1941 Bulgaria formally acceded to the Tripartite (Axis) Pact and allowed German troops to pass through the country en route for Greece and Yugoslavia. Bulgarian troops moved into Yugoslav Macedonia and the Aegean coastlands of northern Greece, reviving memories of the "Big Bulgaria" which had emerged from the Treaty of San Stefano in 1875. Although deeply committed to the Axis cause, and virtually under German occupation, Bulgaria did not declare war on Russia. Pan-Slav sentiment was strong and the government no doubt feared that an open attack on Russia would be unpopular. Because of her geographical position Bulgaria was outside the main theatre of military operations, and as a consequence suffered far less from the war than any of her Balkan neighbours. Her role was to assist the Germans in the policing of the occupied territories of Greece and Yugoslavia, and to maintain a watching brief on the Turkish frontier. In return for these services Boris was allowed a limited freedom of action at home. The Soviet Minister in Sofia remained at his post throughout the war, and was not seriously hampered in his efforts to maintain contact with anti-German elements. Even the Jews suffered less in Bulgaria than in any of the other countries of Eastern Europe. Most of those who were rounded up and handed over to the Nazi extermination squads came from the Bulgarian occupied parts of Greece and Yugoslavia. The native Bulgarian Jews were treated with comparative moderation.

During 1942 the first moves were made to gather together the anti-Fascist forces into an organisation known as the Fatherland Front. Georgi Dimitrov, the veteran Comintern leader, who remained in Moscow until the end of the war, directed this movement from afar. Within the country the Communists collaborated with the left wing Agrarians, led by Nikola Petkov[1] and a left wing intellectual group known as "Zveno" (the link). After the mysterious death of King Boris in August 1943 a Regency Council was set up to govern in the name of the infant King Simeon. Thereafter the activities of the Fatherland Front increased, and there was even some indication of a Bulgarian Partisan movement. The advance of the Red Army into Rumania during the summer of 1944 stimulated the activities of the resistance movement, and also threw the Regents into a panic. When Soviet troops appeared on the Danubian frontier they hastily formed a pro-Western coalition government and attempted to make a separate peace. This did not prevent the Soviet Union from declaring war and marching into the country. On September 9th the Fatherland Front seized power and welcomed the Soviet troops as allies. The new government arranged for Bulgarian troops to assist the Yugoslav Partisans and the Red Army in driving the Germans out of Yugoslavia. After the fall of Belgrade in October 1944 they went on to fight through Hungary and to participate in the liberation of Vienna. Bulgarian losses[2] in these campaigns were heavier than any which had been sustained during the previous three years of the German alliance. They were nevertheless small in comparison with the sufferings of other East European countries. Bulgaria had experienced a comparatively easy war, and emerged materially almost unscathed. Nevertheless, their flirtation with the Axis had cost the leaders of

---

[1] Petkov was executed in 1947 as a result of his opposition to the Communist-led Fatherland Front.

[2] About 30,000 killed.

the old régime all their privileges and powers. Their obsession with the real or imagined wrongs of the past had led them into a ruinous alliance with Nazi Germany which produced a few temporary territorial gains, as a poor consolation for the eventual loss of everything for which they stood.

Rumania

Bulgaria's northern neighbour, Rumania, was not a revisionist power. She had good reason to be satisfied by the Versailles settlement. During the inter-war period she had been one of the members of the Little Entente, and even after war broke out she clung to her links with Britain and France. She soon realised that these links would be of little help to her in withstanding the combined pressure of Germany and Russia. Her geographical position across the southern approach road to the Russian steppes, and her important oil reserves, were the two main attractions which she had in both Soviet and German eyes. In the summer of 1940 she had a sharp reminder of the precariousness of her position. This was the period of the Nazi–Soviet alliance, and one of its fruits was annexation to the U.S.S.R., with German consent, of the Rumanian provinces of Bessarabia and northern Bukovina. Later in the same year King Carol was forced to agree to the occupation of southern Dobrudja by Bulgaria and a large part of Transylvania by Hungary. The Vienna Award (or Diktat) by which Hitler effected these territorial changes produced an upheaval in Rumania which led to the overthrow of King Carol. Paradoxically this did not result in a move away from Germany. Michael, Carol's young son, who came to the throne, found himself with a pro-Axis premier, General Antonescu, supported by the Fascist Iron Guard movement. Antonescu, who took the title of "Conducator" (Führer), invited German troops into his country, joined the Tripartite (Axis) Pact, and enthusiastically introduced anti-Semitic legislation on the model of the Nazi Nuremberg Laws. After the German invasion of Russia,

Rumania became fully involved in the war, her troops taking part in the fighting all along the Black Sea coast from Odessa to Rostov. They were mainly responsible for the conquest of the Crimea and took a prominent part in the advance towards Stalingrad. In all this fighting they suffered terrible losses — probably as many as half a million dead. In addition, the country was ruthlessly exploited economically, providing oil and grain for the Germans at ridiculously low prices. All that she could show for this sacrifice was the annexation of a part of the Ukraine, including the port of Odessa, to offset the loss of Transylvania and the Dobrudja.

Internally the régime of Antonescu maintained some shadow of independence from the Germans, as was shown by his decision in 1941 to disband the Iron Guard. This movement, which drew its support from the gangster elements which are present in all societies, had become an embarrassment because of its senseless brutalities towards sections of the population which displeased it. Although Antonescu had relied on the support of the Iron Guard, he was really a representative of the old school militarists and he was able to enlist the support of the regular army in the job of suppressing the Fascist thugs. A curious feature of the Conducator's régime after the suppression of the Iron Guard was its apparent toleration towards representatives of the pre-war political parties. Men like Iuliu Maniu, the veteran Peasant leader, Petru Groza, the Left-wing leader of the Ploughman's Front, and prominent Liberals, continued to engage in political activities. Communists like Gheorghiu-Dej remained outlaws, of course, for Antonescu, like Carol, was obsessed with fear of Bolshevism. As the strain of war began to tell on the Rumanian people, efforts were made to organise an effective resistance movement which would break the German connection and make a separate peace. Maniu was approached by the Communists to lead such a movement, but he hesitated until finally the King took the initiative. In August 1944 he ordered the arrest of Antonescu, announced the withdrawal of Rumania from the war, and set up a coalition government in which both Maniu and the Communists participated. The Germans bombed Bucharest and attempted to set up a "Free Rumanian Government" under the Iron Guard. The Rumanian army joined the Red Army in driving out the Germans from their territory, then proceeded to expel the Hungarians from Transylvania. To their losses of half a million on the Russian front they now added a further 150,000 dead in fighting the Germans and their old enemies the Hungarians. This eleventh-hour change of front, in which the King played an important role, may explain why Michael was the last King to reign in Eastern Europe, surviving for more than two years after the war as the titular head of a people's democracy. Of course, he no longer had any real power after his country had been occupied by the Red Army. All the important decisions about the future of Rumania were made by the Soviet patrons of the new ministers.

In the end the result for Rumania was the same as that which we have already described in Hungary and Bulgaria. The old rulers were swept aside.

CHAPTER V

EASTERN EUROPE TODAY

The Aims of the Communists

The events of the Second World War shattered the old social and political framework of Eastern Europe. There was no possibility of a return to pre-war conditions. Nevertheless, the form which the new social order was to assume throughout the area was determined less by the conscious will of the peoples concerned than by the over-riding security needs of the Soviet Union. In most countries Communism had shallow roots amongst the people. Only in Yugoslavia and Albania was there a significant Communist-led movement. In all the other countries the Communist leaders were brought in almost literally in the baggage train of the Red Army, as it swept westward in pursuit of the retreating Germans. Men like Rákosi, Bierut and Dimitrov had been working in the U.S.S.R. for most of the previous two decades, and were better known outside their homelands than within them. They accepted Stalin's thesis that the defence of the Soviet Union was the first duty of the good Communist, and their primary loyalty was to the Soviet Communist Party. The facts of geography and history and the realities of world power politics ensured that the dominant influence in the lives of the East European nations would henceforth flow from the east. To the Soviet Union the main importance of Eastern Europe was as a bulwark against the possibility of future German expansion. In view of the history of the previous forty years the Soviet view was understandable, for twice in the twentieth century Russia had felt the fury of the German drive to the east. Both during and since the Stalin era, the Soviets have shown that their principal pre-occupation in dealing with their neighbours was that of security rather than of ideology. It is against this background that we should examine the policies which were initiated by the new leaders when they came to power during the final stages of the war.

The first task of the Communists was to secure control of the machinery of government, and to exclude from office the representatives of the non-Communist parties. In the immediate post-war period the Communists, despite the support of the Red Army, were not strong enough to accomplish this task in one move. There were also powerful international reasons to justify a "step by step" approach. International agreements, to which Britain and America as well as U.S.S.R. were parties, required the

> holding of free and unfettered elections as soon as possible on the basis of universal suffrage and secret ballot in which all democratic and anti-Nazi parties shall have the right to take part and to put forward candidates.[1]

The appalling devastation of European Russia and Eastern Europe required an immediate programme of relief and rehabilitation, and the chief source of aid came from the U.S.A. All the countries of Eastern Europe as well as the Soviet Union were in receipt of this aid in the years immediately following the end of the war, and this no doubt exercised a restraining influence. For tactical reasons, therefore, the Communists were prepared to accept coalition governments in which leading non-Communists held high office, and to hold elections in which candidates from the old pre-war parties were permitted to stand against the representatives of the Communist Party. In some cases they even permitted the kings to remain for a time on their thrones. Rumania, Bulgaria, and Yugoslavia had been monarchies before the war. Under pressure from the Allies, Tito's provisional government merged with that of King Peter, but the King never returned

---

[1] This quotation from article IX of the Potsdam Declarations refers specifically to Poland, but similar statements were made concerning other East European countries.

to Yugoslavia, and the monarchy was abolished at the end of 1945. King Simeon of Bulgaria was deposed in 1946, but King Michael remained on the throne of Rumania until 1947. The first elections which were held after the war conformed in most cases to the general line of the Allied directive concerning freedom of political life. In most countries the Communists and their associates did not receive a majority of the votes. This resulted in the formation of coalition governments. In Poland, for example, Communists held the posts of Public Security, Industry, Communications, and National Defence. One of the two Deputy Premiers was Gomulka, whose duties also involved responsibility for the administration of the territories reclaimed from Germany. The Peasant leader, Mikolajczyk, who was the other Deputy Premier, also held the portfolio of Agriculture. Other posts were given to Socialists, and to members of the Democratic and Peasant Parties. The levers of power were in the hands of the Communists, however, and the others were included merely to give an air of respectability.

Professor Seton-Watson has classified into three categories the stages by which the Communists took over power. There was at first a stage of genuine coalition involving a number of parties whose range of support extended from the centre to the far left of the political spectrum. In the second phase, the coalitions remained in being in name only. The non-Communist parties were subordinated to the policies of the Communists, and their more independent-minded representatives were excluded from public life. The technique of isolating the leadership and winning over the rank and file was pushed to the point at which it became possible to merge the party organisations into one Communist-led front — the Polish United Workers Party, for example, or the Bulgarian Fatherland Front. Mátyás Rákosi, the "Muscovite" leader of the Hungarian Communists, used the phrase "salami tactics" to describe these manoeuvres.

During the evolution towards monolithic, one-party rule, the theoreticians of the Marxist–Leninist movement began to define the basis of the new form of government, to which the name

"Peoples' Democracy" was given. Marx and Lenin had foreseen that the first stage in the establishment of a new society would be that of a dictatorship of the proletariat, or more correctly of the Communist Party acting in the name of the proletariat. In the Soviet revolution, no attempt was made to operate behind a façade of parliamentary forms, with the nominal existence of other political parties who shared office with the Communists. The new form of Peoples' Democracy was described in the Soviet Encyclopaedia of 1954 in the following terms.

> The experience of history has shown that the system of Peoples' Democracy successfully fulfils the aims of the dictatorship of the proletariat, even when there exist several parties and social and political organisations, on the one indisputable condition that the only leading and directing force of all political life is the Communist party, which does not and cannot share leadership with anyone.

Throughout Eastern Europe this situation had become explicit long before 1954, the process being quicker to develop in some countries than in others — for example, East Germany started its post-war political life in the second stage of bogus coalition, whilst Czechoslovakia was ruled by a genuine coalition, based on free elections, until the crisis of February 1948.

The process was occasionally given an overt push forward by the intervention of the Soviet Union, especially in the ex-enemy states of Hungary, Rumania and Bulgaria, where Soviet occupation forces played an important part in the politics of the immediate post-war period. Thus, in February 1947 the Soviet military police arrested Béla Kovács, the Hungarian Peasant leader, because he had shown too great an independence. In Rumania, the direct intervention of Vyshinski forced King Michael in 1945 to appoint the Soviet client, Groza, as Premier in place of the less pliant Redescu. Even where Soviet intervention was less obvious, there is no doubt that the forms of government which the East European states acquired after the war were determined by the fact that the Red Army had entered the country and imported with it the idea of Peoples' Democracy. This is not to suggest that the peoples of Eastern Europe would have wanted a return to the old régime, or that the Communists and their allies were not genuinely popular in some areas. In Czechoslovakia, for example, the free elections of 1946 gave the Communists 38 per cent of the total vote, making them the largest single group in the Parliament. In Yugoslavia the leadership by Communists of a genuine movement of national resistance, the Partisans, gave them a position of great strength and enabled them to move further and faster than any other East European country in the direction of a one-party state. The Yugoslav and Albanian revolutions owed little to direct Soviet influence, but in the other countries the presence of the Red Army was decisive. In the 1930's the Polish Communist Party had been wilfully, and as was admitted in 1956, wrongly, liquidated by Stalin, no doubt because its existence would have been inconvenient to the authors of the Nazi–Soviet Pact. The Hungarian and Rumanian Communist leaders were virtually unknown to their compatriots in 1944. Some, like Rákosi, had been away from their countries for so long that they had even become Soviet citizens, and they were nicknamed "Muscovites".

The certainty that Eastern Europe would fall under Soviet hegemony after the war was tacitly admitted by the Western leaders at Yalta. Only a political innocent could imagine that the Soviet Union would throw away the chance to push her sphere of influence westward to the Elbe, in order to place a *cordon sanitaire* between herself and the consequences of a future revival of German expansionist ambitions. Eastern Germany was under direct Soviet military control, and Hungary, Poland and Rumania continued to have Soviet troops on their soil long after the military situation demanded it. In addition, Soviet economic penetration ensured that the economies of the countries were made to serve the needs of Russia. In Rumania, for example, the oil industry was run by "Sovrom" companies, in which the Soviet Union had a controlling interest. As Khrushchev admitted in 1956, the Polish economy was milked to the tune of 500 million U.S. dollars between 1946–1953 by the forced delivery of coal to Russia at prices well below the world level. It was in furtherance of this policy of Sovietisation that pressure was put on Yugoslavia in an attempt to subordinate her army and her economy to the needs of the Soviet Union. Tito's resistance to this pressure precipitated the expulsion of the Yugoslav Communist Party from the Cominform in 1948.

Although there exists in some countries of Eastern Europe the shadow of former political parties, the essence of the political life of a People's Democracy is the paramount role of the Communist Party "which does not and cannot share the leadership with anyone". As Rákosi put it, Peoples' Democracy is "the dictatorship of the proletariat without the Soviet form". The stages by which the Communist Party acquired complete control varied from country to country, but by the end of the nineteen-forties the pattern was clearly established. Thus, article 86 of the Rumanian Constitution of 1948 states that "the Rumanian Workers Party is the directing force of all workers organisations, as well as of the state organs and institutions". The Polish Constitution of 1952, and the Hungarian of 1949, were consciously modelled on the Stalin Constitution of 1936, and although they did not specifically mention the overriding power of the party, they used phrases like "mass social organisations of the working people" and forbade the setting up of associations "whose aims or activities are directed against the political or social system". These were interpreted in such a way as to ensure the domination of political life by the Communist Party. After the dissolution of the bourgeois parties, the emasculation of the Peasant parties and the creation of "Front" organisations under Communist leadership, the next stage was to bring under Communist control the parties which still claimed the allegiance of some industrial workers. The Social Democrats merged with the Communists in a number of countries to form such bodies as the East German "Socialist Unity Party", the Polish "United Workers Party" and the Hungarian "Workers Party".

Thus, political life in the sense in which it is understood in the parliamentary democracies of Western Europe did not exist. There never had been anything resembling liberal democracy in

most of Eastern Europe during the inter-war period. Czechoslovakia was the notable exception which proves the rule. East
Germany shared for a time in the doomed Weimar Republic,
and several of the other states concealed the realities of their
authoritarianism behind the fig leaves of constitutional correct-
ness. The concepts of loyal opposition, unfettered voting and
freedom of political association were almost completely absent,
however. After the war there was a brief period of political
activity before the monolithic rule of the party was established.
Since the death of Stalin there has been a relaxation in some
countries. In Poland, elections were held in 1957 in which 722
candidates stood for the 459 seats in the Sejm. As Gomulka had
said, "The election law must enable people to elect and not
merely to vote." The new Polish parliament included sixty-three
deputies who belonged to no party, as well as the representatives
of the three government parties — the United Workers, the
United Peasants and the Democratic Party. Of course, there was
no question of a return of candidates fundamentally opposed to
the new social order, but there was a recognition that the limits of
free expression had been too rigidly drawn during the Stalinist
period. A striking illustration of the tenacity of the old political
parties in Hungary was demonstrated during the Nagy revolution,
when literally overnight the Smallholders, National Peasants and
Social Democrats resumed their political activities. Since Soviet
intervention restored the power of the Communists these parties
have again been submerged. Despite these exceptions, support
for parties whose philosophy is opposed to that of the Communists is regarded as treason. This is not to say that some form
of political activity does not go on within the framework of the
Communist and allied parties.

Economic Policies

Thus, under the guidance and leadership of the Soviet Union
the Peoples' Democracies embarked upon their programmes for

economic and social transformation. The tasks which faced them were the industrialisation and modernisation of the predominantly peasant economies, whose already low level of productivity had been further reduced by their appalling sufferings and losses of the war years. UNRRA aid provided a stop-gap to enable organised life of some kind to begin again. The next stage was the inauguration of economic plans which would implement the Communists' dreams. The problem was to create as quickly as possible the foundations of an industrial economy, and to draw from the countryside the surplus labour which under the old agricultural system had been only half-employed on the inefficiently run farms. The first requirement was a heavy rate of investment in the basic industries — fuel and power, steel and heavy engineering, mining and transport.

After years of privation due to the war, the people now had to face the enforced saving for the future which a programme of major capital investment required. Even a nation in which political literacy had reached a high level would find it hard to carry out such a programme in these circumstances by methods of consent. The Communists believed that the job could only be done by strengthening the power of the state and arming it with the weapons of enforcement which would enable it to override the demands of the people for consumer goods and their desire for a respite from austerity. In the Soviet Union the job was done in the 1920's and 30's at a terrible cost in terms of human life and happiness. Some would argue that the cost was too great, and that gentler methods would have been more efficient in the long run. Eastern Europe between 1945 and 1953 experienced nothing like the liquidation of the *kulaks* or the Stalin purges of the 1930's. This may be explained by the fact that, unlike the pre-war Soviet Union, they were not alone and surrounded on all sides by enemies. Nevertheless, although played in a lower key, the themes echoed those of the Soviet Union. The Soviet model was slavishly copied. Stalin's *Shorter History of the CPSU(B)* was obligatory reading amongst the party members. The author recalls conversations with Yugoslavia at the time of the 1948 Party Congress when, despite the quarrel with Russia, problems were still being discussed within the context of the Stalinist blueprint. By 1949 centralised state plans had been adopted for all the countries except Eastern Germany. These ranged from the Rumanian one-year plan of 1949 to the Yugoslav five-year plan (1947–52). In the second stage, the planning period was in all cases for five or six years, at the end of which it was assumed that the foundations of heavy industry would have been firmly laid. In all cases the techniques of planning were based on the centralisation of all power in the hands of the government and party. This was the phase of the dictatorship of the proletariat. There is no doubt that some increases in production were achieved under the various plans, but one begins to look more critically at the claims which were made at the time when one reads the comments of Gomulka in 1956 concerning the Polish situation.

> Generally speaking, after the conclusion of the Six Year Plan which according to its promises was to raise high the standard of living of the working class, we are now faced with immense economic difficulties, which grow from day to day.

The Polish United Workers Party, at its Seventh Plenary Session in July 1956, expressed a view which is probably true in outline of other East European countries.

> In the course of the implementation of the Six Year Plan, an excessive centralisation of the planning and administration of the economy has taken place, as well as an excessive growth of the state apparatus . . . and the bureaucratisation of the methods of leadership. These phenomena have hampered the initiative of the masses . . . have caused waste and have retarded technical progress and economic expansion in general.

At about the same time, similar revelations of bureaucracy and waste were being made in Hungary. The Polish Party also complained of the shortcomings of planning in the sphere of agriculture.

Co-operative and state farms, according to Gomulka, had yields far below those of the privately owned farms, despite the preferential treatment in matter of credits, subsidies and purchase of equipment which the public sector of agriculture enjoyed.

The Peasant Problem

The difficulties encountered in industry were small compared with those which arose when the new governments attempted to tackle the chronic ills of the countryside. Throughout Eastern Europe the majority of the population earned their living from the land. Only in Czechoslovakia and East Germany did the proportion of peasants in the total population fall below half. Elsewhere the peasant element in the population varied from 55 per cent in Hungary to 80 per cent in Bulgaria. Although there were some areas, such as the plain of Hungary, where peasant farming was prosperous, the general picture was one of poverty, squalor and overcrowding. Yields of the staple grain crops were from a third to a half of those in Western Europe, but the land was expected to support a much greater density of rural population than was found in other European countries. The land was parcelled out into innumerable smallholdings which were unable to provide a decent living for the large families which depended on them. Although the pre-war régimes had made some effort to redistribute land taken from some of the larger estates, land reform had been partial and inadequate, and in the absence of alternative sources of income arising from the development of industry, little could be done to reduce the population working in agriculture.

The Communists earned support from the peasantry in the early post-war period by promising to break up the large estates and to reform the system of ownership, so that the land would belong to those who tilled it. Once firmly in power, however, they attempted to tackle the agricultural problem by inducing or compelling the peasants to join some form of collective or co-operative farm. Stalin had faced this problem in the Soviet Union in the 1920's and had accomplished the collectivisation of Soviet agriculture by the most brutal methods of coercion. The East European Communists were nowhere as ruthless as Stalin in the implementation of their farm policy. Although some direct coercion was used, the most common method was to offer material inducements to the peasants, and to mount propaganda campaigns to put pressure on those who refused to join collective farms. The resistance of the peasantry was sufficient either to hamper or even in some cases to wreck the plans of their leaders. Poland and Yugoslavia, after attempting to bring the peasants into collectives, reversed the policy, and today most of the land in these countries is farmed privately. Czechoslovakia, Hungary and Bulgaria, on the other hand, have pressed ahead despite setbacks and resistance. They now claim that most of their land is farmed either by collective or state farms. This does not seem to have contributed much to the solution of the agricultural problem. In Hungary, for example, production from the land fell short of its planned target in 1961 by 9 per cent, and food had to be imported. In Czechoslovakia the drive for collectivisation was halted for a while in 1954, because of the opposition of the farmers. At that time Premier Široky admitted that pre-war yields for potatoes, flax, sugar beet, grain, beef and milk had not yet been reached, and he announced that "co-operatives will be established only where conditions are suitable and where small and medium farmers have been convinced of the advantages of co-operative farming". In 1961, after the transition to co-operative farming had been virtually completed, the Central Committee of the Czech Communist Party complained of the failure of co-operative farms to reach their production targets. Czech newspapers during the summer of 1961 were full of complaints about food shortages and queues. In Poland, however, where most of the farms are privately owned, there appears to be less anxiety about the performance of agriculture, although yields are still very low compared to those of Western Europe. In both Poland and Yugoslavia education and persuasion are being used, rather than direct pressure, in an effort to convince the private farmers that co-operative methods are the most efficient. In these countries hostility of the peasantry to the régime is less intense than it was during the earlier collectivisation drives, but there is still a good deal of suspicion. On the Communist side, Lenin's views on the peasantry still influence the thinking of many of the Party members:

> The peasant holding continues to remain small-scale production. It is here that we have a boundlessly broad and very deep-rooted basis of capitalism. It is on this basis that capitalism preserves itself and regenerates in the fierce struggle against Communism.

Religion in Eastern Europe

Communism is a materialist philosophy which cannot in the long run be reconciled with any religious view of the world. Thus, wherever Communists have come to power they have sought to eradicate the influence of religion, particularly amongst young people. They realise that this aim cannot be accomplished quickly, and that for some time to come they will have to accept some form of co-existence with the churches. They have concentrated, therefore, on reducing the social and political influence of the churches rather than on the prohibition of religious observances as such. Throughout Eastern Europe the churches are open, and worshippers attend services, generally without molestation. Church marriage is not recognised by the law, but couples can take part in religious ceremonies if they wish, provided that they also comply with the laws regarding civil registration of marriage. The churches have been stripped of their landed estates and deprived of much of their property and income. Their role in education has been drastically reduced, and their social and cultural societies have been wound up. The position varies from country to country and from church to church, but in general it can be said that the Roman Catholic Church has had the greatest difficulty in its relations with the East European states, and the Orthodox and Moslem communities the least difficulty.

E

The Roman Catholic Church

Before the war the Roman Catholic Church had great power and influence in many parts of Eastern Europe. It was strongest in Poland, Hungary and northern Yugoslavia, and in total claimed the allegiance of almost half the population of Eastern Europe. During the war some of its leaders collaborated directly with the Nazis and their satellites. Thus, Mgr. Tiso became the puppet ruler of Slovakia, Archbishop Sarić of Sarajevo was an enthusiastic supporter of the Croat Fascist dictator Pavelić, and the attitude to Archbishop Stepinać of Croatia was, to say the least, equivocal in the face of the unspeakable brutalities of the Ustaši. On the other hand, many Roman Catholic leaders made no secret of their detestation of Communism, and spoke out clamantly against the policies of the new régimes which were established after the war. Professor Seton-Watson has written of Cardinal Mindszenty of Hungary

> A brave and obstinate man, a narrow Hungarian nationalist, and a conservative with little understanding of social issues, Mindszenty was an almost medieval figure, a prelate from the heroic times of the Turkish invasions. He antagonised not only Communists but the large number of Hungarian democrats who at first believed that collaboration with Communists was possible, and in any case wished as strongly as the Communists themselves to transform the semi-feudal and chauvinist Hungary which the Cardinal seemed to defend.

In Poland, where the Roman Catholic Church claimed the vast majority of the population, the Primate, Cardinal Hlond, was by no means the Right-wing reactionary that Mindszenty appeared to be. Nevertheless, he felt it necessary through pastoral letters to denounce "the atheistic and materialistic philosophy of communism". The situation was not made easier by the policy of the Vatican at this time. The late Pope John's pronouncements about the possibility of ideological co-existence are far removed from the policies of his predecessor. In July 1949, all Catholics who belonged to the Party were excommunicated. Later in the same year it became clear that the Holy See would not recognise as permanent the new Western frontier of Poland along the Oder–Neisse line. This was particularly embarrassing to the Polish Church and caused grave dissensions amongst Polish Catholics. Some of them gave support to the government-sponsored "Social Catholic" movement which sought to find common ground in political and social activity between Catholics and Communists. One of the first acts of the new Primate, Archbishop (now Cardinal) Wyszynski, was to issue a pastoral letter denouncing the "many who have strayed". Despite these difficulties, Catholicism in Poland has had a somewhat better relationship with the régime than has been the case in any other East European country. This may be due to the massive support which the Church has managed to retain amongst the Polish people, and also to the more realistic attitude of Polish Catholic leaders in comparison with that of their Hungarian and Yugoslav brethren. Nevertheless, Wyszynski was under detention from 1953 to 1956. He was released after the triumph of Gomulka, and used his influence to assist in the consolidation of the new line which was inaugurated after the upheaval of 1956. The period of improved relations lasted until 1961, when further trouble broke out partly because of a government decree ending religious instruction in state shools. The Primate replied by an onslaught on the bad faith of the government, and expelled from the priesthood the leader of the government-supported "National Church" Father Maximilien Rode, who controlled the Catholic social organisation "Caritas". Despite all these difficulties, the Roman Catholic Church is still a major force in Polish life, and whatever the government may think of its teachings, it cannot ignore its existence.

In Yugoslavia the attitude of the Roman Catholic Church to the Croat Fascists during the war made any *modus vivendi* like that reached in Poland out of the question as long as Archbishop Stepinać was alive. Catholicism is strong in Slovenia and Croatia and amongst the Hungarian minority in the Vojvodina. Most of the churches are still open, and one has only to visit a Slovene or Croatian village on Easter Sunday, or look in Ljubljana Cathedral on almost any day of the week, to realise that the individual is free to worship. But, as the Jesuit Father Cavalli has written,[1] the Catholic Church makes a distinction between freedom of worship and freedom of religion. In his meaning of the term, freedom of religion does not exist in Eastern Europe because the Church has lost its former status in education and social and political life, and is no longer able to engage in religious propaganda. There have been times when professional men and teachers have felt that church attendance would work against them in their prospects of promotion, but the atmosphere of recent years has been more relaxed.

Other Religious Communities

The Orthodox communities, whose greatest strength is in Bulgaria, Rumania and Yugoslavia, have had less difficulty than the Roman Catholics. This is partly because they have always been closely identified with the national aspirations of their people, and have had only the most tenuous organisational links on the international plane. They were never open to the accusation that they formed part of an international conspiracy. The East German Protestants, however, have suffered because of their attempt to maintain contact through West Berlin with their co-religionists in the Federal Republic.

As with the Roman Catholics elsewhere, the German Evangelicals have been deprived of their former income from church properties, and their role in education has been virtually eliminated. Efforts have been made from time to time to set up anti-religious youth organisations, often using former church premises for their meeting places. In general the attitude of the East European governments to citizens who wish to maintain their religious practices is to ignore the older people and to hope that the younger generation will be won over to a materialist philosophy of life. The Communists realise that they must co-exist with the Churches at least for another generation, and that they may during this period find it to their advantage to co-operate with the less reactionary religious leaders. Many Christian priests

[1] *The Church of Silence.*

are willing to reach a *modus vivendi* with the governments, hoping
that if they preserve something of their organisation and authority
by making compromises on social and political matters, they may
keep open the possibility of some religious revival in the future.[1]
Thus many Orthodox priests have supported the "peace movements" of recent years, the pace setter in this respect being the
Patriarch of Moscow, who has been described as one of Russia's
best diplomats.

The non-Christian religious communities — the Moslems in
the Balkans and the Jews who are scattered throughout the area
— have had less difficulty than the Christians. In the last days
of Stalin's life an anti-Semitic drive, related to that taking place
in Russia, affected both Czechoslovakia and Rumania, but on
the whole the Jews who remain have been less persecuted as a
community than ever before in East European history.

The Effects of De-Stalinisation

For the first ten years after the war the economic policies of
all the East European countries strove to lay the foundations for
economic autarchy. This involved concentration on basic heavy
industry at the expense of the production of goods for immediate
consumption. Often this policy led to economically wasteful
distortions which could only be justified in terms of political and
social objectives. Thus, the establishment by the Poles of a new
industrial complex at Nowa Huta near Krákow involved an
enormous capital expenditure, but the return in terms of the
production of much-needed heavy iron and steel products was
not commensurate with the effort which was made. The fuel
and raw materials all had to be brought from some distance away,
and the costs of production were excessive. The social trans-

[1] It should be mentioned, however, that church-going is far more common
in Eastern Europe than it is in most countries of Western Europe. An English
vicar who had congregations as large as those in many East European
parishes would consider that a mass religious revival had taken place.

formation of the Kráków area was considered more important than the economic value of the project. Since 1956 this attitude has been criticised by the leaders of the Polish Party, and it is unlikely that costly experiments of this kind will be attempted again. Professor Vajda, the distinguished Hungarian economist, has made similar criticisms of Hungarian development before 1956:

> We did not recognise in time that for the new mines, foundries and machine shops we needed people, who were satisfied and enthusiastic about their work, who could gauge the fruits of their labour not only by the rising walls and giant steel structures, the production statistics and government statements, but also in the improvement of their own living standards. . . . All in all, basic disproportions arose between the size and the efficiency of the investments. . . . We did not prosper as hoped because our mistakes were very costly.[1]

Until after the death of Stalin in 1953 the discontent of the peoples of Eastern Europe could find no outlet. The new régimes had been conceived in the image of Stalin's Russia, and their leaders copied the methods of the Soviet Union in suppressing even the genuine doubts and criticisms of devoted Communists. The few brave men who dared to consider political, economic or even artistic questions in the light of the national interest of their countries, and who refused to submerge their critical faculties in a flood of sycophantic praise of Stalin and the Soviet Union, were hounded from public life. Some, like Gomulka in Poland and Nagy in Hungary, survived Stalin, but many were executed as Titoists and traitors, like Rajk in Hungary, Slanský in Czechoslovakia and Kostov in Bulgaria.

Stalin's death was followed by a period of confusion in Eastern Europe, which reflected the struggle for power in the Soviet Union. By 1956 Khrushchev was firmly in the saddle, and felt strong enough to make his speech at the twentieth Congress of the Soviet Communist Party, which denounced the brutality of the Stalin régime not only because of its effect on the Soviet Union, but also because of its trampling on the rights of the

---

[1] *The Second Five Year Plan in Hungary. Problems and Perspectives*, Budapest 1962, p. 8.

East Europeans. He affirmed the right of other countries to find their own way to Communism, according to their own traditions and national characteristics. Shortly afterwards he dissolved the Cominform, the international organisation of Communist parties which had been one of the instruments of Stalinist control in Eastern Europe. For a quarter of a century nothing but praise of Stalin had been heard in Russia, and for nearly a decade the people of Eastern Europe had been subjected to the same flood of Stalinolatry. The author vividly recalls the atmosphere of the International Student Congress in Prague in 1950, when every speech by an East European delegate ended with a hymn of praise to Stalin and the U.S.S.R., which was punctuated by bursts of applause lasting for several minutes, during which the audience shouted the name Stalin! Stalin! Stalin! The posthumous dethronement of the man of whom Khrushchev had said was ". . . the best that humanity possesses. For Stalin is hope; he is expectation; he is the beacon that guides all progressive mankind", was bound to create confusion in the minds of Communists. For a time the parties in Eastern Europe lost the initiative and even their nerve. They stood by whilst the ferment produced by Khrushchev's speech began to work amongst the mass of their people. In Hungary the pressure of discontent was strong enough to force the "Muscovite" Rákosi from power as early as July 1953. He climbed back for a brief period between the spring of 1955 and the summer of 1956 before he was finally forced into exile. The pace of de-Stalinisation was uneven, varying according to the circumstances in each country. It was most complete in Poland and Hungary as a result of the upheavals of 1956. It did not become effective in Czechoslovakia until 1963.

An interesting feature of the process was the re-establishment of contact between the Yugoslavs and their former comrades in Eastern Europe and the U.S.S.R. In June 1955, Khrushchev and Bulganin flew to Belgrade, and even before they had left the airport for the beginning of their state visit, they startled the Yugoslavs assembled to welcome them by publicly recanting and apologising for their earlier attacks on Tito. One of the effects of this reversal of policy was the rehabilitation of the many East European Communists who had been punished for Titoism during the last five years of Stalin's life. One of the first to receive a posthumous vindication was László Rajk, whose ashes were removed in October 1956 from the criminal's grave in which they had rested for seven years, and were re-interred after a state funeral attended by thousands of mourners. It was not until the summer of 1963 that the Czech "Titoists", Slanský and Clementis, were exonerated (alas for them, also posthumously). Once the right of the Yugoslavs to follow their own road to communism was recognised, it was impossible not to admit that others had the same right. Henceforward the main preoccupation of the Soviet Union in its relations with Eastern Europe was that of security. Experiments in communism were not thought to threaten that security unless they led to changes in military and foreign policy. Thus, it was not until Imre Nagy spoke of taking Hungary out of the Warsaw Pact that Russia moved in to crush the Hungarian revolt of 1956. Gomulka in Poland never denied the right of Soviet troops to use routes across Poland to reach their bases in East Germany, and never suggested that he might take Poland out of the Warsaw Pact. The Soviet leaders, although naturally anxious about the turn of events in 1956, were apparently satisfied that the new course in Poland did not threaten their security.

Since 1955 the main instruments of Soviet influence in Eastern Europe have been the Warsaw Pact and the economic organisation known as COMECON.[1] Direct interference and control, such as existed during the Stalin period, is hardly ever used, except in times of extreme crisis. As a result, the divergences in outlook and needs between the various countries, which had been blanketed by the rigid uniformity imposed by Stalin, have now come into the open. The visitor to Eastern Europe in 1950 hardly noticed whether he was in Hungary, Czechoslovakia or Poland in terms of the political atmosphere. Today, the differences are striking,

[1] Council for Mutual Economic Assistance.

the variety of approach to political problems reflecting the national characteristics of the countries concerned. In the economic sphere, COMECON is trying to persuade its members to abandon economic autarchy in favour of a co-ordinated plan for the development of the whole area, in which each member concentrates on what it can best produce. The aim is to promote economic growth throughout Eastern Europe and to avoid the wasteful competition which resulted from the policies of the post-war period. Not all the countries concerned are equally enthusiastic about COMECON's plans, and there is some suspicion that the resistance of the Bulgarians and Rumanians to the role assigned to them is being supported by China, as a move in the Russo-Chinese struggle for the soul of Communism. Albania, China's open ally in Europe, has been expelled from COMECON.

The effect of the political changes on the economic life of Hungary are described by Professor Vajda:

> We realise that our country is small and our possibilities are limited; our aim is to join in the economic co-operation among socialist countries, to find and occupy our proper place on the world market, and to establish lively and growing trade relations with countries outside the socialist world system.

These sentiments are echoed in varying degrees by many of the leaders of the other COMECON countries. In practical terms the fruits of COMECON planning are as yet unimpressive, but as the machinery of technical and financial co-ordination begins to operate, it is likely that COMECON will be as important to Eastern Europe as E.E.C. is to the West. Some progress has already been made in the vital matter of power distribution. The "Friendship oil pipeline", which at the moment takes oil from the Carpathian foothills of the Ukraine to Budapest, is to be extended until by 1970 East Germany, Czechoslovakia and Poland will also receive oil from Russia and Rumania. It is also hoped to link the electric power lines of the COMECON countries into an integrated grid system by the 1970's. Equally important are the political implications of COMECON, for the Soviet Union clearly intends to use the organisation as a weapon in its ideological struggle with the Chinese. The admission of Outer Mongolia to membership in 1962 is obviously of greater political than economic importance. The exclusion of Albania, coupled with the development of closer links with Yugoslavia, also has obvious relevance to the course of the Sino-Soviet dispute.

CHAPTER VI

SOME PROBLEMS OF CURRENT INTEREST

1. The German Problem and Berlin

The role which Germany has played in the affairs of Eastern Europe has frequently been mentioned in the preceding pages. It will be apparent that the word "Germany" has somewhat different connotations at different periods in history. At times the area inhabited by German-speaking peoples has extended far to the east of their original homeland on the Baltic shores of the great European plain. There are even pockets of German colonists as far east as the Volga, and until a generation ago, large areas now governed by Poland and the U.S.S.R. were under German rule. Hitler's Third Reich was the most recent manifestation of the long standing German aim of including within the borders of one state all the scattered German-speaking communities of Eastern and Central Europe. During the five years which followed Hitler's occupation of Austria in 1938, the realisation of the slogan "Ein Reich, ein Volk, ein Führer" was virtually complete. Like all other attempts to form a united Germany, Hitler's Reich was short-lived because its creation could only be achieved at the expense of the peace of Europe. To-day, the efforts of a thousand years of German pressure eastwards have been undone by the consequences of the reaction which Hitler's "Drang nach Osten" provoked. The German colonies in Eastern Europe were forcibly expelled at the end of the Second World War, and the frontiers of Germany were pushed back over 100 miles by the westward expansion of Poland.

It is the misfortune of the German people to inhabit an area which has few clear natural boundaries. This is particularly true in the east, where Germans and Slavs meet in the open spaces of the great northern plain. Here the frontier has seldom remained stationary for more than a generation since the Middle Ages. Even within their frontiers, the German people have enjoyed only brief periods of internal unity under a single political authority. Frequently unification has been achieved by force, and has often expressed itself through aggression against Germany's neighbours. In view of the recent memory of Germany's disastrous attempt to win "lebensraum" for herself at the expense of the nations on her borders, one can understand why so many people view with equanimity the prospect of a permanently divided Germany.

To-day there are in fact two Germanies occupying part of the historic lands of the German nation. The settlement after the Second World War resulted in a contraction of the total area under German rule and a concentration of Germans from beyond the new frontiers within the area which remained. East and West Germany together make up about two-thirds of the area held by the Third Reich, before the annexation of Austria in 1938. The biggest changes have been in the east, where Poland and Russia have acquired over fifty thousand square miles of former German territory, with a pre-war population of about nine million. East Prussia has disappeared altogether from the political map of Europe, and the Polish–German frontier has been pushed back up to 200 miles west of the former line. It now runs along the Oder and its tributary, the Western Neisse. It has been estimated that approximately seven million Germans have left the territories acquired by Russia and Poland, and most of these have settled in Western Germany. The territory which remained after these frontier changes was divided by the Allied powers into four zones of occupation, in accordance with agreements reached at the wartime conferences of Yalta and Potsdam. The division of Germany was seen as a temporary measure pending the creation of a democratic, all-German government which would then sign a peace treaty with its conquerors. But the victors have been unable to agree, and in place of the intended all-German government, there have emerged two German governments based on fundamentally different concepts. The three western zones have been merged and an independent state, politically, economically and militarily linked to its former occupiers, has been created. The Federal German Republic, led for the whole of its existence from 1949 to 1963 by Dr. Adenauer, claims to be the rightful government for the whole of Germany, and refuses to recognise the existence of the German Democratic Republic which was set up in the former Soviet zone of occupation. Thus each German state mirrors the social and political ideas of its former occupiers. Each has also entered into alliances with them. The Federal Republic is a member of NATO, the West European Union and E.E.C. (the Common Market), whilst the Democratic Republic adheres to the Warsaw Treaty and COMECON. We must accept the fact that there are now two Germanies, and realise that as time passes, the differences between them will grow even deeper, making German unification increasingly unlikely as a real political objective, at least in the foreseeable future.

The German Democratic Republic (East Germany)

The Soviet occupation zone, which developed into the East German state, was the least industrialised part of the Third Reich. The Silesian coalfield area and the port of Stettin were taken by Poland, so that what remained of Eastern Germany was predominantly agricultural, and less densely populated than Western Germany. In 1950 there were $18\frac{1}{4}$ million inhabitants in an area of 41,380 sq. miles, whilst the Federal Republic had a population of over 50 million living in an area of 95,737 sq. miles. The Eastern zone contained only 3 per cent of the coal, iron and steel potential of the Reich, and under one-third of its agricultural output. Its economic capacity was further reduced by the drastic Soviet policy of dismantling industrial plants and transporting the equipment to the U.S.S.R. during the first few post-war years.

The German Democratic Republic came into existence in October 1949, three weeks after the Western occupying powers had announced the setting up of the Federal Republic. At first both states were denied full sovereignty, but in 1954 the Western powers announced the ending of the occupation statute and the admission of the Federal Republic to NATO. Shortly afterwards, the Soviet Union took similar steps in the Eastern zone, and a sovereign German Democratic Republic was admitted to the Warsaw Treaty, the East European counterpart of NATO. As the Federal Republic became involved in the movement for West European integration, which culminated in the formation of E.E.C. in 1957, the G.D.R. formally acceded to COMECON, and further steps were taken to integrate her economy with that of its eastern neighbours.

Since its inception the G.D.R. has been led by Walter Ulbricht, a veteran of the Communist Party who spent a good deal of the inter-war period in the Soviet Union, and who was trained in the Lenin Institute in Moscow. Like Rákosi, Dimitrov and many of the East European leaders of the immediate post-war period, Ulbricht is regarded by many of his people as a "Muscovite" — an impression which was confirmed by his appearance in Berlin in 1945 in the uniform of a Red Army colonel. Unlike his colleagues, Ulbricht has survived the de-Stalinisation process, although he admitted in 1961 that Malenkov and Beria had planned to abandon him if an agreement could have been reached in 1953 with the Western powers over a German treaty. Under Ulbricht's guidance, a merger was effected between the Communist and Social Democratic Parties in 1946 to form the Socialist Unity Party, and the Christian Democrat and Liberal Parties, whilst remaining nominally in existence, submerged their political identity in a front organisation led by the Communists.

The economic development of the G.D.R. followed the pattern of the other Peoples' Democracies. By 1948, most of the industries had been brought under state control, and there had been a land reform which redistributed over six million acres taken from the big estates and the "kulaks"[1] amongst over half a million small

---

[1] "Kulak" is the Russian term for the middle-class farmers. Details of the land reform and the industrial plans are given in *Der Deutsche Zwei-jahresplan* published in 1948 by the Socialist Unity Party (S.E.D.).

farmers. From 1948, until the mid-1950's, economic planning aimed at industrial autarchy. Investment in heavy industry, even where this was not a realistic economic proposition, resulted in a restriction of immediate consumption which created great resentment amongst the workers. In 1953, when the Communist leaders were temporarily confused by the aftermath of Stalin's death, this resentment boiled up into an open revolt, which the government was unable to deal with. Soviet troops were called in to restore order, and there was a temporary relaxation in the severity of the work "norms" required by the planners.

During the early Two and Five Year Plans, attempts were made to replace the Silesian coal lost to Poland by the exploitation of the brown coal deposits of Saxony. To this end, plant for turning brown coal into metallurgical coke and chemicals was started in the Leipzig and Spreewald areas. Blast furnaces were built which depended partly on imported Soviet iron ore. The labour force for the new industries was sought from the countryside, where it was hoped that collectivisation of agriculture would release workers from the farms. In all these matters the G.D.R. followed a similar pattern to that of the other Peoples' Democracies. There was, however, one vitally important difference. The existence of the western sector of Berlin made it possible for dissatisfied East Germans to migrate into the Federal Republic, where there was not only the attraction of a booming economy, but where there was no linguistic or cultural barrier to assimiliation. The loss of manpower through "Republikflucht" has been a major headache for the Ulbricht Government. Between 1945 and the erection of the Berlin Wall in 1961, over three million East Germans fled the country. More than half the refugees have been under 25 years of age. Thus the G.D.R. not only has a smaller population than it had in 1948[1] but over 41 per cent of those who remain are over 45 years old. The greatest losses of manpower have been from the rural areas, where opposition to collectivisation has

[1] In 1948 the estimated population was 19 million. The latest figure is 17¼ million.

been a major factor in persuading young people to risk the penalties awarded to those caught in the act of "Republikflucht".

The current Seven Year Plan (1958–65) reflects the new economic thinking of COMECON which has been summed up in the phrase "the socialist division of labour". The G.D.R. has abandoned its expensive attempt to achieve autarchy, and is now concentrating on those types of production for which it is best equipped. Under a trade agreement with the Soviet Union, it will receive most of its import requirements in coal, coke, iron ore, petroleum and grain. With this help the G.D.R. will be free to concentrate on the development of chemical and engineering industries for which it has both the raw materials and the skilled labour force. The petro-chemical plant at Leuna and the Buna synthetic rubber works, both survivals from pre-war days, are being expanded to provide large export surpluses to meet the needs of other COMECON countries. Better communications are being provided, including a new loop railway round Berlin to cut out the short length of the existing line which runs through the western sector. A new autobahn will link East Berlin with the Rostock–Warnemünde port area on the Baltic, as the former outlet at Stettin is now in Polish hands.

Little is said about agriculture, which still employs nearly half the population. The collectivisation programme is officially completed, but there are many reports that production is below expectations, largely because so many farms have been abandoned by families who have fled to the West.

However, the new plan is more realistic than its predecessors, and there are already signs of economic progress leading to better living standards and a wider range of consumer goods. It was obviously with the intention of stopping the drain of manpower via West Berlin that a high concrete wall was built along the frontier in 1961. Had emigration continued at the rate of four thousand a week, the success of the plan would have been undermined. In this sense, therefore, the building of the wall was a contribution to the economic development of the G.D.R.

Berlin

One of the strangest survivals from the Second World War is the Western sector of Berlin. Two and a quarter million Berliners are governed by a city council headed by Herr Brandt, the Social-Democratic Mayor, whilst one and a quarter million of their citizens live in the adjoining eastern sector which contains the seat of government of the Communist G.D.R. Between the two halves of the city runs a concrete wall, flanked to the east by a fortified no-man's land, several hundred yards wide. British, American and French troops are stationed in West Berlin, to which they have access by a number of land and air routes across G.D.R. territory, from various points over a hundred miles away on the frontiers of the Federal Republic. This bizarre arrangement has come about because a temporary expedient devised in the last stages of the Second World War and only workable on the assumption that the major allies would continue to co-operate with each other, has survived into the new era of the cold war. Originally the city was under four-power control, with freedom of movement between all four sectors. In 1948 the four power control ceased to function after the Soviet representative had walked out in protest at the currency reform by which the western powers introduced a new West German mark into their zones. Shortly afterwards, in June 1948, the Soviet Union blocked all the land routes between Berlin and Western Germany, and the Western Powers replied by organising a massive air lift which involved over a quarter of a million flights into Berlin during the eleven months of the blockade. During this period, the administration of the city was split, and two city councils came into being. In May 1949 the blockade was suddenly lifted, but the mistrust which it had engendered prevented the re-creation of a unified administration.

Gradually since 1949 the links between the two halves of the city have become more and more tenuous, each step in the process of separation being accompanied by a major world crisis. In the summer of 1961 the G.D.R. authorities, who now control the border, built a wall to seal off their sector from that of the West.

The flood of refugees was now reduced to a trickle. Those who dare to attempt the crossing run the risk of being shot if caught in the act by the Volkspolizei who guard the wall.

The tragedy of divided Berlin symbolises the awful irrationality of the cold war. Western politicians have not been slow to appreciate the propaganda value of the inhuman wall, and few can resist the temptation, when visiting Berlin, of mounting one of the look-out platforms to peer into the eastern half of the city, whilst the television cameras register their shock and horror for the benefit of their constituents back home. On the less frequent occasions when Mr. Khrushchev and his friends visit East Berlin, the wall is referred to as a "wall of peace" which keeps out Western saboteurs. The tragic absurdity of the whole situation was vividly demonstrated in June 1963. The late President Kennedy found, when he mounted his platform to look across the Brandenburg Gate into East Berlin, that his view was obstructed by huge curtains of red drapery in front of which were posters proclaiming Communist slogans. A few days later, Mr. Khrushchev came to East Berlin to convey his birthday greetings to Herr Ulbricht, the latter having survived for seventy years. In his speech to the gathering of East European leaders who accompanied him, the Soviet leader announced that the only united Germany which he would countenance was a socialist one. A few months after Khrushchev's speech a tentative step was made which appeared to offer the possibility of an improvement in the situation. Agreement was reached that for a brief period at Christmas 1963 West Berliners could visit their relatives on the other side of the wall. Any hope that this grudging concession to the Christmas spirit implied a change of heart was soon dispelled. Although hundreds of thousands of West Berliners did pass through the wall, young East Germans were shot whilst attempting to pass in the opposite direction by climbing over it. In September 1964 a second agreement was made, this time permitting a number of visits over a longer period. This was followed by the news that an East German guard had been shot while attempting to prevent a group of his fellow citizens from using an escape tunnel under the wall.

These incidents serve to focus the attention of the world on the dangerous potentialities of the Berlin situation, but they make no contribution to its solution.

Solutions of the Berlin Problem

The Berlin problem cannot be solved outside the context of a general settlement of the much bigger German problem, and this can only be achieved with the consent of the major contestants in the cold war. In fact it may only be possible to settle the German question within the framework of a general disengagement in Europe. Any partial settlement, restricted to Berlin only, would be no more than a temporary first step to a more general agreement.

The attitude of the Western powers is, at first sight, straightforward and simple. Their position is that, as with the Austrian State Treaty of 1955, where the problem was superficially similar to that of Germany, free all-German elections should be held under international supervision. The resulting all-German government would then be asked to sign a peace treaty with its former enemies, and would be free to resume its place in the community of nations. This line of thinking begs a number of questions which are considered by the Soviet and East European leaders to be vital to their security. Mr. Molotov went so far as to admit in 1955 that the holding of free elections would result in the return of an anti-Communist government. Would such a government take a united Germany into NATO? The Western powers refuse to bind a future German government in the matter of its foreign alliances. It is hard to see what objections there are in principle to the imposition of restrictions of this kind. Austria, Finland, Laos and a number of other countries have been so restricted with the agreement of the Western powers. Mr. Macmillan's offer, that if Germany were united and chose to remain in NATO, western troops would promise not to move further east than the present frontier between East and West Germany, can hardly have been intended seriously. It would certainly never be accepted by the Russians, Poles and Czechs as an adequate guarantee of their security.

What would be the position of the new Germany in regard to the Oder–Neisse line? This line is recognised by Poland, Russia and the G.D.R. as a permanent frontier. The Western governments regard it as a temporary demarcation line pending a German peace treaty. Dr. Adenauer always insisted that it was an unjust frontier, which must be rectified at Poland's expense before a lasting peace could be ensured. Dr. Erhard appears to share this view. Can the miseries inflicted on the millions of Germans who were forced to leave their homes in 1945 be rectified by the expulsion of a similar number of Poles, who have settled there since the war? Will many of the German refugees, and especially their children, really want to abandon their comfortable homes and well-paid jobs in the West to return "home" to towns and villages which they abandoned nearly twenty years ago? Until these questions are answered there is no hope of gaining Soviet acceptance for the implementation of the Geneva agreement of 1955 which stated:

> The Heads of Government, recognising their common responsibility for the settlement of the German question and the re-unification of Germany, have agreed that the settlement . . . by means of free elections shall be carried out in conformity with the national interests of the German people.

The proposals put forward by the Soviet Government during the long process of international debate which has proceeded almost ceaselessly since 1949 involve the recognition by the big powers of the two German Governments and the holding of direct negotiations between them. The role of the big powers in these proposals is to create a climate in which talks between the two Germanies might succeed. This could be achieved, in the Soviet view, by a general agreement on disengagement of forces which would involve a NATO withdrawal from West Germany, and possibly other countries, in return for a Soviet withdrawal from Poland, Czechoslovakia and Hungary. A plan on these lines was put forward separately by Mr. Rapacki, the Polish Foreign

Minister, in 1957. The Rapacki Plan dealt initially with the creation of a nuclear free zone in which both Germanies and a selected group of Eastern and Western countries would be included. If this succeeded, it could be extended to cover conventional weapons.

In this way, a zone of disengagement would be created which would link the Rapacki Plan countries with the already non-aligned nations of Yugoslavia, Austria and Switzerland in the south, and Sweden and Finland in the north. The Polish proposals would obviously not have been made public without prior consultation with the U.S.S.R., and they are in harmony with the Soviet plans for settling the German question. Within the framework of the Soviet proposals, a suggestion is made that, in view of the likelihood that agreement between the two Germanies may take some time, as an interim measure Berlin should become a Free City under international control. They are willing to consider a United Nations "presence" or even a token force of Western troops.

If agreement cannot be reached on these lines, the Soviet government has expressed its determination to sign a separate treaty with the G.D.R. Government. As Mr. Gromyko put it in 1961:

> If we are to speak frankly, the Soviet Government considers the creation of a free city far from being an ideal solution of the Berlin question. The most equitable solution to this question would be, of course, the extension to West Berlin of the full sovereignty of the German Democratic Republic. I think that the G.D.R., whose capital the division of the city continues to mutilate, could with the fullest justification demand such a solution of the question.

The reply of the Western powers to these proposals is to argue that they are legally in Berlin as a result of the wartime agreements, that they do not recognise the legality of the G.D.R., and cannot recognise any treaty which the Soviet Union may sign with Herr Ulbricht. They suggest that the Soviet and Polish plans for disengagement are a device to get the Americans out of Europe and West Germany out of NATO, and that until a more acceptable set of proposals are produced they will stand on their existing rights. Dr. Adenauer frequently said that he would withdraw recognition from any country which established diplomatic contact with the G.D.R. He regarded the Federal Government as the rightful government for all Germany, and declared that "the correct postal address for the East German government is via Moscow". All leading West German politicians, including Dr. Erhard, have committed themselves to the same general line as Dr. Adenauer on this point.

Thus, unless some new initiative is taken, it would appear that a stalemate exists. Neither side is prepared to make the concessions which the other regards as essential. The situation may change as a result of changes of government in West Germany and Britain, as both the British Labour Party[1] and the West German Social Democrats are thought to be more flexible in their approach than either the Christian Democrats in Germany or the Conservatives in Britain. Nevertheless a change of policy in either country could only be effective if it were acceptable to both the U.S.A. and the U.S.S.R.[2] It may be that only a summit agreement of a far-reaching kind between the leaders of the two major powers offers any hope. Until such an agreement is reached, we must be prepared to live with two Germanies, and face the prospect of continuing crises over the anomaly of Berlin.

2.   Hungary since 1956

The year 1956 saw the beginning of a new phase in the history of Eastern Europe. In that year, two nations experienced violent upheavals, each of which originated from the discontent of ordinary people at the failure of their Communist leaders to live up to their promises. At the end of the year, the revolt in Poland appeared to have achieved its objectives, whilst that in Hungary

---

[1] It remains to be seen whether the new Labour Government in Britain can make any progress over the German question.

[2] Shortly before his fall from power, Mr. Khrushchev had accepted an invitation from Dr. Erhard to visit West Germany.

seemed to have failed utterly. The streets of Warsaw were full of cheering crowds, hailing their new idol, Gomulka, whilst in the blood-soaked streets of Budapest, Soviet tanks rumbled past under the sullen gaze of the defeated Hungarians. First impressions can be misleading, however. On closer examination, it seems that Poland has not seen the fulfilment of all the hopes of its people, or the promises of its leaders, whilst Hungary has gained a great deal more than any observer could have forecast in the grim winter of 1956.

Hungary was one of the first countries in Eastern Europe to see political changes arising out of the death of Stalin. This may have been because the Hungarian leader of the time, Mátyás Rákosi, was one of Stalin's most devoted followers. The pressure for his removal became irresistible during the summer following Stalin's death. The workers were tired of the austerity imposed by planners who were obsessed with the need to build heavy industry at all costs.[1] The programme for rapid collectivisation of agriculture aroused the implacable hostility of the peasants. The deportations from Budapest of professional men and their families, often in circumstances of great brutality, created an atmosphere of fear and hatred in the capital. Any hint of criticism, even from loyal Communists, was answered by savage police repression. There were ugly rumours that Rákosi took a sadistic interest in the tortures and beatings practised by the AVO[2] on the erring comrades whose arrest he ordered. The opportunity for a change came during Malenkov's brief tenure of office in the Soviet Union.

With the concurrence of the Soviet leader, Rákosi was replaced by Imre Nagy in June 1953. Rákosi continued to hold office in the party, but did not take a prominent part in public life during the next eighteen months. Nagy followed a policy similar to that of Malenkov in Russia. The pace of industrialisation was slowed

[1] The steel works at Stalinváros (Dunapentele) was one of the monuments left by Rákosi's planners. It was sited in an area where both coke and iron ore had to be fetched from long distances away. Some of the iron ore was imported from Yugoslavia. The project was a costly failure.

[2] Secret Police.

down, forced collectivisation was abandoned, and the worst
excesses of the police and the bureaucrats were kept in check.
An attempt was made to brighten the life of the ordinary people
by providing a wider range of consumer goods in the shops.
Nagy's new course ran for nearly two years until it was abruptly
terminated in 1955 by the return to power of Rákosi. It seems
strange that the old Stalinist should have climbed back at a time
when Khrushchev was in the first flush of his de-Stalinisation
campaign, after his secret speech to the twentieth Congress of the
Soviet Party. He cannot have believed seriously Rákosi's per-
functory "self-criticism", in which he confessed to his past
failures, and promised that he would in future abandon the cult
of personality. At the time when Rákosi staged his comeback,
pressure was building up for a more rapid liberalisation than even
Nagy was prepared to allow, and it may be that Khrushchev felt
that a strong hand was needed to restrain the hotheads. If so,
this was a foolish move, for Rákosi's return to power did not
prevent further criticism. The critics only became more bitter
and more determined.

One centre of disaffection was the club of young intellectuals
known as the Petöfi circle.[1] Early in 1956 they held a meeting
which was addressed by the widow of László Rajk. Rajk had
been Minister of the Interior immediately after the war. He was
one of the few Hungarian Communists who had spent most of
the war years in his homeland, part of the time in a German
prison. In 1949 he was arrested and was made to sign a confession in which he pleaded guilty to being "an instrument of Tito
. . . of the same Tito who followed in Hitler's wake . . . and who
was backed by the American imperialists, his ruling masters".
After a grotesque show trial he was condemned to death and
executed. His widow told the Petöfi circle that the trial was a
miscarriage of justice, and demanded that her husband's mur-
derers should be punished. A few weeks later Rákosi admitted
that "the entire Rajk trial had been based on provocation". This
was the first sign that the régime was bowing before the storm of

[1] Petöfi was a Hungarian national poet of the nineteenth century.

protest. The next success for the opposition came during the summer when the Writers Congress elected a new executive, most of whom were known to be anti-Rákosi men. As the pressure increased, the name of Imre Nagy was mentioned as Rákosi's successor. Eventually the Soviet leaders intervened to secure the removal of Rákosi, but he was not immediately replaced by Nagy. For a few months Ernö Gerö held the fort for the Stalinists, until he, too, was swept aside by the October revolution.

The ferment in Hungary coincided with a similar movement in Poland, and there is no doubt that the success of Gomulka had its effect on the Hungarians. The statue of General Bem, the Polish hero of the 1848 revolution, became a rallying point for young demonstrators in Budapest. The Hungarians have a strong sense of history, and throughout the hectic days of October and November 1956, echoes of the independence movement of the previous century were frequently heard. History does not repeat itself, but historical memories often influence political movements. In 1956 the demonstrators sought inspiration from the heroes of 1848, and the mythology of earlier revolutions was woven into the mystique of the new revolutionaries. The names of Kossuth, Bem and Petöfi were as often on the lips of the demonstrators as was that of Nagy. Thus it was from the foot of Bem's statue on October 23rd that the President of the Writers Association addressed a huge crowd. After referring to the significance of their meeting place, he read out a declaration which said:

We want an independent national policy based on the principles of socialism. Our relations with all countries, and with the U.S.S.R. and the People's Democracies in the first place, should be regulated on the basis of the principle of equality.

He also demanded the democratisation of the party, the removal of Stalinists from public life, the ending of forced collectivisation and the granting of a great degree of control to the workers in the running of their factories.

Gerö's reaction to these and similar demands from other sections of the public was to agree to the return of Nagy to the

Premiership, while at the same time asking for Soviet help under the Warsaw Treaty. Gerö held on to his position as First Secretary of the Party, which is a far more important post than that of Prime Minister. The Soviet leaders Mikoyan and Suslov then visited Budapest, and decided that the storm of protest could not be kept back as long as Gerö remained in power. They ordered his removal to Russia and replaced him by János Kádár, a former "Titoist" who had seen the inside of Rákosi's jails and was thought to be in sympathy with Nagy's ideas. During the last week of October fighting broke out in Budapest and other cities, hundreds of political prisoners were released by armed parties of young students and workers, and members of the AVO were attacked and killed. Nagy's first reaction was to give way. In the space of a week Hungary ceased to be a one-party State. The Social Democrats, Liberals and Smallholders were allowed to resume activities and their newspapers were soon on sale in the streets of Budapest. Anna Kéthly, the veteran Social Democrat leader, joined the government and was sent to represent her country at the United Nations. Cardinal Mindszenty, the Primate of Hungary who had been imprisoned for over seven years, was released and allowed to take up his ecclesiastical duties again. On October 28th Nagy announced that Russian troops would leave Hungary, and on November 1st he went even further and declared his intention to make Hungary a neutral country. This involved her resignation from the Warsaw Treaty. The announcement came a few hours before the delivery of the British and French ultimatum to Egypt.

It is likely that the preoccupation of the Western powers with the Suez crisis helped to tip the scales in favour of Soviet intervention, although it is hardly likely that the Soviet Union would have tamely accepted the withdrawal from the Warsaw Treaty of one of its members, even if they had been prepared to acquiesce in the reappearance of the old political parties in Hungary. To many Communists the latter event was as shocking as the former, for it implied that the post-1945 revolution had failed. Nagy had struck a blow at the political cohesion of Eastern Europe as well as threatening the military security of the Soviet Union. It was apparent to Khrushchev that Nagy was no longer in control of the situation. Who knows what further concessions he might be forced to make? The American propaganda radio had urged the Hungarians to rise. Did this mean that American troops would move in to help the rebels? Many Hungarians expected American help. Who can blame Mr. Khrushchev for jumping to the same conclusion? We shall probably never know exactly what happened in the Soviet Union at this time, and we can only suggest that the factors mentioned above may have weighed in the minds of the Soviet leaders, causing them to take their decision to intervene in great strength in Hungary shortly after they had announced the beginning of negotiations for a Soviet withdrawal in response to Nagy's earlier request.

The Soviet attack began on November 4th. Tanks, heavy artillery and aircraft were used, and some reports suggest that as many as fifteen armoured divisions were employed. Nagy's last act as Prime Minister was to broadcast the following message:

"In the early hours of this morning, Soviet troops launched an attack against our capital city with the obvious intention of overthrowing the lawful, democratic Hungarian Government. Our troops are fighting. The Government is in its place. I hereby inform the people of Hungary and world opinion of the situation."

Before the first Soviet tanks reached Budapest, Nagy and many of his supporters were in hiding in the Yugoslav Embassy. A new government was announced, headed by János Kádár. Its first act was to request Soviet help in restoring order. There was no danger of this request being refused. For the next few months Hungary was under direct Soviet occupation, the Red Army remaining until all traces of resistance had been eliminated. Anna Kéthly, who by this time had reached the United Nations headquarters on her mission from the Nagy Government, declared that Kádár was a prisoner of the Russians, and that she could not believe that he would have accepted his post voluntarily. Kádár is still in power in Hungary, and in view of his past record of courageous opposition to Rákosi, it seems strange that he should have remained in office for so long if he was an unwilling tool of the Russians. He could surely have found a way of retiring before now if he had no stomach for his task. It may be that he was convinced that he could make some contribution to the healing of the terrible wounds inflicted in 1956.

Shortly after Kádár came to office, Imre Nagy was lured out of the Yugoslav Embassy by a shabby trick, and deported to Rumania by the Soviet authorities. Eventually, he was tried and executed as a traitor. The martyrdom of Nagy came long after the revolution had been crushed, and seems to have been a pointless act of revenge against a man who could no longer do any harm, but again we are very much in the dark about the details of the affair. Many of Nagy's supporters have now been rehabilitated and have resumed their public activities after periods of imprisonment and disgrace. The execution of Nagy would have been more comprehensible if it had occurred in the heat of the moment, immediately after his arrest, for at that time the streets of Budapest were soaked in the blood of Hungarians who had supported him. Another puzzling feature is the apparent indifference of the Soviet and Hungarian authorities to the effect which their treatment of Nagy had on relations with Yugoslavia. The Yugoslavs made no secret of their horror at the course of events, and Soviet–Yugoslav relations deteriorated considerably at a time when Khrushchev's policy of reconciliation had just begun to show results. During the winter of 1956–7, production in Hungary came almost to a complete standstill. The workers in the heavy industrial plants near Budapest, the miners of Pecs and the steel workers of Dunapentele went on strike, demanding the setting up of "Workers' Councils" on the lines of those introduced in Yugoslavia after 1950. Gradually they were persuaded to return to work, and by the middle of 1957 production was back to normal. Then began the slow process of recovery. It is only just beginning to be realised in the West that Hungary is undergoing a process of change which has resulted in many of the demands of the revolutionaries being met in ways which would have seemed impossible in 1957. The Hungarian writer, George

Mikes, writing at that time, spoke of the possibility of Hungary being kept in subjugation "by brute force, starvation and martial law". That is how the situation looked in 1957. To-day it is apparent that many Hungarians are materially better off than they have ever been. It is certainly not starvation which is keeping Kádár in power. George Pálóczi-Horváth, one of the Hungarian rebels, who now lives in exile in Britain, said in the course of a B.B.C. broadcast in 1962:

> When we were marching on that revolutionary protest march . . . if anyone had told us that in five or six years life will be in Hungary as it is now, we would have been very pleased, because it would have accomplished a great deal, if not everything we wanted to achieve.

In the same programme, another anti-Communist refugee, Paul Ignotus said:

> Even those who feel strongly against the present regime . . . I think would all agree that nothing of the sort of . . . semi-feudalist capitalism of pre-war Hungary or even of capitalism as we know it . . . should be restored. . . . Those who sparked off the 1956 revolution were against the then existing régime, not because they found it too socialist, but because they did not find it genuinely socialist.

These statements may sound strange to those in the West who automatically associate the name of Hungary with the political refugees streaming into Austria whilst Soviet tanks bombard the streets of Budapest. They accord, however, with the views of most recent western observers in Hungary. Thus, Eric Bourne, writing in the *Christian Science Monitor* on July 26th, 1962, states that:

> Few Hungarians these days talk about the uprising of November 1956. Many — with varying mental reservations — fall in with the régime's general effort at conciliation and accept the "guided" liberalisation from the top with relief. But it is evident that the liberalisation has its calculated limits and that the régime, which has gone further than any other in Eastern Europe with destalinisation, is concerned to keep the process from getting out of hand.

Kádár has declared that "he who is not against us is with us", and to implement this slogan he has permitted the release of almost all the political prisoners taken during the first months of his régime. Selection for posts of responsibility is now based on merit rather than upon party membership, and a serious and apparently successful effort has been made to win over the professional middle class. Contacts with the West have been opened up in the realm of ideas as well as in trade. There is a refreshing lack of dogmatism in the speeches and writings of many Hungarians who have been permitted to engage in discussions with their western counterparts. Mistakes are frankly admitted, and difficulties are not glossed over. In 1961, for example, a group of Italian journalists attended a press conference addressed by leading Hungarian Catholics. One of them admitted that "We are a long way from affirming that the situation of Catholics here is ideal. But there are possibilities for Catholics, and it is our task to profit by them. . . ."

In a country where two-thirds of the population belong to the Roman Catholic Church, it is of course a serious matter that the Primate, Cardinal Mindszenty, is still unable to act. His work is in the care of an Apostolic Administrator appointed by the Vatican in 1959. Mindszenty has lived in the American Embassy in Budapest since 1956, and he apparently refuses to accept the government's offer to allow him to leave the country to take up an appointment in Rome. In the eyes of many Hungarians, Mindszenty is associated with the old régime, and he is in no sense a popular figure, like Cardinal Wyszinski in Poland.

The Hungarian Church, is of course, financially dependent on the State because it lost its estates and properties after the war. Its role in education, to which Catholics attach so much importance, has been drastically cut, but it is still able to function. Many church leaders no doubt feel that a situation like that which exists in Poland would be to their advantage, and they see in Mindszenty's stubborn refusal to compromise a stumbling block to the achievement of a *modus vivendi* with the régime.

The economic development which has occurred since 1956, under the Three Year Plan (1958–60) and the current Five Year Plan (1960–5), has been greatly helped by the Soviet Union. The Soviet leaders appear to have learned the lesson of

1956. The revolution revealed the massive discontent of the workers at the drabness of living standards imposed by the over-weighting of the investment programme in favour of heavy industry. The new plan still puts a high priority on the growth of heavy industry, for Hungary still needs to expand in this sector.[1] However, the emphasis has changed. As Professor Vajda put it:

> Our stand in support of priority for heavy industry development should not be interpreted to mean that we wish to justify the neglect of industries producing directly for consumption — thus the neglect of human consumption. We mean nothing of the sort; this must not be the aim of socialist government, and we consider it most regrettable that there were years when this did actually happen in Hungary.[2]

Thus, although it is intended under the present Five Year Plan that the machine building industry should increase output by 65 per cent, chemicals by 76 per cent, mineral oil by 63 per cent and electric power by 57 per cent, it is also planned to increase the amounts of food, clothing, furniture and other consumer goods. The planners talk about "a wide range of choice, accommodation to changes in taste and culture". In the words of Professor Vajda: "Far-reaching flexibility of planning in this sphere is a major and indispensable requirement; the discriminating tastes of the public are not a burden, but a gratifying sign of progress." Such a remark would have been unthinkable from a Communist economist ten years ago.

The effects of the new approach are already evident in the greater range of goods in the shops, and the much more comfortable existence which the town dwellers at least, now enjoy. The changes are less noticeable in the countryside.

Forced collectivisation had been one of the major complaints of the peasantry under the Rákosi régime. As a result of their resistance, food production declined, and a country which had once been one of Europe's major food exporters became an

[1] In 1959, 54·5 per cent of her industrial development lay in the field of heavy industry, compared with 61 per cent in this sector in the more developed industrial economies of Western Europe.

[2] Imre Vajda, *The Second Five Year Plan in Hungary*, p. 28.

importer of basic foodstuffs. In 1938 over half a million tons of grain were exported from Hungary. Since the war there has been a net balance of imports over exports. In 1960, for example, imports of grain exceeded exports by almost a quarter of a million tons. The total area under cereals has fallen from 2·3 million hectares to 1·3 million. To offset this, there has been some improvement in yields, but total output is well below pre-war levels. Since 1956 the Soviet Union has been supplying large amounts of food to Hungary, no doubt hoping that a well-fed population will be less likely to indulge in revolutionary adventures like that of 1956. If the Hungarian planners are successful, aid of this kind will become unnecessary, for it is hoped that total agricultural production will increase by over 4 per cent a year, and that the pre-war emphasis on grain production will be replaced by a more healthy balance in the rural economy. Fruit, vegetables, milk, eggs and meat will be given a higher priority, and grain production will be maintained at about its present level of two million tons a year, although from a reduced acreage.

The first step in the plan was the bringing under co-operative management of the remaining private farms. Now over 96 per cent of the productive area is under some form of communal management. This remarkable feat has been achieved by the Kádár régime without recourse to the cruder methods of coercion which were employed before 1956. One of the factors which has helped to reconcile the peasants to the new system has been the generous latitude allowed to the members of the co-operatives in the matter of the so-called "household farms". These are plots of about an acre which co-operative farmers can manage privately, selling the produce on the free market. In 1962 a quarter of the milk, a half of the eggs and a sixth of the pork products marketed in Hungary came from this private sector. It would seem that this compromise between collective and private farming has been successful, and that, given reasonable weather conditions during the remainder of the period of the Five Year Plan, the agricultural targets may be reached.

To-day the Kádár régime appears to be gaining in strength as it moves forward to a more liberal form of communism. The black night of Rákosi is now a distant memory, and even the bitterness of 1956 is fading. Hungarian intellectuals who were imprisoned after the revolution are now at liberty, and some, like Tibor Déry and Gyula Hay, have even been permitted to travel to Western Europe. The rigid censorship of literature by administrative order has been abandoned. Many writers have used their new freedom to expose the excesses of the Rákosi régime and to criticise the Soviet Union. If they appear to go too far, they may be attacked in the party press, but at least the issues are publicly ventilated. For example, when Sandor Csoori gave an objective report of his visit to Cuba in 1962 the official press ran a series of articles attacking his "non-conformism", but at least his "Cuban Diary" was published in Hungary, and the author is still able to write. According to László Tikos, a young writer who left Hungary in 1956 and who now teaches in America, Hungarians now enjoy "greater personal, spiritual and political freedom, an increased measure of national independence and economic well-being, and an end to isolation from the West — all things that the 1956 revolution stood for and that are now more in evidence than at any other time since the Communist takeover . . .".[1]

3. The New Course in Poland

Poland not only experienced a political transformation at the end of the war. She also changed physically. By the acquisition of 44,000 square miles of former German territory in the west, and the loss of 69,000 square miles to Russia in the east, her geographical position shifted bodily westward. Her present area is about four-fifths that of pre-war Poland, but her population is

[1] Article in *Problems of Communism*, May/June 1964, "Hungary — Literary renascence".

F

now approaching that of the 1930's.[1] The new Western frontier follows the line of the Oder and the Western Neisse rivers, thus giving Poland control of the whole of the Silesian coalfield, the important industrial region round Wroclaw (formerly Breslau) and the Baltic port of Szczecin (formerly Stettin). The Western powers do not recognise the Oder–Neisse line as a final frontier between Poland and Germany, but regard it as the limit of a *de facto* Polish occupation which must ultimately be settled by a German peace treaty. The Soviet Union and her allies, including the East Germans, express no such reservations, and have always supported Poland's claim to full sovereignty of the area taken from Germany. Now that over nine million Germans have left the area, and a somewhat smaller number of Poles have moved in, it is unlikely that any major revision of the line could be achieved short of war. As time passes, the strident claims of West German politicians for a revision of the frontier are gradually subsiding, and are now only uttered for the benefit of the large, but declining, numbers of unassimilated East Germans who belong to the refugee organisations in the Federal Republic. Nevertheless, many Poles feel real anxiety about the prospect of a united Germany in alliance with the Western powers, and they see in friendship with Russia their only hope of maintaining control of the newly acquired Western provinces. A minor but psychologically important factor in a still predominantly Catholic country is the decision of the Vatican, after long hesitations, to permit the appointment of Polish bishops to administer the former German dioceses in the regained territories.

The eastern frontier with the Soviet Union was fixed approximately along the line suggested by Lord Curzon in 1918 as the fairest ethnic boundary between Poland and Russia. By

[1] In 1931 the population was 32 million in an area of 149,000 sq. miles. The first post-war estimate for the population within the new frontiers gave a figure of 25 million in an area of 120,000 sq. miles (roughly the area of the British Isles). By 1960 a figure of about 30 million was recorded, indicating that the cruel losses of the wartime period had almost been made good because of the high post-war birth rate and the virtual cessation of emigration.

this change Poland lost a predominantly agricultural region, much of it marshy and infertile, containing a population of eleven million, of whom half were non-Polish in origin. No serious objection has been raised in the West to the Soviet Union's recovery of territory which was taken from her by force of arms in 1918. Nor has there been any complaint outside extremist circles in West Germany at the partitioning of East Prussia between Poland and U.S.S.R.

As a result of all these changes, the new Poland is ethnically more homogeneous and economically stronger than she has ever been in modern times. In this sense the Poles have reason to be grateful to the Russians. On the other hand, they may feel that some of the other consequences which flowed from the association with the Soviet Union during the Stalinist period were less to their advantage. For almost a decade Poland was treated as little more than a Soviet colony. Her government was led by "Muscovites", and her forces were placed under the control of a Red Army officer of Polish origin, Marshal Konstantin Rokossowsky. The only prominent Polish Communist who had remained in the country during the war, Władisław Gomulka, was removed from his position as party secretary and expelled from the government because of his "Titoist" leanings. Gomulka had been an exponent of "national Communism" long before the expulsion of Tito from the Cominform in 1948. In 1946 he had declared:

> We have chosen our own Polish road of development, which we have named a Peoples' Democracy. Along the road . . . the dictatorship of one party is neither essential nor is it necessary . . . Poland can follow its own path.

Gomulka was removed from power at the instigation of the Soviet Union in 1948, and was later placed under arrest, but he was too popular to share the fate of the Czech, Hungarian and Bulgarian "Titoists" who were liquidated as traitors. For the next seven years, Poland was governed by men whose loyalty to the U.S.S.R. was stronger than their devotion to the interests of their own people. The Polish economy was subordinated to that of the Soviet Union and Polish coal and raw materials were exported at prices well below the world level, in return for Soviet goods bought at inflated prices. In 1956 Mr. Khrushchev admitted that this form of exploitation had robbed Poland of over $500 million during the previous seven years. A grotesque reminder of this period is the palace of culture which Stalin presented to the people of Warsaw. Its pompous vulgarity was regarded by the citizens engaged in the heroic task of rebuilding their shattered capital as a joke in the worst possible taste.

As in all the other Peoples' Democracies, economic planning was highly centralised, and gave rise to wasteful bureaucratic excesses. The concentration of capital investment in heavy industry was to some extent necessary, but it was pursued with a single-minded disregard for all other considerations. Although some successes were recorded, there were also many expensive failures, like that at Nowa Huta referred to on p. 125. Between 1949 and 1955 real wages actually fell. The lack of consumer goods and the drabness and austerity of life, and the concentration on production at the expense of human beings, led to serious discontent amongst the workers. The constant promises of better things to come, which never seemed to be translated into reality, caused widespread disillusion and alienated the Party from the mass of the people. The truth about this situation began to be expressed even by devoted Communists. Thus, Jerzy Putrament, writing in *Przegled Kulturalny* two months before the Poznan riots in 1956, described the effects of the economic plan on the workers who were supposed to benefit by it:

> Non-fulfilment of the Plan has become something so terrible that people will do anything to avoid it. A mason foreman reports artificially increased results of the work of his gang as otherwise he will not gain a bonus. The book-keeper accepts the return because he is also interested in avoiding the catastrophe of non-fulfilment. The director pretends not to notice anything. Another article in the youth paper *Po Prostu* described how twelve times a year the last ten days of each month become a virtual hell of production in many engineering works. . . . It is the production which should have taken place during the first twenty days of the month. The Plan is Law. . . . The Plan means bonuses. The Plan means for many workers the achievement of a minimum standard of living.

Poland was primarily an agricultural country before the war, and even to-day almost 40 per cent of the Polish working force is employed in farming. The Communists attempted to make agriculture more efficient in order to release workers from the land to provide the labour force for the new industries. The Polish leaders were no more successful than the other East European governments in their efforts to persuade the peasants to accept communal methods of farming. Direct force was not generally employed, but all kinds of social pressures were used, and material inducements were offered in the form of quotas of low-priced industrial consumer goods to peasants who agreed to join collective farms. None of these methods worked. In 1956 Gomulka admitted that the value of farm produce per hectare was more than 25 per cent less on the collective farms than on those in private hands, despite the much higher capital investment on the collectives. On the State farms, which were mainly found in the former German territories in the west, the situation was even worse. The state and collective farms together accounted for 21 per cent of the farmland of Poland, but they produced only 16 per cent of the crops and supported only 9 per cent of the total livestock. Thus, in a country which depended so much on its agriculture, food shortages and high prices were a shocking testimony to the failure of the government's farm policy.

In the years immediately after the war, the Polish people could expect little but hard work and austerity, whatever the policy of the government, for until the appalling material and human losses of the war were made good, there was no basis for an improvement in living standards. At first people were prepared to accept the assurances of their leaders that things would get better in the near future, but as time passed and no noticeable improvement occurred, disillusion and cynicism began to spread throughout the Polish society. The Party drifted further and further from the working masses it was supposed to represent, and in its isolation it produced ever more unreal plans. Because honest critics were often branded as traitors, mistakes which could have been rectified went uncorrected. As in the Soviet

Union, during Stalin's ascendancy, a heavy-handed bureaucracy, backed by a vicious political police, shielded the party hierarchy from the consequences of their folly.

The dead hand of the Party machine cramped and stultified the creative work of Polish writers and artists. This was particularly tragic in a nation which has given so much to European culture. The Writers' Club in Warsaw became a hotbed of dissension against the Party, the ringleaders being disillusioned Communist intellectuals. Gradually the discontent began to find expression even in official publications. Thus, Jan Kott wrote in *Nowa Kultura* in March 1955: "The writer is paralysed when he knows that every word he writes will be scrutinised and examined carefully according to one decisive criterion — whether or not he has exposed himself." A few months later a major sensation was caused by the publication in the same literary journal of Adam Wazyk's[1] *Poem for Adults* which savagely attacked the dishonesty of the Party leaders, and made an eloquent plea for "the bread of freedom". In January 1956 the youth paper *Po Prostu* published an article by Jerzy Urban in which he said: "In the name of higher aims the most normal human emotions were being suppressed. For the good of Socialism I was deprived of my most effective weapon — my sensitivity." In view of these cries from the heart by disillusioned young Communist writers, it is not surprising that Gomulka spoke of the need to "shake off the poisonous fumes of deceit, falsehood and duplicity" and of "violence, distortions and errors which affected every single sector of life".

It is encouraging to note that all the criticisms quoted in the above paragraphs are taken from Polish sources, and that their authors are still active in Polish cultural and political life. Many of them had the courage to make their criticisms before the great change which came over Polish society, and which they helped

[1] Wazyk was one of the thirty-four prominent Polish writers who signed a letter to Mr. Cyrankiewicz in March 1964 protesting against the censorship of literature. When the letter became public knowledge abroad, the signatories were put under heavy pressure to withdraw, but most of them, including Wazyk, have refused.

to achieve, in 1956. The change came about because the Party leaders were frightened by the growing volume of criticism which expressed itself in all sections of the community. The breaking point came in June 1956 when the workers at the Zispo engineering works in Poznan went on strike and paraded through the town, demanding higher wages and lower prices. A few days earlier a delegation had gone to Warsaw to put the workers' grievances before the Prime Minister, Mr. Cyrankiewicz. When the delegates returned empty-handed, their angry comrades staged a spontaneous demonstration of protest. The police and the army were called in to restore order, but this only provoked the workers to make further demands. At first the slogans had been confined to the purely economic issues of wages and working conditions. Now new slogans appeared, which called for an end to "Soviet occupation" and "dictatorship". The town jail and the offices of the Security Police were stormed, shots were fired, tanks sent to quell the riots were captured, and a number of people were killed on both sides. All this occurred during the time when the town was full of foreign visitors who were attending the International Trade Fair, and it was therefore impossible to keep the news of what had happened from reaching the pages of the world press. At first, the government put out the story that the riots had been fomented by western agents, but they quickly dropped this version. As Gomulka said six months later to his comrades on the Central Committee of the Party,

> The attempt to present the painful tragedy of Poznan as the work of imperialist agents and provocateurs was a great political naïveté. . . . Comrades, the causes of the Poznan tragedy and of the deep dissatisfaction of the entire working class lie within us, in the Party leadership and in the Government.

The Poznan riots brought to a head the anger which had been seething below the surface for many years. The Party had the sense to see that they must change their ways if they were to survive. Fortunately for the Party, a leader was waiting who could command the respect of the nation, and who had the ability to channel the discontent into constructive courses. Also fortunately,

the leaders of the Soviet Union were at this time willing to allow
Poland to undertake an experiment in liberal Communism,
provided that the new course did not endanger the security of the
U.S.S.R. For a time it seemed as if the Soviet leaders would not
allow Gomulka to resume his place as Party secretary after his
eight years in the political wilderness. It is possible that the
Chinese Communists intervened to tip the scales in favour of
Gomulka, however strange this may seem in the light of recent
events. Certainly the Poles believed this, for when Mr. Chou-en-Lai
visited Warsaw in January 1957 they gave him a tumultuous
reception and hailed him almost as if he were the saviour of their
country.

On October 19th the Communists elected Gomulka to the
position of First Secretary, thus completing the process of rehabilitation which had commenced with his readmission to the
Party two months earlier. Mr. Khrushchev, who had never
before met the new Polish leader, flew to Warsaw in company with
a number of senior Soviet dignitaries, and conferred with his
Polish colleagues. After a stormy meeting, the Soviet comrades
acquiesced to the changes, even if they did not appear to be very
enthusiastic about them. Once in power, Gomulka conducted a
searching examination, much of it in full public view, into the
shortcomings of his predecessors. The Party was purged of its
leading Stalinists — known in Poland as the Natolin group, after
the name of the village in which they held their caucus meetings.
Marshal Rokossovsky was sent home to Russia, and was replaced
by General Spychalski, a former Minister of Defence who had
been imprisoned with Gomulka during the Stalinist period.
Gomulka's return to power came a few days before the Hungarian
revolt, and his reaction to the tragic events in Budapest suggests
that whilst he did not approve of the Soviet intervention he was
enough of a realist to appreciate that if he publicly denounced it
he would endanger the gains which had just been won in Poland.
When it was all over, he reluctantly expressed his support for the
Kádár Government. At all times during the ferment of 1956,
Gomulka and his associates were careful to insist that they had

no intention of leaving the Warsaw Pact, and that they were prepared to accept the presence of Soviet troops in Poland. Gomulka never allowed himself to be pushed into the position which Imre Nagy took when he declared the neutrality of Hungary. Gomulka proved himself to be a master of the art of political tightrope walking, balancing precariously between the security demands of the Soviet Union and the pressure for reform from the Polish people.

By February 1957 he felt himself strong enough to permit elections in which there was a genuine choice of candidates. The limited freedom of choice which the elections allowed was in furtherance of a promise which Gomulka made immediately after his election to leadership of the Party. He promised them an electoral system "which allows people to elect and not merely to vote". The new law permitted the nomination of up to two-thirds more candidates than the number of seats available. As well as Communist lists, candidates were put forward by the Peasant and Democratic Parties — both of which had previously functioned in a common front with the Communists — and a number of non-party candidates, including several prominent Catholics, were also able to stand. Although there was no danger of the government losing the election, the moral effect would have been great if a large number of Communist supporters had been pushed into bottom place on the lists in favour of non-Communist candidates. When the results were declared the Communists received 237 seats in the Sejm, giving them a majority of 18 over all other parties. 63 non-party members were elected, of whom 12 were supported by Catholic organisations. In Gomulka's own Warsaw constituency, where he headed the poll, the next two places went to non-party candidates, one of whom was a Catholic writer. The remaining Communist candidates occupied the three bottom places.

Four years later, in 1961, another general election was held. On this occasion the list of candidates was smaller than in 1957, but there was still an element of choice. The Roman Catholic Church, which in 1957 had advised its members to vote, remained silent in 1961 because it felt that the government had failed to honour the promises made to Cardinal Wyzsynski after his release from imprisonment. Nevertheless, a number of Catholic candidates stood, and 11 were elected. One of the Catholic candidates, Professor Stomma, headed the list in Mr. Cyrankiewicz's[1] constituency of Krákow, the Prime Minister being in sixth place. In most constituencies there were large numbers of electors who registered a protest by crossing some or all of the names off the voting lists.

One of the most difficult problems which faced Gomulka when he took office was the relationship between the régime and the Roman Catholic Church. Despite over ten years of Communist rule, Catholicism in Poland remained a powerful force, claiming the alliegance of 90 per cent of the population. Since 1953 the Primate, Cardinal Wyszinski, had been under arrest. One of Gomulka's first acts was to release him and to permit him to resume his ecclesiastical functions as head of the Polish Church. The two men had little in common except their patriotism and their sense of the realities of the situation. They each realised that it was in the interests of their country to work out a *modus vivendi* which would permit them to operate in their separate spheres with a minimum of friction. An open quarrel between Church and State might lead to a situation in which the new freedom of action which the events of 1956 had made possible would be endangered. In the nine years since the Cardinal's release, relations between Church and State have not always been harmonious, but they have been considerably better than during the previous nine years. The Cardinal has made several journeys to Rome, most recently to attend the Oecumenical Council

[1] Joszef Cyrankiewicz, a former Socialist leader who made his mark in Polish politics as a young man in the 1930's, had remained in Poland during the war, and suffered a period of imprisonment in Auschwitz as a result of his activities in the resistance. After the war he led a group of Socialists into an alliance with the Communists to form the United Workers' Party. Since that time he has been continuously in office as Prime Minister, regardless of the political changes which have taken place. It is rumoured in Poland that even if the Habsburgs ruled, Cyrankiewicz would still be Prime Minister!

convened by Pope John in 1962. At the time, there were rumours of a new agreement between the Church and the Polish Government, but this has not yet materialised. In fact, relations worsened as a result of what Wyszynski described as a "religious war that has begun in Poland". The issues concerned the role of the Church in education and medical care. Wyszynski denounced the government for closing schools run by monks and nuns, alleging that this action was contrary to the agreement he made with Gomulka in 1956. Although he has been attacked in the party press, no action has been taken by the government to restrict his freedom of action.

In other spheres of Polish life the events of 1956 resulted in a great relaxation of tension. Writers and intellectuals who had been stifled by the oppressive atmosphere of the Stalinist period suddenly found that they could write as they wished without incurring disciplinary penalties. The result was a great wave of creative activity, a ferment of political discussion and an opening up of contacts with the West.

The Party has occasionally shown concern lest the movement should get completely out of hand, and there have been mild attempts from time to time to restrain the more outspoken critics. Nevertheless, the gains of 1956 have been maintained, and Polish intellectual life is probably freer to-day than it has ever been in recent history. Polish writers and artists are now able to contribute once more to the mainstream of European culture, instead of wasting their talents in the blind alley of "beetroot and tractor" culture from which they escaped in 1956. One of the most striking manifestations of this new freedom has been the great contribution which Poland has made in recent years to the art of the cinema.

When he outlined the tasks before Poland in 1956, Gomulka was careful to point out that he could not promise an immediate improvement in the economic situation.

I am unable to give any concrete answer to the question of when it will be possible to save further resources for the stepping up of the living standards of the working class. This depends primarily on two factors: in the first place on an improvement in the management of industry and in the entire national economy, and in the second place on the workers, that is on an increase of productivity and on the lowering of output costs.

After analysing the mistakes of the past, the government began cautiously to move forward to a more liberal economic organisation. Problems were looked at in a pragmatic way, the intention being to produce results rather than, as in the past, to prove dogmas. In agriculture, the peasants were given real freedom of choice concerning membership of collectives, and the result was a wholesale reversion to private farming. In 1962 there were only 1700 collective farms in the whole country, and their acreage of arable land was less than 1 per cent of the total. Another 12 per cent, mainly in the West, was held by State farms. On the other hand, there were over three and a half million private farms. As in Yugoslavia, the government is encouraging the formation of voluntary co-operative organisations for handling machinery, seed, marketing and the dissemination of agricultural education, but collectivisation has been dropped from the immediate programme of the Party. Although there have been good and bad years for agriculture since 1956, the general level of production is rising, and with improvements in methods of distribution and storage, food shortages in the towns are a rare occurrence. In the late 1950's, a great contribution was made to the food situation by the American decision to permit dollar credits to Poland for the import of surplus food from U.S. stocks.[1] The decision of Congress in November 1961 to suspend all aid to Communist countries, including Yugoslavia and Poland, meant that this source was not to be available, save in exceptional circumstances.

Industrial production has been growing steadily in recent years, increases of 10 per cent in overall output being recorded in both 1961 and 1962. Planning is on a much more realistic basis than before, and there is a willingness to experiment with new forms of management and control in the factories. Although Gomulka hinted in 1956 that Poland might learn from Yugoslav experience in workers' self-management, nothing as radical as this has

[1] Between 1957 and 1960, U.S. dollar credits amounted to $360 million.

appeared. There has been some decentralisation of control and more initiative has been given to both management and workers. Criticism of faulty planning and bureaucratic distortions still appear in official publications, but this in itself is probably a healthy sign that these tendencies are being watched and corrected. In 1963 an experiment was started with the aim of increasing production in a number of factories engaged in the vitally important export trade. The factories were given complete freedom to run their affairs in accordance with their own assessment of the market, their success being measured in terms of the profit showing on the balance sheet at the end of the year.

The Five Year Plan which started in 1961 was geared to the current Soviet Seven Year Plan, in accordance with the decisions of COMECON. Poland's economy is now being integrated with that of the other East European countries in such a way as to avoid the wasteful duplication of effort which characterised the period of economic autarchy. The Plan envisages an 80 per cent rise in industrial output during the five years, and a 30 per cent rise in agricultural production. There seems more hope that the industrial targets will be reached, in view of the progress already made in steel, coal, shipbuilding, oil and chemicals. Success in agriculture depends partly on favourable climatic conditions, and the bad harvest of 1962 was a serious set-back.

In connection with the recent discussions within the Communist world which have arisen out of Russia's quarrel with China, Gomulka has reaffirmed that "every party is fully autonomous, independent, and bears full responsibility for the country it rules". However, no ruler of Poland can ignore the limitations on his freedom of action which are imposed by the facts of political geography. It is vitally important to Poland's existence as an independent nation that conflict should be avoided between her two powerful neighbours, Russia and Germany. Since the Second World War the German menace has subsided, but in view of Poland's recent experience it is understandable that her leaders should be wary of a possible revival of German expansion at Poland's expense. Her fate is now linked to that of Russia by political, economic and military ties which many Poles would perhaps like to see loosened, but which few would consider breaking completely. It was appropriate therefore that the Polish Foreign Minister, Mr. Rapacki, should have been the author of the plan for the relaxation of tension in Europe by the creation of a nuclear free zone which would include Poland, Czechoslovakia, Hungary and both Germanys. This was seen as the first stage in a much wider disengagement which might pave the way for a solution of the German problem. The Western Powers were not prepared to accept the Rapacki Plan, mainly because it envisaged the withdrawal of NATO forces from Western Germany. In the absence of any other proposals acceptable to them, the Poles have been enthusiastic supporters of Mr. Khrushchev's as yet unrealised intention to sign a separate Peace Treaty with East Germany, and to declare the whole city of Berlin to be an integral part of the German Democratic Republic. Until this problem is solved within the framework of a general *détente* between the big powers, Poland will continue to cling to the Russian alliance, and to accept the military obligations of membership of the Warsaw Treaty Organisation.

4.   Albania

The only European Communist Party to align itself with China in the great schism which divides the disciples of Marx and Lenin is that of the tiny Balkan state of Albania. In foreign affairs the quarrel is concerned with the big issues of peace and war, and in this sphere the role of Albania has been that of a ventriloquist's dummy, piping in shrill falsetto the words which its powerful master has put into its mouth. In domestic politics the Albanian Communists have remained unrepentant Stalinists, as yet untouched by the liberalising influences which have developed elsewhere since the death of Stalin. Enver Hoxha still rules with the aid of crude police terrorism, and continues to use show trials to purge his party of dissident elements. The cult of personality continues to flourish in Tirana long after it has been discredited in Moscow, Prague and Budapest. It is the anomalous survival of Stalinism in a remote corner of the Balkans which directs the interest of the world to the otherwise insignificant state of Albania.

Albania is obviously too poor and too small to be able to stand alone in the world. Most of her people are still occupied in the day to day problems of wresting a precarious living from the inhospitable land. Many of them are semi-nomads, herding flocks of sheep on the poor pastures of the limestone mountains. Others farm the marshy coastal lowlands, large areas of which are still undrained and malarial. A small amount of industrialisation has occurred as a result of the exploitation of the oilfield between Valona and Berat, and the chromite mines along the Yugoslav border in the mountainous north and east. Such development as has occurred has been as a result of foreign intervention. During the inter-war period the main source of capital and technical assistance was Fascist Italy. In recent times first Yugoslavia, then the Soviet Union, and now China have occupied the role of Albania's "Big Brother". Since she achieved her independence from Turkey in 1913, she has never been free of outside inter-ference.

Her very existence as an independent state came as a result of a decision of the great Powers, meeting in London in 1913, after the Second Balkan War. Her frontiers were drawn so as to leave nearly half the Shqiptar-speaking people under Yugoslav or Greek rule, a dispensation which has produced innumerable incidents between Albania and her neighbours. It is still a source of friction, border raids along the Yugoslav frontier adding additional heat to the already strained relations between the two countries. In 1913 the powers also introduced a head of state, Prince Wilhelm of Wied, a nephew of the Queen of Rumania, and a member of one of the minor German royal houses. A few months after he first set foot on Albanian soil, the First World War broke out, and he hurried home to join the German Army. For the next few years Albania was under military occupation, Italy eventually becoming the predominant influence. The

Italians hoped to be given a protectorate over Albania, but at Versailles the promises made to them under the secret Treaty of London in 1915 were whittled down, under pressure from President Wilson. They eventually obtained a naval base at Valona and the nearby island of Saseno. Until 1928 Albanian affairs were dominated by the struggle for influence between Italy and Yugoslavia, the Italians eventually gaining the upper hand, largely because of their greater resources and their possession of the base at Valona. Occasionally there were rumours of Communist influence entering by way of the Bulgarian terrorist organisation, IMRO, whose plans for the reorganisation of the Balkans included a place for an enlarged Albania at the expense of Yugoslavia. The Yugoslav interest in Albania first expressed itself in support for a Gheg[1] tribal leader, Ahmed Zogu, who became Prime Minister in 1922. His chief rival, the Orthodox Bishop, Fan Noli, was supported at this time by the Italians. Noli, who had been educated at Harvard, and later became an American citizen, entered Albanian politics by a curious route. He was elected under an arrangement which permitted the expatriate Albanians in U.S.A. to choose a member of parliament for their mother country. After the elections of 1924, Fan Noli replaced Zogu as Premier, and the latter fled to Yugoslavia, where he organised an expeditionary force with the connivance of the authorities in Belgrade. He returned to overthrow Noli's government and proclaim himself President of an Albanian Republic. Three years later he changed his title to King Zog I. During these three years he disowned his Yugoslav friends and placed himself under the guidance of Fascist Italy. An Albanian bank was established in Rome, and the economic development of the country was placed in the hands of an Italian company. In 1939 Mussolini rang down the curtain on the farce of Albanian independence by a formal act of annexation, and King Zog was forced to retire into exile in Egypt.

During the Second World War, Italy used Albania as a base for her attack on Greece, and heavy fighting occurred in 1941 in

[1] There are two main linguistic divisions in Albania, Gheg and Tosk.

the region known to the Greeks as Northern Epirus and to the Albanians as the Prefecture of Gjinokaster. Fighting also occurred along the northern borders with Yugoslavia. The frontiers of Italian-occupied Albania were extended to take in the Shqiptar-speaking population of what is now the Yugoslav region of Kosmet. When Italian resistance collapsed in 1943, an independent Albanian Government came into being, but German troops from Greece soon moved in to occupy the strategically important coastal area. Nevertheless the Albanian Government did exercise some degree of internal self-government, as the Germans were only interested in ensuring the free use of the ports and communication for their troops. During the course of the war two Albanian resistance groups emerged. One was led by the newly formed "Party of Labour" (i.e. Communist Party), whose chief figure was a French educated schoolmaster called Enver Hoxha. His associates were mainly men like their leader, whose political ideas had been formulated whilst they were students in other countries. Some had fought with the Albanian contingent in the International Brigade in Spain. The Conservative resistance movement, "Balli Kombetar", lost a great deal of its influence because it participated in the government formed during the German occupation. The Communists not only benefited by the tactical mistakes of their rivals, but they also drew great strength from their association with the Yugoslav Partisans. It is perhaps projecting western political ideas into a foreign environment to use terms such as "Conservative" and "Communist" to describe the divisions within the Albanian Resistance Movement. In a sense they reflected the social and cultural divisions based on much older concepts. "Balli Kombetar" drew its strength from the intensely nationalistic Gheg chieftains of the mountain regions, whilst the Communist-led National Liberation Movement was composed predominantly of Tosks from the lowlands. Both social groups had scarcely emerged from medieval ways of life. The Ghegs were organised in tribes and accepted the authority of their hereditary chiefs rather than that of any government. In religion some were Roman Catholic, many others adherents of the Sunni branch of Islam. In the lowland areas many of the Tosks were little better than serfs on the estates of Moslem beys. The Tosks also provided the majority of the workers in the towns, where the limited amount of industrialisation was beginning to produce an urban proletariat — more akin to that of Stalin's Georgia in the late nineteenth century than to the towns of Western Europe. The Tosks included many members of the Greek Orthodox Church, whose Albanian branch became self-governing in 1937. Thus language, religion, social organisation and even personal rivalry and blood feuds are as important as political ideology in understanding the divisions amongst the people of Albania. This may explain also the peculiar ferocity with which the quarrels between different groups of Albanians have always been conducted — a feature which is apparent to-day in the behaviour of Enver Hoxha towards his political opponents.

When the Germans finally left the country in 1944, the National Liberation Movement had no difficulty in taking over the country and establishing, with Yugoslav assistance, a government modelled on that of its Slav neighbour. The new régime was recognised by the Allies and Albania was admitted to the United Nations. It was soon in trouble, however, because of its behaviour both at home and abroad. In 1946 a major international crisis resulted from the mining by Albanians of the international waters of the Corfu Channel. Two British destroyers H.M.S. *Saumarez* and H.M.S. *Volage*, were badly damaged and over thirty ratings were killed. The International Court judged Albania to be guilty, and awarded substantial damages to Britain, which have yet to be paid. As a result of this incident Britain broke off diplomatic relations with Albania, and to-day the only Western Embassy which functions in Tirana is that of France.

For a time it seemed possible that Albania might be absorbed into a Balkan Federation, headed by Yugoslavia. Bulgaria and Yugoslavia were both in favour of such a scheme, and Stalin is reported to have encouraged the Yugoslavs to "swallow Albania". But Stalin changed his tune in 1948. After criticisms in *Pravda* the Bulgarian leader, Dimitrov, hastily disowned the idea, and after the breach between Yugoslavia and the Cominform, Hoxha added his voice to the indignant protests of the other Communists at Tito's "imperialist" ambitions. Only a few weeks before, Hoxha had been loudly applauding the Yugoslav leader for the help which he had given in the form of credits, the loan of technicians and the granting of scholarships to Albanian students attending Yugoslav universities. Immediately after the Cominform resolution of June 1948, Hoxha broadcast over Tirana radio a bitter condemnation of Tito's "Turkish terrorist" régime and ordered the expulsion of Yugoslav technicians. The students were hastily recalled home, and many of them later completed their studies in Moscow.[1] At home, Hoxha ordered a purge of suspected "Titoists", the chief victim being Koçi Xoxe, the Minister of the Interior, who was unfortunate enough to have been Hoxha's emissary to the Yugoslav Partisans during the war. Xoxe was executed in 1949, along with a number of other heretics. Having repudiated Yugoslav patronage, Albania had no alternative but to place herself under Soviet protection, and during the next few years she became virtually a Russian colony. The Red Fleet took over the naval base near Valona, and Soviet technicians replaced the Yugoslavs in the oilfields and the copper and chromite mines. Albania became the main base for aid to the Greek rebels who were fighting under Communist leadership against the Royalist régime in Athens. She also became a centre of intrigue against Yugoslavia, the existence of an Albanian minority in the Kosmet area providing plenty of scope for espionage, border violations and anti-Tito propaganda.

Relations between Albania and the Soviet Union began to deteriorate after the visit of Khrushchev and Bulganin to Yugoslavia in 1955. At first, the only sign to the outside world was the stubborn refusal of Hoxha to abate his attacks on Yugoslavia, despite the obvious desire of the Soviet leaders to heal the breach caused by Stalin's policy in 1948. There was a brief pause in the

[1] The author recalls meeting some of the students in Zagreb in 1948. Some of them decided to stay in Yugoslavia.

development of the Soviet–Albanian quarrel after Khrushchev's visit to Tirana in 1959, but the improvement did not last more than a few months. During 1960 there were two important international Communist meetings, one at Bucharest and the other in Moscow. At these meetings the Soviet–Albanian affair became submerged in the much more explosive disagreement between China and the U.S.S.R. The Albanian leaders were the only Europeans to support China's case. For the next two years Soviet attacks which were really intended for China were addressed to Albania, and the Chinese replies referred to Yugoslavia when the obvious target was the Soviet Union. The Soviet attacks were backed up by economic sanctions against Albania, which led in 1961 to a complete break in diplomatic and trade relations. Since that time Albania has been excluded from the work of COMECON. In reply, Hoxha staged a show trial at which the pro-Soviet elements within the Albanian Communist Party were accused of plotting with Yugoslavs, Greeks and Americans in an attempt to overthrow the government. Several leading figures, including the head of the navy, were later executed as traitors. The Soviet submarines were ordered out of the base at Saseno at about the same time. Hoxha savagely attacked the Soviet leaders for "attempting to impose their opportunist conceptions on all the Communist Parties", and warned them that "our people have friends and comrades . . . who will not leave them in the lurch". These comrades were obviously Chinese, for in the summer of 1961 it was announced in Canada that $3 million worth of Canadian grain, paid for by China, was being diverted to Albania, and later in the same year Chinese technicians began to arrive to take over the posts vacated by the Russians.

As long as China is prepared to underwrite Hoxha's régime, the Stalinists will remain in power in Tirana. Albania is a tiny country, and China can no doubt afford to keep her going if it suits her purposes to do so. There is a possibility that this will not be for much longer. Chou-en-Lai's visit in January 1964 may prove to be the last occasion on which Hoxha shared the limelight with his Chinese overlord. If the successors to Mr. Khrushchev attempt to heal the breach between Russia and China, there will no longer be any need for Pekin to maintain an expensive puppet in Tirana. Hoxha's main value was to voice Chinese attacks on Khrushchev and the "revisionists" during the period between 1960 and 1963, when Sino–Soviet differences could not be openly stated. His importance immediately declined when the dispute became public knowledge. On the face of it, the situation in which Albania is kept afloat by hot air pumped from the far side of the world is absurd and in the long run untenable. Hoxha has isolated himself at the end of a very weak branch which is in imminent danger of being sawn off.

As the most backward and underdeveloped country in Europe, Albania's living standards are closer to those of Asia and Africa. As an index of her relative industrial development it is interesting to note that her energy consumption per head of population is about one-tenth that of the Soviet Union, but only half that of China. The countries whose Communist Parties take the Chinese side in the great schism are predominantly those with low living standards and a recent history of foreign exploitation. Those whose industrialisation has begun to show results, and who have therefore more to lose by international conflict, tend to take the more moderate line of the Soviet leaders. It is significant that Albania fits more appropriately into the former category, and this may help to explain the attitude of her leaders.

From what has been said of recent Albanian history, and of her economic plight, it is apparent that she cannot survive unless aid is forthcoming from more wealthy friends abroad. Common sense would suggest that in the long run it would be better for her people if these friends were also her geographical neighbours. There are, however, obvious political and national difficulties. Greece still persists in claiming "Northern Epirus" from Albania, and the Albanians have not forgiven the Yugoslavs for setting up an autonomous Albanian region in Kosmet, instead of handing the area over to them. Ultimately it would seem that the best solution would be a Balkan Federation in which Greece, Albania, Yugoslavia, and possibly Bulgaria participated. It would be possible for such a framework to guarantee Albanian cultural and political autonomy, whilst at the same time giving her the economic benefit which would come from an association with a larger unit. For example, her great hydro-electric potential could best be developed in co-operation with Yugoslavia, and an improvement of communications across northern Albania would be to the advantage of both countries. In such a Federation, border disputes would generate less heat, and it may be possible to effect some kind of union between the Albanians and their brothers in Greece and Yugoslavia. The question of course is not whether such a federation would be ultimately desirable, but what is to be done in the short run when passions run too high for any talk of common-sense arrangements to receive a hearing.

5.   Czechoslovakia

Czechoslovakia is in many ways different from her neighbours in Eastern Europe, and her situation raises a number of interesting questions. In the inter-war period Czechoslovakia was regarded as a beacon of democracy in the authoritarian twilight of Central Europe. The Czechs are a Slavonic people, but they have many cultural links with the West. They owed their nationhood to the sympathetic help of Woodrow Wilson and the Allied peace-makers at Versailles. The new state was seen as a bridge between East and West. As the most highly industrialised and politically mature of all the new nations of Eastern Europe, Czechoslovakia was thought to have the best chance of demonstrating the virtues of liberal democracy in an area where the tradition of government by consent had but shallow roots. Her greatest weakness was the presence of large alien groups, but even here it was hoped that her intelligent handling of national minorities would set an example to her more illiberal neighbours. All these hopes were shattered when Czech democracy collapsed like a house of cards, after her Western friends had abandoned her at Munich in 1938.

At the end of the war the old illusions revived for a time, and

Czechoslovakia was again looked upon as the bridge between different social systems and ways of life. When elections were held for the Constituent Assembly in 1946 the Communists emerged as the largest single party, with 38 per cent of the popular vote. In accordance with normal constitutional practice President Beneš called upon the Communist leader, Klement Gottwald, to form a government. In the new cabinet only nine of the twenty-six ministers were Communists. The rest were representatives of the various parliamentary parties which had participated in the pre-war governments. The appearance of continuity with the old liberal republic was strengthened by the fact that the President, Edvard Beneš, wore the mantle of Thomas Masaryk, the father of Czechoslovak independence. The founder's son, Jan Masaryk, held the post of Foreign Minister. It seemed as if the Czechs were going to demonstrate the possibility of peaceful co-existence between Communists and liberal democrats in the tasks of post-war reconstruction. The Czech Communist Party had functioned legally until the end of 1938, and leaders like Gottwald, Zápotocký and Široky had been well-known members of the old Parliament. Relations between them and the representatives of the other parties were reasonably good, and there seemed to be no reason to doubt that the two groups could work together. The situation in Czechoslovakia was quite different from that in the other Peoples' Democracies, where the new Communist leaders were almost unknown when they returned home under the protection of the Red Army after years of exile in the Soviet Union.

The events which led to the overthrow of the parliamentary régime and its replacement by a dictatorship of the proletariat are really part of the history of the Cold War. One of the clearest signs that the wartime coalition between Russia and her Western Allies was not going to survive into the era of peace was the rejection by the Peoples' Democracies of America's plan for Marshall Aid. When the proposal was first put forward in 1947 the Czech Government responded favourably, but their policy changed abruptly after Gottwald had been summoned to Moscow and ordered to withdraw his acceptance of the American invitation. Stalin personally conveyed his displeasure to the Czech leader, who told Jan Masaryk when he emerged from the interview, "I have never seen Stalin so furious". As if to emphasise Czech dependence on Moscow, Gottwald was compelled a few weeks later to ask for Soviet help to prevent a serious food shortage occasioned by the disastrous harvest of 1947.

In February of the following year a government crisis was precipitated by the withdrawal of the non-Communist ministers from the coalition government, in protest against the actions of some of their Communist colleagues. With the help of Left-wing Social Democrats, Gottwald was able to secure a parliamentary majority for a new government, of which he was again the Prime Minister. A wave of demonstrations in favour of the Communists unnerved the opposition, many of whose leaders were in any case under arrest. The names of some of the old parties were retained, and in fact are still in use to-day, but the political activity of the groups they represent is purely nominal, and they have no influence on the course of events. Jan Masaryk remained in office as Foreign Minister, and one or two minor posts were held by non-Communists, but all the key positions of power were in the hands of Party members. The Social Democrats were reunited with the Communists after a divorce which had lasted for almost thirty years. The fusion was celebrated as a return to the fold of the separated brethren, for the Communist Party had come into existence in 1921 as a result of a split within the Labour Movement.

Within a few months of the February coup both Beneš and Masaryk[1] were dead, and the last links with the old republic seemed to have been broken. Gottwald moved up into the Presidency, and the Slovak Communist Vladimir Clementis[2] took over the Foreign Ministry. Almost bloodlessly, though with vigorous protests from some of the students in Prague, Czecho-

[1] Masaryk was found dead outside the window of his apartment, and it is not known whether he committed suicide, or was murdered.

[2] Clementis was executed as a traitor in the Titoist purges of 1952. His soul no doubt rests in peace since his posthumous rehabilitation into the Party in 1963.

slovakia became the newest recruit to the ranks of the Peoples
Democracies.

Even before 1948, considerable progress had been made towards a socialist economic system. The Kosiče programme,
agreed by all the coalition partners in 1944, provided for the
nationalisation of the major industries. In many cases this had
meant simply a transfer of power from the German occupying
forces to the new Czechoslovak Government. The Germans had
kept Czech industry running throughout the war and had even
built a number of new factories. New industries had also been
started by the "independent" Slovak government of Mgr. Tiso.[1]
Most of the industrial undertakings owned by Sudeten Germans
were confiscated when the owners were forcibly deported to
Germany after the war. Later, all factories employing more than
fifty workers were nationalised. The Two Year Recovery Plan
1947–1949 provided for a large programme of investment in the
government-owned basic industries, whilst the consumer goods
industries and agriculture were starved of capital. High priority
was also given to the development of the Slovak economy, which
had hitherto been backward in relation to the level of the western
Czech lands.

The Two Year Plan had not been completed when the Communists assumed full power, but it was replaced by a Five Year
Plan which accelerated the process of socialisation, and placed
even greater emphasis on heavy industry and on the development
of Slovakia. As much as 25 per cent of the national income was
allocated to investment. The aim was to make Czechoslovakia
the industrial power house for the whole of Western Europe.
Her traditional commercial ties with the West were weakened,[2]
and her trade was orientated in the direction of the U.S.S.R. and
the Peoples' Democracies. Although there was no overt protest
from the Czech people at these changes, it soon became apparent
that the spirit of the *Good Soldier Švejk* (Schweik) had not been

---

[1] The national income had actually increased during the occupation.
[2] She nevertheless continued to do more trade with the West than any of
the other Peoples' Democracies.

forgotten.[1] It is understandable that workers who had been schooled in the trade union struggles of pre-war days should have found it difficult to adjust themselves to the new approach to labour discipline which the Communists introduced. The new legislation required unions to co-operate with the management in raising productivity, strengthening labour discipline and damping down wage demands which were not justified by increased efficiency. In other East European countries, where the new labour force in the industries was mainly recruited from the peasantry, old-fashioned trade-union attitudes were less of a problem than in Czechoslovakia. There is abundant evidence from the pages of Czech newspapers since 1948 that the régime has been seriously concerned at the lack of spontaneous co-operation from the class in whose interests it claims to act. Absenteeism has been a recurrent problem, all the more serious because of the chronic shortage of labour which has afflicted the Czech economy since the wholesale expulsion of hundreds of thousands of skilled Sudeten Germans. An official concerned with the textile industry, writing about the problems which arose after the expulsion of the Germans, stated that

> the main reason for lack of success . . . has been the lack of skilled workers, due to the transfer of the Germans. I can readily say that 100,000 of the 180,000 working on textiles to-day have never seen a textile factory before 1945.

Agriculture has been in an even worse state than industry. Collectivisation was officially completed by 1961, but the farmers still retain small private plots. As in Hungary, the productivity of the private plots is higher than that on the collective land, and pilfering from the produce of the collective is a serious problem, despite the severe penalties imposed on the culprits. Some of the targets set by the Five Year Plan 1961–5 were little better than the results actually achieved in the years before the war.

---

[1] Švejk (Schweik) was the hero of a popular novel. During the Austro-Hungarian times he had perfected the arts of passive resistance and dumb insolence in the face of authority. "Schweikism" is held by many to be a national characteristic of the Czechs.

For example, it was hoped that the number of cattle would reach 4·8 million in 1965, compared with the 1938 figure of 4·7 million. In 1962 there was a serious food shortage. A Minister admitted that wholesale watering of milk was being practised, and that egg deliveries had fallen short of expectations by 134 millions. President Novotny blamed poor labour organisation and irresponsibility for the food shortages which were causing serious unrest in the towns. The student demonstrations of 1962, which led to a number of arrests, were a protest against the régime's failure to satisfy the material expectations which its own propaganda had aroused. The riots of 1953 against the currency reform were of similar origin. It is apparently no comfort to the Czechs to know that their standard of life is higher than that of the other Eastern European countries, for this has always been the case. They are more concerned by the fact that real wages have risen more slowly than they had been led to expect. They view with considerable cynicism the boast of their leaders that by 1965 "Czechoslovakia will be far ahead of the United States, Great Britain, the German Federal Republic and France, and she will be a model for these states, not to speak of other capitalist countries, insofar as the standards of living are concerned". This announcement in the Slovak *Pravda* of January 1960 contrasts pathetically with the admissions of failure which a committee of the National Assembly made two years later when reviewing the progress of the Five Year Plan.

From time to time the upper ranks of the party hierarchy have been decimated by purges directed against former leaders, whose alleged crimes have ranged from Titoism to criminal conspiracy and embezzlement. The most spectacular of these purges was in 1952, when Rudolph Slansky, the Secretary of the Party, and Vlado Clementis, the Foreign Minister, were executed, along with a number of lesser officials. The Czech Communist Party can claim the dubious distinction of employing more distasteful methods against its fallen comrades than were used by any of the other East European parties during the Stalin period. Perhaps the lowest point was reached when *Rudé Právo* published a letter from the son of one of the accused to the judge who was trying his father.

Dear Comrade,

    I demand the heaviest penalty, the penalty of death, for my father. Only now do I see that this creature, whom one cannot call a man because he did not have the slightest feeling and human dignity, was my greatest and vilest enemy. Hatred towards my father will always strengthen me in my struggle for the Communist future of our people. I request that this letter be placed before my father. . . .

One wonders, with deep pity, what young Comrade Frejka now feels about his father in view of the government's announcement in 1963 that the trials were based on fabricated evidence, and that the accused were wrongly executed. Posthumous readmission to the Party is a somewhat grotesque form of consolation.

Since the death of Gottwald in 1953, shortly after that of Stalin, there have been fewer political trials, and imprisonment rather than death has been the more common penalty. Nevertheless, the Party leaders have been reluctant to allow de-Stalinisation to go too far. Although they supported the Soviet Union on all the major international issues which arose since the death of Stalin, they did not show much enthusiasm for Mr. Khrushchev's policy of friendship with Yugoslavia, or for his denunciation of the cult of personality. Although they grudgingly acknowledged that Stalin's campaign against Tito was misconceived, they were quick to voice doubts about the reliability of the Yugoslavs when there was a temporary estrangement between Tito and Khrushchev as a result of the Soviet intervention in Hungary.

Unlike Gomulka, who made no secret of his doubts about the handling of the Hungarian crisis, the Czech leaders were solidly behind the Soviet intervention. They even obstructed the transit of medical supplies from Poland to Hungary. There were no visible stirrings of sympathy for the Hungarians from the people of Czechoslovakia, although in Poland and to a lesser extent in other East European countries there were many signs of widespread concern.

In 1962 the first significant steps toward de-Stalinisation were taken. Rudolf Barak, the Deputy Premier and former Minister of the Interior, was expelled from the Party for "abuse of office" and was later imprisoned for fifteen years on charges of embezzlement. Barak had been a vigorous prosecutor of alleged deviationists. His rise to high office in the Party and government had begun during the last years of Gottwald's Presidency. In the summer of 1962 Gottwald's ashes were removed from the Museum built to perpetuate his memory and were reinterred in more modest surroundings. At about the same time work was started on the demolition of the huge Stalin monument in Prague. The cult of personality, with its bizarre mythology, was officially disowned, but President Novotný and Premier Široký were at pains to warn the Party that the Charybdis of "revisionism" was as dangerous a heresy as the Scylla of Stalinism. The true Communist, they urged, should chart a course which avoided both of these hazards. "Revisionism" seemed to be strongest amongst the young intellectuals of the Slovak branch of the Party, and during 1962 and 1963 Novotný frequently found it necessary to denounce them for their attacks on his leadership. In September 1963 the malcontents secured a great victory in driving Široký from office. He was replaced by a young and previously little-known Slovak Communist, Josef Lennart. It is not clear how far the liberalising movement draws strength from the revival of Slovak nationalism, once such a powerful disruptive force in the days of the pre-war republic, and not apparently eradicated by Stalin's "proletarian internationalism". Whatever the causes, it is unlikely that the reformers will cease their pressure on the few remaining Stalinists. The most prominent representative of the old guard is President Novotný, who has shown great skill in knowing when to move over to the winning side. It will be interesting to see if he is adroit enough to ride the approaching storm.

One of the features which stands out in recent Czechoslovak history is the apparent passivity of the mass of the people during the upheavals of the post-Stalin era in Eastern Europe. One might explain the lack of sympathy for the Hungarians in 1956 as a survival from the pre-war days of bitter Slav–Magyar antipathy,[1] but how can one account for the way in which an enlightened and progressive people have borne with so little open protest the consequences of the mistakes of their leaders? Edward Táborský, a former colleague of President Beneš, and now a Professor in America, suggests that the answer may lie in the Czech national character.

> Among the major traits of the Czechoslovak mentality are a down-to-earth realism, a mistrust of doctrinaire shibboleths, an overdose of caution, a dislike for doubtful risks, and a lack of romantic heroism. When confronted with what he thinks to be a superior power, the average Czech resorts to devious manoeuvring covered up by a pretence of submission, rather than to an outright frontal opposition. He prefers to bend and preserve his strength rather than to break in a gesture of bold defiance.[2]

Referring to Czech attitudes during the occupation, Elizabeth Wiskemann makes a similar point. She believes that "tradition, temperament and geography" caused Czech resistance to the Nazis to be "passive on the whole". The abstraction of "national character" is difficult to define, and generalisations which are true of metropolitan Prague may be meaningless when applied to the backward rural areas of Slovakia. One experience in which the whole nation shared, however, and which seems to have a bearing on the present attitudes of the Czechoslovak people, was the humiliation of Munich. It is not easy for an Englishman to gauge the effects of what the Czechs regarded as a cynical betrayal by their so-called friends in the West. In the first shock of disillusionment many temporarily embraced Nazism, on the rebound from their broken romance with liberal democracy. The Nazi occupation soon made it plain that Hitler had nothing to offer them. At the end of the war, they realised that their future existence depended on an accommodation with the Soviet Union, and the obvious people to achieve this were their own Communists. Their experiences during the previous decade convinced many Czechs that friendship with the U.S.S.R. was their only guarantee against

---

[1] It has been suggested, however, that many Czechs wished to show their solidarity with the Hungarians, but were prevented from doing so.

[2] Táborský, *op. cit.*, p. 129.

a revival of German aggression. Even to-day, many who are indifferent or even hostile to Communism view with anger the policies of the Western Powers which have led to the rearmament of Germany and the steady increase of her influence in world affairs. The Communists have not been slow to exploit these feelings, and in this they have often been aided by the tactlessness of many Western leaders.

The disillusion and apathy which seem to have affected Czechoslovakia since the collapse of the liberal republic have had their impact on the country's economy. Throughout Eastern Europe one hears complaints of the shoddiness and bad workmanship of imported Czech industrial goods. Even *Rudé Právo*, the Party newspaper, tells the same story. Thus, when a spot check was made of clothing offered for sale in shops in 1959 it was reported that "65 per cent of the checked merchandise was deficient and should not have appeared on the market". Such revelations are shocking when one thinks of the high reputation once enjoyed by Czech industrial goods. The volume of output may have gone up dramatically since 1948, but there has apparently been a serious decline in quality. Part of this may be ascribed to the loss of skilled German workers as a result of the expulsions from the Sudeten land, but one cannot think that this is the whole story. The sad fact is that Czechoslovakia has failed to progress under communism in the way that one might have expected from the most advanced industrial nation in Eastern Europe.

During 1964 the "revisionists" succeeded in establishing bridgeheads in the universities, the literary press and other spheres of cultural activity. Economists have attacked "the cult of the plan" and one has gone so far as to suggest that it was necessary to "begin to criticise socialism as a social system".[1] Historians have started to correct the myths and distortions which passed for historical truth in official party accounts of the post-war period. As yet the intellectuals do not seem to have roused the

[1] Article by Professor Haba of Bratislava University, quoted by Táborský in *Czechoslovakia — out of Stalinism?*, "Problems of Communism", May/June 1964.

mass of the people, but it is likely that their onslaughts on the cherished dogmas of the old guard who still cling to power will prepare the way for more radical changes at the centre.

Josef Lenart may be the first swallow heralding the spring thaw which will reawaken the people of Czechoslovakia and enable them once more to play a leading role in the life of Eastern Europe.

6. Yugoslavia between East and West

The year 1948 will be remembered by future historians of Eastern Europe for two dramatic developments. In February, the Communists assumed full power in Czechoslovakia, and in June the Yugoslav Communist Party was expelled from the Cominform. Of the two, the latter was perhaps more important in its effects on the future course of events. Before examining the causes of the break between Yugoslavia and her former friends, it is necessary to dwell for a moment on the factors which made it possible for her to succeed in her determination to pursue an independent line of action.

There are, first of all, the simple facts of geography. She shares only 1300 miles of her 3000-mile-long frontiers with other Communist states. In the north she has a common frontier with Austria, which in 1948 was under Allied military occupation. In the north-west there is a short land frontier with Italy, which terminates at the Adriatic coast near Trieste. In 1948 Anglo-American forces occupied "Zone A" of the Free Territory of Trieste. Yugoslavia's long coastline gives her access through international waters to the ports of the Mediterranean and to the open oceans beyond the Straits of Gibraltar and the Suez Canal. Thus her geographical position made her less dependent on Soviet goodwill than was the case with any of the other Peoples' Democracies. None of the others could have broken the economic stranglehold of the Soviet Union by redirecting their trade westward as Yugoslavia did after 1948. If geography made the break physically possible, historical circumstances made an independent stand politically feasible. Throughout the war Tito had remained with his people, and had become the leader of the most important resistance movement in Eastern Europe. Rákosi, Bierut, Gottwald and the rest of the "Muscovites" did not have the mystique of the Partisans to raise their status in the eyes of their people. Tito was the only East European leader whose position did not depend on the support of the Red Army. Although led by Communists, the Partisans had drawn in Yugoslavs of all political opinions, and Tito knew that in defying Stalin he could count on the support of the majority of his people.

If these circumstances made it possible for the Yugoslav leaders successfully to resist Cominform pressure, one must now ask why such defiance was necessary. Between 1945 and 1948 Yugoslavia had moved further along the road towards a Peoples' Democracy than any of her neighbours. A Communist-led provisional government was set up at Jajce in November 1943, and introduced the framework of a new social order into the areas under its control even before the last German soldiers had been driven out of Yugoslavia. In 1946 this provisional government purged itself of the few representatives of the non-Communist Parties whose participation had been a condition of Western recognition. The new constitution of 1946 gave the state full power over the conduct of economic affairs, and charged the government with the responsibility for drawing up a general economic plan based on the nationalisation of all mineral wealth, power resources, communications, finance and foreign trade. In Tito's own words, the new constitution ensured "a high degree of concentration of authority in the central organs of the state, and the direct management of the state mechanism by the party". Once in full control of the state machine, the party was able to introduce the economic, social and political changes associated with their concept of "the dictatorship of the proletariat". In all that they did they gratefully acknowledged their debt to the Soviet Union, and the guidance which they had received from the inspiration of Lenin and Stalin. If there was any difference between Yugoslavia and the other Peoples' Democracies during

G

the first post-war years it was only that she moved faster than most of the others towards the complete socialisation of the economy. There seemed to be little cause for dissension over domestic policies between her and the Soviet Union.[1]

In foreign policy also there seemed on the surface to be no reason for a quarrel. Relations between Yugoslavia and the West were at their lowest ebb in 1948. The chief bones of contention were the Trieste situation and the civil war in Greece. Yugoslav troops faced those of Britain and America in the hills a few miles from the city of Trieste, and there was constant tension, which almost reached breaking point in 1948 when the Yugoslavs shot down an American plane which crossed the border. The Yugoslav attitude was fully supported by the Soviet Union. In Greece, the Anglo-American supported government was fighting for its life against Communist-led guerrillas. The Yugoslavs gave every assistance to the rebels, sending them arms and equipment, caring for their wounded and permitting their troops to cross the Yugoslav frontier when the enemy pressed too hard. Bulgaria and Albania were giving similar help, and the whole operation was backed by the Soviet Union. On all other major foreign policy issues there seemed to be a complete identity of views. An outside observer might have detected one tiny grain of dissension when a paragraph in the Soviet Party organ, *Pravda*, referred to the abandonment of the proposed Balkan Federation which Bulgaria and Yugoslavia had suggested in 1947. The Bulgarian leader, Dimitrov, hastily withdrew his support for the scheme on learning of Stalin's displeasure, but Tito refused to make a gesture of submission.

In June 1948, however, it was revealed that the public appearance of unity was a façade concealing a bitter quarrel which had been raging behind the scenes for several months. For example, in March 1948 Tito received a letter signed by Molotov and Stalin which began "We consider your answer (i.e. to previous

[1] After the dispute became public the Soviet leaders did make criticisms of Yugoslavia's internal policies, but these were self-contradictory and obviously put out as a smoke screen to conceal the real reasons for the quarrel.

criticisms) untruthful, and therefore wholly unsatisfactory." The letter accused the Yugoslav leaders of being Trotskyists, slanderers of the Soviet Union and "dubious Marxists". After the expulsion of the Yugoslavs from the Cominform, following Tito's refusal to go to Bucharest to answer the charges made against him, the lengthy correspondence between the two Parties was published. Even the Russians admit to-day that the arguments they used were false. One can disregard the finer points of Marxist theology which were developed at great length by the writers of the letters The real core of the dispute lay in the refusal of the Yugoslavs to acquiesce in the conversion of their country into a Soviet colony. They believed that they knew better than the Soviet leaders what was good for the Yugoslav people, and whilst they were prepared to listen to comradely advice, they were not prepared to see Soviet "experts" running their army and their economy.

Stalin and his associates undoubtedly picked the quarrel deliberately, assuming that they would be able to engineer Tito's downfall if he did not submit to their browbeating.

Djilas records Stalin as having said "I will shake my little finger, and Tito will be no more."[1] However, after months of violent fist shaking, Tito appeared to be stronger than ever. For the remaining years of Stalin's life Yugoslavia was subjected to a campaign of hysterical abuse from her Eastern neighbours. "Titoism" became a major crime in the Communist calendar, and any suspicion of sympathy for the Yugoslavs led to swift and terrible punishment. The chief victims of the anti-Tito purges included the Prime Minister of Bulgaria, and the secretaries of the Hungarian and Czechoslovak Parties, all of whom were executed. In addition men like Gomulka in Poland and Kádár and Nagy in Hungary were removed from public life and suffered terms of imprisonment for their supposed sympathy with

[1] Djilas has since been twice imprisoned for political offences. Ironically, on the second occasion it was for publishing a book called *Conversations with Stalin*, which recorded his impressions of the Soviet leader, drawn from his personal experience as Tito's representative.

G*

Yugoslavia. It is probable that in many cases "Titoism" was used as a convenient term of abuse for men who had fallen out of favour for quite different reasons. The definition of the term may have been as wide and imprecise as the term "Trotskyite", which Stalin used so indiscriminately during the Soviet purges of the 1930's. Nevertheless, some of the leading victims of the anti-Tito drive undoubtedly shared the Yugoslav view that the Peoples' Democracies should be given greater freedom from Soviet domination. The facts of political geography meant that they were unable to act upon their convictions.

In Yugoslavia the effect of the break with the Cominform was to force the Party to make a fundamental re-examination of its position. As Tito told a meeting of the Central Committee in 1959:

> The campaign against our country . . . which for the last decade has been waged by leaders of the countries of the Eastern bloc . . . has so far inflicted great damage on us, particularly in the material respect. But it has also brought some benefits, particularly in the field of Marxist ideology; in the more rapid liberation from dogmatism and in the better recognition of negative features in the development of Socialism, thus enabling us to avoid such shortcomings ourselves.[1]

At first, however, the problem was simply one of survival. Until 1948 the Yugoslav economy had been geared to trade with Eastern Europe, but one of the first consequences of expulsion from the Cominform was the almost complete suspension of commercial relations with the Eastern bloc. In view of the very bad relations which existed at that time with the Western countries, it was not possible for Yugoslavia to make a rapid readjustment in the direction of her trade. For two years there was great hardship. Bad harvests necessitated the import of wheat, but there was almost no possibility of earning the foreign currency to pay for the imports. Fortunately for the Yugoslavs, the leaders of Britain and America recognised a common interest in supporting the bid for independence from Soviet control. Despite their dislike of many aspects of Tito's internal administration, the

[1] *Forty Years of the C.P.Y.* Text of a speech by Tito to the Central Committee. Belgrade, 1959, p. 40.

Western Powers agreed to send both economic and military aid. Although fluctuating with the vicissitudes of international politics, dollar aid has been a major factor since 1951 in helping Yugoslavia to meet her chronic balance of payments problem. In the seven years 1955–61 the average annual trade deficit was approximately 44,000 million dinars, and U.S. dollar aid during the same period was running at a rate of over 27,000 million dinars a year.

As the worst effects of the Cominform blockade were gradually overcome, the Yugoslav Communists began to examine their economic plans for the future. The first Five Year Plan, launched in 1947, had to be abandoned before the end of its second year. For several years "One Year Plans" were introduced, which were in fact improvisations in the face of exceptional economic difficulties. These Plans showed an increasing tendency to break away from the old methods of centralised state control, and to experiment with machinery which was designed to place a greater emphasis on regional and local initiative in economic planning. In 1950 the first law on workers' self-management was enacted. This introduced the concept of the "working collective" as the group responsible for the management of publicly owned enterprises. The working collective is in fact the whole body of workers in a factory. They were authorised to set up Workers' Councils, composed of elected representatives whose authority was as great as that of a board of directors in any private concern in a capitalist country. The basic law of 1950 has undergone many changes in the light of the experience gained since that time. The most recent constitutional changes envisage further decentralisation, by placing even more responsibility in the hands of both the working collective and the communal organs of local government. The principle of rotation of office has been applied to all offices save that of the Presidency of the Federal Government. The intention is to give the opportunity for as many citizens as possible to take part in the direction of economic and political affairs at all levels of society. In order to encourage this participation, the adult education movement has been mobilised to train workers in the exercise of their new functions. There are, of course, large sections of the community who do not yet take part. The most important of these are the private peasants, who still constitute the largest single occupational group in Yugoslavia. In other spheres the degree of active participation varies greatly from region to region and even within a given industry. Much depends on the quality of local leadership, and the strength of the League of Communists in a particular area.

It is obvious that if workers are given some measure of control over investment policies, distribution of surpluses and the fixing of incomes, problems will arise in co-ordinating the economic effort of the nation to fit within the framework of a general plan. There are two main instruments of central authority which make such co-ordination possible. One is the power of the Federal Government to influence the rate and direction of investment through its taxation policies and its control of the National Bank. The other is the unifying role of the League of Communists, whose members play an active part on all Workers' Councils, Peoples' Committees and similar representative bodies. Another tendency which helps to iron out local differences is the growth of large industrial combines by the amalgamation of a number of smaller enterprises. In 1958, after some years of experience in running the new system, the League of Communists discussed its ideological consequences at their Congress in Ljubljana. They expressed the view that the dictatorship of the proletariat is only the first stage in the construction of a socialist democracy. Although necessary in order to smash the power of the capitalist class, it is a transient phase which must be completed as quickly as possible. It contains the seeds of many harmful tendencies, which if allowed to grow will stifle democracy beneath a mountain of bureaucratic restrictions. At first the Party must run the State machine, but gradually both Party and State will begin to shed their powers, and an independent commonwealth of self-governing institutions controlled by the workers will emerge. The Yugoslav Communists believe that they have taken the first steps towards the "withering away of the state" and its replacement by more democratic forms of workers' self-management. Their criticisms of the Soviet Union for failing to understand this process led to a mass walk out of the East European observers at the Ljubljana Congress.[1] In 1960 their revisionist views were condemned at an international meeting of Communist Parties, but since then, as the Sino-Soviet struggle has developed, Mr. Khrushchev and his friends have been much more polite towards the Yugoslavs. During his state visit to Yugoslavia in 1963 the Soviet leader acknowledged the right of the Yugoslavs to call themselves socialists, and promised to study their system, although confessing that there were aspects of it with which he did not agree.

Since the introduction of Workers' Councils, Yugoslavia has undoubtedly made great economic progress, although one might argue as to whether the latter is a consequence of the former. In the period 1956–60 the rate of economic growth was the highest of any country in the world, but during the next two years there was a sharp fall in the rate of increase, and a serious rise in the trade deficit. Some of the causes of these difficulties are not directly concerned with internal policies in Yugoslavia. They are simply consequences of the cutting down of American dollar aid and of the problems of Yugoslav exporters in face of growing competition in Western Europe. Italy and West Germany are Yugoslavia's biggest customers, and the trade policies of both have been affected by their membership of E.E.C.

Agriculture is the Achilles' heel of the Yugoslav economy. Almost half the population are engaged in agriculture, but their contribution to the national income is only about one quarter. Every few years there is a partial failure of the harvest, and this adds greatly to the balance of payments difficulties. From 1960 to 1962 there were three bad harvests in succession, and it is significant that these were years of slow economic growth. In the early post-war years there was an attempt to force the peasants into collective farms, but, as in other countries, the effort failed. Since 1953 the peasants have been allowed to take their land back from

[1] Only the Polish representative remained in his seat.

the collectives and to farm it individually. Most of them exercised this right, but more and more are now being persuaded to join voluntary co-operatives of a general type. In these the peasants still retain private ownership of the land, but agree to join with their neighbours for the purchase of seed, the use of machinery and the pooling of knowledge about new farming methods. In 1963, 27 per cent of the wheat produced came from collective and state farmers, 14·5 per cent from private farmers working in some form of general co-operative, and the remainder from private farmers outside the co-operatives. The yields (in quintals per hectare) averaged 36 for the socialist sector, 24 for the co-operative sector and only 14·5 for the private sector. Before the war, the average for the whole country was 11 quintals per hectare.

Although the attitude of the authorities to the private peasant is less hostile than in the past, there is still a great deal of mutual suspicion. However, Yugoslavia has handled its peasantry more intelligently than has been the case in some other Peoples' Democracies, and the results are now beginning to show in greater agricultural efficiency.

The shock of expulsion from the Cominform not only forced the Yugoslavs to think again about their domestic affairs, it also initiated changes in foreign policy. They badly needed Western economic aid, but they were not prepared to sacrifice their freedom of action in order to obtain it. They calculated correctly that their bargaining position was strong enough for them to ask for aid without having to accept political conditions. There were, however, some tactful shifts of emphasis which removed the worst irritants in the eyes of the western powers. For example, aid to the Greek rebels was ended, and very soon afterwards the Greek revolt collapsed. In 1953 Yugoslavia signed the Balkan Treaty with Turkey and Greece, both members of NATO. This pact never developed into a military alliance, as had been originally intended. Within a short time after signature it was virtually a dead letter because of the Turkish-Greek dispute over Cyprus. In 1955 there was a dramatic change in the attitude of the Soviet

Union. Mr. Khrushchev and Marshal Bulganin publicly apologised in Belgrade for the anti-Yugoslav campaign, which they said had been the fault of Beria and Abakumov, both of whom had been liquidated. Normal relations between the two countries were resumed, but Tito was careful not to go too far in re-establishing contacts at Party level. There was brief estrangement again over Hungary in 1956, but by 1960 relations were again cordial, and have steadily improved ever since. In the summer of 1963 Khrushchev spent a "working holiday" in Yugoslavia, during which he made it plain that he utterly rejected China's attacks on Yugoslav "revisionism". Perhaps more important, the Soviet Premier brought promises of orders for Yugoslav ships, industrial goods and raw materials and agreed to the extension of credits to help the Yugoslavs in their trade with the COMECON countries. Shortly after Khrushchev's return home, there was a visit from the Hungarian leader, János Kádár, and the unpleasant memories of 1956 were forgotten in an exchange of mutual cordialities. The Yugoslavs have long been accustomed now to manipulating the delicate mechanism of international bargaining between East and West. An apparent shift of interest on their part in the direction of the Soviet Union is immediately followed by a reaction from the United States. There was little surprise, therefore, when an announcement was made in September 1963, that on his way home from a tour of Latin America Tito would call on President Kennedy in Washington. As long as the Yugoslavs are sought after by both America and Russia they will find it possible to survive economically.

However, the Yugoslav leaders can claim to be the first to demonstrate the possibility of Communist governments living in peace with their capitalist neighbours. The most striking example of this is afforded by the dramatic improvement in Italo-Yugoslav relations which followed the signing of the Udine agreement of 1955. Two years before the signature of this pact relations between the two countries were so bad that war over Trieste seemed a possibility. The long tradition of hostility, invigorated by the memories of the Italian occupation during the Second

World War, seemed to preclude any hope of a settlement. Today the roads and railways which connect Trieste with its hinterland in Yugoslavia are crowded with passengers and freight, and frontier formalities are reduced to a minimum. Yugoslavia is now hoping that she can make similar arrangements with her other neighbours, both Communist and Capitalist.

A further demonstration of Yugoslavia's refusal to permit either bitter memories from the past or present political differences to interfere with economic necessities was her willingness to accept credits from West Germany as part of a long-term trade agreement signed in 1964. On the German side, the agreement also showed that the absence of normal diplomatic relations is no obstacle to trade.[1] The time may come when such developments are too commonplace to deserve mention, but in the present situation Yugoslavia can claim to be the only Communist country whose economy depends on the maintenance of good relations with the leading capitalist countries of the world.

7. Rumania in the 1960's

Until the early 1960's, Rumanian Communism stood out as a rock of orthodoxy amid the storms and stresses of the Khrushchev era. Gheorghiu-Dej and his close associates were amongst the most loyal followers of the Soviet Union to be found anywhere in Eastern Europe. It seemed to matter little to them whether the orders from Moscow bore the signature of Stalin or of Khrushchev. The Rumanians always toed the line. In 1948, when Stalin launched his thunderbolt against Yugoslavia, the Cominform headquarters were moved to Bucharest and the Rumanian leaders played a prominent part in the anti-Tito campaign. Four years later, when Anna Pauker, the Foreign Minister, was removed from office, Gheorghiu-Dej happily denounced her as a Titoist. The charges were presumably

---

[1] West Germany broke off diplomatic relations when Yugoslavia accorded recognition to the East German Government.

framed with Stalin's approval, but few people outside the Communist Party even pretended to believe them. In 1961, when de-Stalinisation was the popular cry throughout Eastern Europe, Gheorghiu-Dej suggested that the purge of Mrs. Pauker in 1952 was the first step along the new lines. If so, Rumania's early lead was not maintained, for there were no other discernible changes in either domestic or foreign policy during the first turbulent five years of the post-Stalin period. During the Hungarian rising of 1956 Rumania gave full support to the Soviet Union. When Imre Nagy was lured out of the Yugoslav Embassy in Budapest, he was imprisoned in Rumania and probably remained there until his execution.

For fifteen years the rulers of Rumania showed no sign of dissatisfaction with the subordinate and often ignominious role to which they were assigned by their Soviet masters. This was not surprising, for they owed their positions to the power of the Red Army. During the first few years after 1944, when the country was under Soviet occupation, the weak and inexperienced Rumanian Party had to be given overt assistance in order to establish itself in a commanding position within the country. For a time the Rumanian economy was controlled by joint Soviet and Rumanian companies, the partnership being one in which Rumania provided the capital and labour, whilst the Soviet Union took the lion's share of the output. She was in all but name a colony of her big neighbour, supplying at the cheapest possible prices the oil, wheat and raw materials so desperately needed to rebuild the war-torn Soviet economy.

The first signs that Rumania was dissatisfied with her position within the Communist world came in 1962. COMECON's plans for the achievement of "an international socialist division of labour" appeared to perpetuate for Rumania the old pattern of economic exploitation. They completely ignored the Rumanian Six Year Plan which had been adopted by the 1960 Congress of the Workers Party. The Rumanian Plan envisaged a rapid industrial development which would use to the full the rich, and hitherto untapped, mineral resources of Transylvania. The oil industry was to be expanded, and some of its output diverted to home use as the basis for a petro-chemicals industry. Agriculture would be made more efficient by a programme of mechanisation under collective management. The aid of non-Communist countries was to be sought in the construction of new industrial plants, and to assist this process, new markets for Rumanian exports were to be developed outside the countries of COMECON. Up to 1960, over 60 per cent of Rumanian exports had gone to the U.S.S.R. Before any substantial reorientation of trade could be accomplished, certain political obstacles had to be overcome. It was necessary, for example, to negotiate a settlement of British, French and U.S. claims for compensation arising out of the nationalisation of foreign oil assets. Until this problem had been solved no increase in trade with the West could be expected. Progress in this direction was made in 1960, and during the next four years a number of important trade agreements were signed. In 1962, for example, an Anglo-French consortium began the construction of a £13 million steel mill at Galati. In 1963 the U.S. Government gave permission for a private company to give technical advice to Rumania on the construction of another steel mill.

Rumania's determination to develop her economy in her own way finally forced COMECON to modifiy its original plans. Gheorghiu-Dej made great play with the resolution passed at the Moscow meetings in 1960 of 81 Communist parties. This spoke of "national independence and sovereignty, full equality of rights, comradely mutual assistance and mutual benefit".

Gheorghiu-Dej's success has lain in his ability to seize the opportunities offered by the Sino-Soviet dispute and to turn them to Rumania's advantage. For fifteen years the situation has offered little scope for manoeuvre. Rumania is a small country, with a population of less than 19 millions. She shares a common frontier of over 500 miles with the Soviet Union. Militarily she is weak, and completely dependent on the Red Army. Her leaders owed their elevation to power after the war to the presence of Soviet troops. In these circumstances it was to be expected that she should have been completely overshadowed by her eastern neighbour. With the opening of the great rift between the two largest Communist powers a new element entered into the situation. Thus in the 1960's it became possible for a small Communist-led nation to resist Soviet pressure without bringing upon its head either the crude bludgeon of military intervention, as in Hungary in 1956, or even the less dramatic forms of economic and political intimidation which had often been employed elsewhere. Gheorghiu-Dej adopted a position of neutrality between China and the U.S.S.R., and assumed the role of honest broker. The Rumanian Press was the first to publish the Chinese letter of June 1963 attacking Khrushchev's "revisionism". The Rumanian line was to give a fair hearing to both sides, and to stress the need for unity within the socialist camp. Trade with China was substantially expanded, and at a time when other COMECON members were following the Soviet lead in reducing theirs almost to vanishing point. In April 1963 Rumania restored her diplomatic relations with Albania, and made a number of other symbolic gestures of goodwill towards China's one European ally. In 1964 the Prime Minister, Ion Maurer, paid an official visit to Pekin, and on his return there were a number of high level meetings involving Tito, Khrushchev and Gheorghiu-Dej, which were seen as part of a Rumanian initiative to prevent the Soviet leader from precipitating a further crisis within the Communist world.

Although Rumania's foreign policy moved at breath-taking pace during 1963 and 1964, there were fewer changes at home. The new programme of industrialisation required heavy capital investment and left little room for the development of consumer goods industries. It also left little scope for relaxation in the political field. Since 1961 Gheorghiu-Dej has combined the posts of President and First Secretary of the Party, thus symbolising in his own person the complete identity of the State with the Party. Although there has been some measure of liberalisation and some of the worst features of Stalinism have quietly disappeared, Rumania has changed less in this respect than Hungary, Poland

H

or Yugoslavia. In the cultural sphere, the changes have been rather in the direction of "nationalism" than "liberalism". Russian is no longer a compulsory subject in the schools and universities. The Hungarian University of Cluj, the capital of Transylvania, has been merged with its Rumanian counterpart, and many of the minority schools for German, Bulgarian, Romany and Magyar children have been closed or "Rumanised". Pride in the Latin origins of the Rumanian language is being fostered, and the long-standing cultural links with France are being revived. Rumanians are once again being reminded, as in pre-war days, that they are different from their Slav and Magyar neighbours, and possibly even superior to them. Nationalism has a stormy and not always reputable history in this part of the world. For a decade after the war it was kept in check by the policies of the Communist Parties. But their "proletarian internationalism" was often a euphemism for policies which placed the interests of the Soviet Union above those of their own people. Instead of stifling nationalism, they probably encouraged it. This was apparent during the late 1950's, when the Soviet grip began to relax. Nationalism of the pre-war variety, often virulently anti-Soviet in character, was an important element in the Polish and Hungarian revolts, and appeared in less extreme form in other countries. Mr. Gheorghiu-Dej has skilfully turned this powerful and often reactionary force into the advantage of the régime. He now appears as a champion of Rumanian interests, and has undoubtedly won support from sections of the population which had previously shown no interest in the new régime. The increase in Party membership to over one million in 1963 is attributable in part to the easing of entry qualifications in order to permit former members of the old Peasant and Nationalist Parties to join.

Gheorghiu-Dej and his leading associates are well placed to take advantage of the upsurge of national feeling. They are almost all of Rumanian origin and many of them remained in the country during the war. Gheorghiu-Dej played an active part in the working-class movement before the war, and acquired a great reputation for his part in the strikes of the early 1930's. In 1933 he was imprisoned and was not released until 1944. During the war he managed to direct a resistance movement from his prison cell. Unlike Rákosi in Hungary, for example, he never became a Soviet citizen. Also, in an area where anti-Semitism is still a significant force, there are few Jews in prominent positions within his government.

In some respects Rumania's experience in the 1960's resembles that of Yugoslavia fifteen years earlier. In both cases Communist Parties led by loyal followers of the Soviet Union were driven too far and reached a point where they refused to compromise on issues where they felt that their national interests were at stake. Gheorghiu-Dej fought his battles in the Khrushchev era, when conditions for a successful stand were more favourable than they had been for Yugoslavia in 1948. He has won without an open conflict, and has emerged, like Tito, as the champion of national rights. Although the Rumanians took an active part in the anti-Yugoslav propaganda campaign before 1955, there has been a rapid improvement in relations during the last few years. The most impressive symbol of the new friendship between Yugoslavia and Rumania has been the agreement to participate in a joint enterprise for the construction of a dam across the Iron Gates Gorge on the Danube. This huge project will not only provide 10 billion kWh. of much-needed electric power to be shared between the two countries, but it will also greatly improve navigation along the Danube. Recent trade agreements provide for a substantial increase in Yugoslav-Rumanian trade, which for ten years had languished because of political differences. In the international sphere there is also great significance in the common policies which are being followed by Tito and Gheorghiu-Dej in their efforts to heal the breach within the Communist world. Both are also committed to the promotion of a nuclear-free zone in the Balkans, but they have yet to convince their Greek and Bulgarian neighbours.

As with Yugoslavia in 1948, the dramatic reorientation in foreign policy was not immediately followed by radical changes within the country. Eventually, however, Yugoslav Communism developed completely new forms. The same may be true of Rumania. Once the old habits of thought are abandoned, a ferment begins to work which affects all aspects of national life. Rumania has moved boldly in foreign affairs and has established her right to follow a Rumanian road to socialism. Already there are signs that her leaders will move cautiously forward on the domestic front.

Author's Note to Chapter VI

Since this book was written, a number of important figures have disappeared from the political scene. These changes appear to warrant a reassessment of the situation as described in Chapters VI and VII. Mr. Khrushchev was removed from office in October, 1964, but the indications are that his successor will follow similar policies in Eastern Europe. Mr. Gheorghiu-Dej died in March, 1965, but the independent line that Rumania took on a number of foreign policy issues during the last few years of his lifetime is being continued by the new leader, Mr. Ceausescu. Mr. Wilson's visit to West Germany in March, 1965, raised no hopes of a fundamental change in British policy over Berlin.

Trade between the two halves of Europe is increasing. West Germany, Britain and France are the chief Western participants in these exchanges. Of particular note in this connection is the agreement between Poland and the West German firm of Krupps. Krupps will supply capital equipment on credit to Poland factories and will have a share in the goods produced. If West Germany and Poland can co-operate in this way, there seems no reason why similar arrangements cannot be made between any suitably placed Western firm and the member countries of COMECON.

April, 1965

CHAPTER VII

CONCLUSIONS

In the foregoing pages an attempt has been made to place recent economic, social and political developments in Eastern Europe in the context of geographical and historical perspectives. The revolutionary régimes which came to power at the end of the Second World War inherited problems rooted in the past, and many of these remain unsolved. No country can forget its own history. Similarly no régime, however revolutionary its aims, can ignore the geographical realities of the country which it governs.

The countries of Eastern Europe lie in the zone of contact between two powerful groups of nations, both of which have shown expansionist tendencies in recent times, and both of which have been governed by authoritarian governments possessed of great military strength. The domination of Eastern Europe by foreign conquerors is not a feature only of recent history. The same pattern recurs again and again when one looks at the events of the last thousand years. Throughout this period the peoples of Eastern Europe have seldom been allowed to express their aspirations freely, without outside interference. In recent times this has meant that the development of the resources of the area has been undertaken less for the benefit of the inhabitants than as a means of furthering the interests of the industrially more developed nations of Western Europe. Apart from a few areas in Poland, Hungary, Bohemia and Slovenia, manufacturing industry on a large scale has only begun since the end of the Second World War. Formerly the role of Eastern Europe in the economy of the whole continent was that of a supplier of food and raw materials to its more affluent western neighbours. The political changes of 1945 severed many of the traditional links with the west, and brought the Soviet Union into a position of commanding political and economic power. The leaders of the western nations acquiesced in this situation, mainly because they knew they had no power to prevent it.

In natural resources Eastern Europe is not one of the richest areas in the world, but its productive capacity is certainly adequate to provide its people with a far higher standard of living than they enjoy at present. Industrial development has been held back by shortages of capital and trained personnel, the failure to develop available power resources and a number of other physical limitations, but misconceived policies and distortions introduced because of the dead hand of Stalinist dogmatism have also played their part. In the absence of foreign capital, the foundations of heavy industry have been laid by compelling the present generation to cut back its own consumption in order to provide the means of capital investment, the fruits of which will accrue to the next generation. This is a process which is painful and unpopular, and cannot be accomplished quickly unless the State wields great coercive power. It is significant to notice that throughout the world, and especially in Africa and Asia, one-party rule is on the increase. As the new nations begin to develop their economies they find that the processes of parliamentary democracy do not serve to further the goal of rapid industrialisation. Without a strong central authority, the popular demands of workers for an immediate improvement in the supply of consumer goods may result in the diversion of resources from investment in new basic industries. However, even Communist leaders began to realise that the growth of a stifling bureaucracy was creating inefficiency and waste, and was defeating the purposes for which the dictatorship had been set up. The first moves in a more liberal direction came in Yugoslavia, after the expulsion of the Yugoslav Communist Party from the Cominform. It required a revolt in Poland and a bloody revolution in Hungary to effect the same sort of change. Other countries, notably Czechoslovakia, are belatedly undergoing a controlled and limited form of de-Stalinisation. The problem, which the Yugoslavs have attempted to solve by their system of "workers' self-management", is to reconcile the needs of overall State planning with the exercise of local initiative at the point of production. This process becomes even more complicated when the general lines of policy are decided at supranational level through the workings of a body such as COMECON. Nationalism, which is far from dead in Eastern Europe, creates problems for COMECON as serious as those which have recently disturbed the leaders of E.E.C. Rumania's resentment at the role assigned to her in the plans for economic integration in Eastern Europe is a recent manifestation of this tendency. Although Mr. Gheorghiu-Dej was no General de Gaulle, he did apparently display the same touchiness and lack of co-operation when he felt that his country's interests were being ignored.

Despite the growth of industry in the post-war period, about half the working population in Eastern Europe is engaged in agriculture. Geographical conditions are such that the area should be able to feed itself and also have agricultural surpluses available for export. Yet the level of efficiency is so low that the contribution of agriculture to the gross national product averages only 25 per cent, and many countries which were once exporters of food have been compelled to spend hard-earned foreign currency on the importation of basic foodstuffs. Modern farming methods cannot be employed until the peasantry have been educated to use them and until larger units of land holding have replaced the millions of tiny farms. The Communists have made many mistakes in their agricultural policies, often because of self-imposed blinkers of Marxist dogmatism, which have prevented them from understanding the realities of the situation. Nevertheless, one cannot doubt the validity of their ultimate goal, which is to improve the efficiency of agriculture by the creation of larger farm units on which the employment of modern techniques is possible. As more and more workers are attracted into the growing towns, those who remain on the land must produce more, and there must be a drastic improvement in the methods of distribution and marketing of food. An agricultural revolution must accompany the industrial revolution if living standards in Eastern

Europe are to be brought up to the level of those in the West. Many human problems arise as the process begins to gather momentum. There are signs that the Communist leaders are facing these problems more realistically than they did during the first post-war decade. They have learned that forced collectivisation, although creating farms large enough to be worked economically by new machines, does not necessarily mean more food production. If the peasants are sullen and resentful there are many opportunities for them to sabotage the most carefully prepared plans of the bureaucrats in the remote capital cities. As methods of persuasion replace those of coercion, and a variety of forms of voluntary co-operation begin to appear, slow and unspectacular progress is being made.

If one reflects on the history of countries like Britain, where the industrial and agricultural revolutions began to make their impact some two centuries ago, it is apparent that this process of economic and social transformation is always a painful one. The Communist might argue that the shock tactics which he employs to force the pace of change are ultimately productive of less human misery than the long-drawn-out agony which was sustained by the working classes of the capitalist countries. One might question the philosophical assumptions behind the view that material prosperity is a pre-condition for the enjoyment of a full life, but most modern societies, whatever the political complexion of their leaders, act upon them. Those societies with the highest standards of living are those which have completed their industrial revolutions. The nations of Eastern Europe are in the middle of theirs, and they are anxious to complete the process. Communism offers a means to this end, but demands the sacrifice of many comforts and liberties in order to ensure that the job is done as quickly as possible.

It is against this background that we should turn to an examination of those features of life in Eastern Europe which have aroused the greatest controversy in the Western World. The whole picture is obscured by a fog of tendentious propaganda. On the one hand the governments of Eastern Europe have painted an idyllic picture of happy, prosperous workers liberated from the burden of past oppression by the magic transformation which occurred in 1945. On the other hand, Western newspapers have tended to concentrate so much on the negative aspects of life behind the "Iron Curtain", that it is even possible for serious politicians to persuade people that they should accept the slogan "Better dead than Red". There is more to the recent history of Eastern Europe than the bleak despair of political refugees, the monstrous wounds inflicted on Hungary in 1956, and the confession of political bankruptcy symbolised by Ulbricht's Berlin Wall. Millions of people who disown the title Communist lead reasonably full and happy lives. Even if they grumble about the behaviour of their governments, and show little enthusiasm for the latest call to action emanating from the Party headquarters, their lives are not ruined by a smouldering hatred of all that the new régime stands for. Few of them would wish to return to the pre-war system, and they accept many of the social and economic changes of the post-war period as irreversible, and in broad outline an improvement on what went before. It is true that there is much less spontaneous enthusiasm than the party propagandists would have us believe, for the party zealots are often completely out of touch with the mood of the mass of the people. Nevertheless, there is little serious opposition, and few of the opponents either inside or outside Eastern Europe appear to have a very clear idea of what they would like to see in place of the present system. Most of the changes which have come about in recent years have been the result of pressures within the Communist Movement, especially from young Communist intellectuals who saw their ideals betrayed by the Stalinist bureaucrats who manipulated the machinery of dictatorship.

Communist Party members are everywhere in a minority in Eastern Europe. In Czechoslovakia, which has the highest percentage membership, 12 per cent of the population belonged to the party in 1960.[1] Only 4 per cent of Soviet citizens belonged to

---

[1] Figures for Czech party membership quoted from *Rudé Právo* (July 8th, 1960) by Táborský, *Communism in Czechoslovakia* 1948–60.

the Party at that time, and the ratio in other countries was nearer to the Soviet than to the Czech figure. One reason for this is that the Party deliberately restricts membership to those it considers worthy to bear the onerous responsibilities which the good Communist accepts as his duty. The Party member sacrifices a great deal of his personal liberty. His private life is subjected to close scrutiny, and he is expected to set an example to his fellow workers in diligence, moral rectitude and attention to civic duty. Ideally, the rank-and-file member should be like the churchgoing pillar of society of middle-class Victorian England. The Party official has some of the attributes of a parish priest. He instructs his members in the faith of the Party, watches over their behaviour, warns them when he detects signs of slackness and hears their confessions of failure. In the new church, the "self-criticism" session has replaced the old confessional. It is, perhaps, significant that the Party training schools are sometimes referred to sarcastically by unsympathetic non-members as "theological seminaries". It is not pushing the analogy too far to suggest that just as the Church, in the days when it wielded great temporal power, attracted hangers-on who paid lip services to its ideals in order to take advantage of the material privileges of membership, so the Communist Parties in Eastern Europe have their share of careerists. There are many who see in the membership card a ticket to advancement at work, or who regard their subscriptions as a form of key money for the securing of a new flat. In the post-1945 period loyalty to the Party was often far more important than technical ability in speeding a man up the ladder of promotion. In recent years the tendency has been to pay greater attention to competence and qualifications, and less to Party membership. There are of course many highly qualified and dedicated Communists whose selfless devotion to the cause cannot be questioned. Some of these were amongst the unfortunate victims of the Stalinist purges. Others survived to participate in the struggles against the old guard "Muscovites" which developed in the post-Stalin period.

Communism has not eliminated class divisions. The Party may

have brought to prominence many sons of the working class, whose status in the old society was one of inferiority. In some respects these new leaders have taken on the attributes of a ruling class. A bitter attack on *The New Class*, in a book of that name, precipitated the fall from grace of the Yugoslav leader, Milovan Djilas. Whilst utterly rejecting Djilas's analysis, the Party has nevertheless warned its members against the temptation to "swim down the stream of petty-bourgeios ambitions . . . " and has felt it necessary to stress that Party members must not "aspire to being a superior élite out of touch with the people". If Party members resist the temptation to regard themselves as an élite, members of the old professional classes and their newer recruits, the factory managers and technocrats, are often less self-denying. The resilience of the old professional middle classes, especially in such spheres as university teaching, medicine and the law, is quite remarkable, considering the pressures put on them immediately after the war. Family traditions in these professions still persist. Often the family has been able to preserve some of the material possessions which it accumulated during the pre-war period — for example, a house and its furnishings, a country villa, a small library or collection of pictures. As social pressures on them have eased during the post-Stalin thaw, the members of this class have begun to assume positions of responsibility by virtue of their abilities. Kádár's announcement that in Hungary, promotion by merit rather than political activity was to be the future policy for all except active opponents of the régime, is already the reality in several countries.

The new class of technocrats and managers is in great measure the creation of the new régime, and so one would expect its members to be active supporters of the Party. However, many are far more interested in technical efficiency than in Party policy, and perhaps even more interested in the material rewards which accrue to them because of their managerial positions. The difference in income between the managers and the workers may not be quite as large as that which exists in some capitalist countries, but it is widened by the many perquisities which the manager enjoys. Expense accounts, company cars and golden handshakes are not exclusive privileges of the Western world.

In all the countries of Eastern Europe, the class which forms the base of the social pyramid is the peasantry. The rural areas are still overpopulated and underproductive, although perhaps less so than before the war. The small private peasant is both materially and culturally underprivileged, and it will take many years of change before he attains even to the standards of his cousins who work in the towns. This in part accounts for the steady drain of young people from the land. A large proportion of the factory workers are the sons of peasants and still retain some of the social habits of the countryside. Their decision to migrate to the town has left the rural areas with an ageing population, a fact which adds to the difficulties of the planners in their struggle to raise the levels of agricultural efficiency.

The coming of Communism has not eliminated private enterprise from large sections of the economy. In several countries, notably Yugoslavia and Poland, private farming is still the rule, and even where collectivisation has been officially completed, as in Hungary, the peasants still retain small private plots, the produce of which they sell on the free market. Public ownership has affected all industrial enterprises except small family craft workshops, each employing no more than a handful of workers. Many small shops and inns also remain in private hands. Although the owners of these businesses are heavily taxed, and are denied some of the social security benefits which public employees enjoy, they find it possible to make an adequate living, and some are even moderately well-to-do. Although the contribution of private enterprise to the total national product is small, the number of people affected is quite large. Thus, in Yugoslavia, over two million people out of a total working population of about eight and a half million fall into this category.

Much misunderstanding exists about the role of the Christian churches in Eastern Europe. Party membership and religious beliefs are, of course, logically incompatible. However, this does not preclude some Party members from quietly attending Christmas and Easter services and even turning a blind eye when their wives insist that the children should be baptised. Thus the Czech party organ, *Rudé Právo*, referred in an article in 1954 to Party members who retained their church membership: " . . . we do not expel from the Party those comrades who have not yet freed themselves of religious prejudices, but on the contrary we help them to shake off such prejudices".[1] To those outside the ranks of the Party no direct obstacles are put in the way of church-going. In fact the churches of Eastern Europe are fuller than those in the West. It is said in Poland many young people go to church less out of religious fervour than out of a desire to demonstrate their sense of revolt against authority. Relations between Communists and Catholics have been particularly bad at times, but recently, especially since the Pontificate of Pope John, there has been a big improvement, which the more responsible Western church leaders now admit.[2] It remains true that a person in Eastern Europe who wishes to go to church can generally do so without incurring any penalties, although if he is ambitious for promotion he will be wise not to advertise the fact of his attendance. His chances are perhaps as slender as those of a Protestant in Spain, a Catholic in Ulster or a Communist in the U.S.A.

Until recently Eastern Europe was a closed world, cut off from most of its former economic and cultural links with the rest of Europe, and dependent almost entirely on its own resources or on those of the Soviet Union. Unlike the former colonial territories of Africa and Asia, whose economies are now beginning to develop, Eastern Europe has been unable to draw on the capital and technical assistance of the industrial West. There has been some economic aid to Poland and Yugoslavia, but in the main the capital required for industrialisation has had to be found from current production. Yet the East European nations were, in an economic sense, something like colonies before the war, and although they had developed further, their problems are of a

[1] Táborský, *op. cit*, p. 134.

[2] As for example in the broadcast by Archbishop Heenan in the B.B.C. programme "Meeting Point" in September 1963.

similar kind to those of the newly independent Afro-Asian countries. There are signs that the "Iron Curtain" is breaking down. The closed circuit of trade relations is being modified by the steady growth of East–West trade.[1] Travel restrictions are being eased, and the exchange of ideas is slowly beginning again. If these changes are to be permanent there must be a solution to some of the major political problems, of which those centring on Berlin and the German peace treaty are the most pressing. The solution of these in turn depends upon agreements between the two major world powers, over which the East Europeans can have little influence. As we have seen so often in the past, the destinies of Eastern Europe are determined by outside forces.

If the major contestants in the cold war are prepared to allow the creation of a zone of uncommitted nations stretching from the Baltic to the Mediterranean, an end to the division of Europe is in sight. The discussion prompted by the Polish Foreign Minister's plan for a nuclear free zone has led to the formulation of a number of schemes for disengagement in Europe. Already Yugoslavia, Austria, Switzerland, Sweden and Finland are, for different reasons, outside the system of military alliances. Can the northern and southern groups of neutrals be joined by a bridge which includes East and West Germany, Poland, Czechoslovakia and Hungary? If the powers could reach agreement over Germany, and persuade the West Germans to accept it, the major problem would be solved. Although West German policy may be more flexible after the departure of Dr. Adenauer, and although German businessmen are anxious not to loose their dominant position in East–West trade, there appears to be no prospect of a reversal of attitude on the major policy questions. Realising these difficulties, there may be some point in attempting to create a zone of disengagement in a less sensitive area — for example, in the Balkans and the Central Mediterranean. The model thus provided of workable co-existence might influence

[1] One recent sign of this was the admission of West Germany and Austria to the Danubian Commission, which has for many years been composed exclusively of Communist States.

other countries further north. Italy and Yugoslavia have already shown that formidable obstacles to co-operation can be removed if the will to co-exist is present. Perhaps Bulgaria and Greece could be induced to settle their differences, and to join with Italy and Yugoslavia in the creation of a southern group of non-nuclear powers.

Until the 1960's any suggestion of this nature would have been regarded in NATO circles with the greatest suspicion. The complete lack of trust between the major powers prevented serious consideration of any proposal which could be represented as involving a concession to the other side. Since the Cuban crisis there has been a more sober realisation of the mutual interest of East and West in avoiding situations which might lead to war. The Sino-Soviet quarrel has also had its effect in bringing Russia and America together to discuss ways of easing tension between them. These developments give ground for the hope than the powers may look afresh at the problem of disengagement in Europe, with some chance of reaching agreement.

It is, however, a distant prospect to imagine a united Europe, in which the whole continent pulls in the same direction to the mutual advantage of its at present artificially separate parts. Perhaps before this ideal is achieved, Europe will have become a backwater in the affairs of the world, as Africa and Asia begin to take the centre of the stage. One factor which may influence Europe's chances of maintaining its influence in the world will be its ability to develop the resources of the whole continent. The "Iron Curtain", which has disfigured the face of Europe since the Second World War, has been a serious hindrance to the rational exploitation of the human and material potential of the continent. If it is to be broken down, there must be greater understanding between the peoples of the two halves. It is hoped that this book will make a modest contribution towards such an understanding.

SUGGESTIONS FOR FURTHER READING

THE following list gives the titles of books which will be of use to the reader who wishes to explore in greater detail particular aspects of East European affairs.

A General Works of Reference

B Geographical Background
     (i) General
     (ii) Political Geography

C History
     (i) Early History
     (ii) The Nineteenth Century
     (iii) The Interwar period
     (iv) The Second World War
     (v) The Post War Period

D Individual Countries
     (i) Yugoslavia
     (ii) Hungary
     (iii) Poland
     (iv) Czechoslovakia
     (v) Rumania
     (vi) Bulgaria
     (vii) Albania
     (viii) East Germany

E Periodicals

F Statistics

A

MACADAM, I S. (Ed.): *The Annual Register of World Events*, Published annually by Longmans. Penguin edition available for some years. Appears in May each year, and covers the events of the previous year in the form of short articles on countries and topics. First published 1758.

KEETON, G. W. and SCHWARZENBERGER, G. (Ed.): *The Year Book of World Affairs*, London Institute of World Affairs. Published annually. Background articles on important events of the previous year, and includes a survey of current books on international problems. Published since 1946.

BARRACLOUGH, G.: *Survey of International Affairs*. (Most recent edition published 1962 covers the years 1956–1958.) (For R.I.I.A.) Oxford University Press.

STEINBERG, S. H.: *The Statesman's Yearbook*, Statistical and Historical Annual of the States of the World. Macmillan. Useful source for official statistics. Published since 1863.

ROSENBERGER, W. and TOBIN, H. C.: *Keesing's Contemporary Archives*, Weekly Diary of World Events. Keesings Publications. An up-to-date record of current events, published since 1 July 1931.

B (i)

HOFFMAN, G. W. (Ed.): *A Geography of Europe*, 1954. Methuen.

GOTTMANN, J.: *A Geography of Europe*, 3rd ed., 1962. Holt, Rinehart and Winston, New York. Written by a French scholar for American university students.

MUTTON, A. F. A.: *Central Europe*, 1961. Longmans. A standard regional geography. Czechoslovakia and E. Germany are the only E. European countries covered. Another volume in the same series by N. J. Pounds will cover the rest of E. Europe.

GEORGE, P. and TRICART, J.: *L'Europe Centrale*, 2 vols., 1954. Presses Universitaires de France. A very complete and orderly geographical account.

B (ii)

WANKLYN, H. G.: *The Eastern Marchlands of Europe*, 1941. George Philip. Geographical background to the political problems of Eastern Europe between the wars.

FITZGERALD, W.: *The New Europe: an Introduction to its Political Geography*, 1945. Methuen.

EAST, W. G. and MOODIE, A. E. (Eds.): *The Changing World: Studies in Political Geography*, 1965. Harrap.

C (i)

McEVEDY, C.: *The Penguin Atlas of Mediaeval History*, 1961. Penguin Books.

DVORNIK, F.: *The Making of Central and Eastern Europe*, 1949. The Polish Research Centre Ltd., London. A standard work on the history of the Slavs to the twelfth century.

DVORNIK, F.: *The Slavs in European History and Civilisation*, 1962. Rutgers U.P., New Brunswick. A major work of scholarship on the history of the Slavs from thirteenth to eighteenth centuries.

OSTROGORSKY, G.: *History of the Byzantine State. Translated by J. M. Hussey*, 1956. Oxford University Press.

C (ii)

HERTSLET, E.: *The Map of Europe by Treaty* (4 vols.), 1875–1891. H.M.S.O. A standard reference book on the nineteenth century.

TAYLOR, A. J. P.: *The Habsburg Monarchy 1809–1918:* A history of the Austrian empire and Austria–Hungary. 1948. Hamish Hamilton.

TAYLOR, A. J. P.: *The Struggle for Mastery in Europe, 1848–1918* (Oxford History of Modern Europe), 1954. Oxford University Press.

C (iii)

SETON-WATSON, H.: *Eastern Europe between the Wars, 1918–1941*, 1945. Cambridge University Press.

MACARTNEY, C. A. and PALMER, A. W.: *Independent Eastern Europe: a History*, 1962. Macmillan.

SNELL, J. L. (Ed.): *The Outbreak of the Second World War: Design or Blunder?* (Problems in European Civilisation), 1962. D. C. Heath, Boston.

C (iv)

TOYNBEE, A. and TOYNBEE, V. (Eds.): *Hitler's Europe* (Survey of International Affairs, 1939–1946), 1954. Oxford University Press. (For R.I.I.A.) A survey of Europe under Nazi occupation.

C (v)

BETTS, R. R. (Ed.): *Central and S.E. Europe 1945–1948*, 1950. Oxford University Press. (For R.I.I.A.)

ZINNER, P. E. (Ed.): *National Communism and Popular Revolt in Eastern Europe: a Selection of Documents on Events in Poland and Hungary. February–November, 1956*, 1957. Columbia U.P., New. York. Chapters by different authors. Gives a survey of the changes introduced immediately after the war.

WATSON, H. SETON-: *The East European Revolution*, 1950. Methuen.

WATSON, H. SETON-: *The Pattern of Communist Revolution; a Historical Analysis*, 1960. Methuen. Covers world communism from the Russian Revolution to the present time.

WATSON, H. SETON-: *Nationalism and Communism. Essays 1946–1963*, 1964. Methuen.

WISKEMANN, E.: *Germany's Eastern Neighbours: Problems Relating to the Oder–Neisse Line and the Czech Frontier Regions*, 1956. Oxford University Press. (For R.I.I.A.)

WALSTON, LORD: *Agriculture under Communism*, 1962. The Bodley Head. A useful survey of agricultural problems since the war and of the attempts made to solve them.

D (i)

HEPPELL, M. and SINGLETON, F. B.: *Yugoslavia* (*Nations of the Modern World*), 1961. E. Benn. A general survey of the history of the South Slavs and an account of modern Yugoslavia.

NEAL, F. W.: *Titoism in Action*, 1958. Cambridge University Press. An objective account by an American scholar of the changes made in Yugoslavia between 1948 and 1957.

INTERNATIONAL SOCIETY FOR SOCIALIST STUDIES: *The Programme of the League of Yugoslav Communists* (Socialist documents and views, No. 1), 1959. The controversial policy statement put before the Ljubljana Congress of 1958. Contains the theoretical background of "revisionism".

I.L.O.: *Studies and Reports*, New Series No. 64. *Workers' Management in Yugoslavia*, 1963. International Labour Office. A detailed study, based on Yugoslav sources, of the system of self-management introduced since 1950. A shorter account is given in:

SINGLETON, F. B. and TOPHAM, A. J.: *Workers' Control in Yugoslavia*, 1963. Fabian Research Series 223, Fabian Society.

KARDELJ, E.: *Problems of Socialist Policy in the Countryside*, 1962. Lincolns-Prager. Mainly concerned with Yugoslav problems. Written by a leading member of the Yugoslav Government.

D (ii)

MACARTNEY, C. A.: *Hungary: a Short History*, 1962. Edinburgh University Press. A concise and readable history of Hungary by the foremost British specialist on Hungarian affairs.

MACARTNEY, C. A.: *October 15th* (2 vols.), 1956. Edinburgh University Press. A detailed study of events, personalities and policies in Hungary from the 1920s to the end of the Second World War.

NAGY, I.: *Imre Nagy on Communism, In Defense of the New Course*. Foreword by H. SETON-WATSON, 1957. Thames and Hudson. A "dissertation" written by Nagy during his enforced retirement in 1955 and 1956. Smuggled out of Hungary after Nagy's arrest following the collapse of the Hungarian revolt of 1956.

U.N.O.: *Report of the Special Committee on Hungary*, 1957. HMSO.

FRYER, P.: *Hungarian Tragedy*, 1956. Dobson. An eye-witness report on events during the Hungarian rising of 1956 by the former *Daily Worker* correspondent in Hungary.

MIKES, G.: *The Hungarian Revolution*, 1957. Andre Deutsch. An account by a prominent Hungarian exile.

Eye-witness Reports on Hungary, a documentary collection, 1962. Hungarian Society of the Friends of UNO, Budapest. A collection of articles from the Western press on Hungary since 1956.

BOGNAR, J.: *Planned Economy in Hungary: Achievements and Problems*, 1959. Pannonia Press, Budapest.

VAJDA, I.: *The Second Five-year Plan in Hungary: Problems and Perspectives*, 1962. Pannonia Press, Budapest.

D (iii)

HALECKI, O.: *A History of Poland*, 2nd ed., 1943. Roy, Publishers, New York. A standard history of Poland by a leading pre-war liberal historian.

DZIEWANOWSKI, M. K.: *The Communist Party of Poland: an Outline of Pistory*, 1959. Harvard University Press.

SYROP, K.: *Spring in October: the Polish Revolution of 1956*, 1957. Weidenfeld and Nicolson. An excellent account of the background to the Polish revolt of 1956.

MONTIAS, J. M.: *Central Planning in Poland*, 1962. Yale University Press. A specialist work of great value to economists. Explains the mechanism of the Polish economy and the changes brought about as a result of the 1956 revolt.

D (iv)

THOMSON, S.: *Czechoslovakia in European history*, 1944. Princeton University Press.

TABORSKY, E.: *Communism in Czechoslovakia, 1948–1960*, 1961. Princeton University Press.

WATSON, R. W. SETON-: *History of the Czechs and Slovaks*, 1943. Hutchinson

D (v)

WATSON, R. W. SETON-: *A History of the Roumanians: from Roman Times to the Completion of Unity*, 1934. Cambridge University Press.

D (vi)

DELLIN, L. A. D.: *Bulgaria*, 1957. Thames and Hudson.

D (vii)

SKENDI, S.: *Albania*, 1957. Atlantic Press. One of a series of books on Eastern Europe written by émigrés in U.S.A.

D̄ₐ(viii)

STOPLER, W. F.: *The Structure of the East German Economy*, 1960. Harvard University Press.

E

Periodicals: The journals mentioned below are some of the more important English and American periodicals concerned with East European affairs:

The Slavonic and East European Review (London).

Slavic Review (Washington).

Problems of Communism (U.S. Information Service).

East European Economics. I.A.S.P., New York.

F

United Nations: *U.N. Statistical Yearbook* and publications of the Economic Commission for Europe on special topics.

INDEX

DEVELOPMENT MEANS PEOPLE

Edited by D. TAYLOR
Governor, Commonwealth Institute; Editor, *New Commonwealth.*

Whilst the quality and availability of trained manpower is a major factor governing the economic growth of a nation, precise information on this subject is non-existent for many of the newly developing countries. This problem, and many others covering all aspects of training people for the developing countries, were discussed in a series of broadcasts, the transcripts of which are contained in this book. The broadcasts took the form of interviews between Mr. Taylor and a number of world-famous authorities in man-power planning, education, industry, management, agriculture, publishing, etc. In all fields, the problems facing the developing countries are discussed, and various solutions are put forward to these problems. The discussions are of special interest to the informed person, and particularly to those who have to deal with the production of trained people.

THE UNITED NATIONS AT WORK

Developing Land, Forests, Oceans . . . and People

JOSEPH MARION JONES

Lecturer on International Development Fletcher School of Law and Diplomacy, Tufts University.

As the brief biography below makes evident, the author has wide experience, and considerable knowledge, of international affairs. In this extremely important and informative book he deals with the needs of the world in the fields of agriculture, forestry, fishing and other activities, and problems such as those of hunger and over-population. He discusses the role of the Food and Agriculture Organization and other related organizations in dealing with these needs and problems. His book is directed towards policy-making, and the policy influencing of people, as well as towards the informing of students of national and international affairs. It will also provide interesting, and thought-provoking, reading for members of the public.

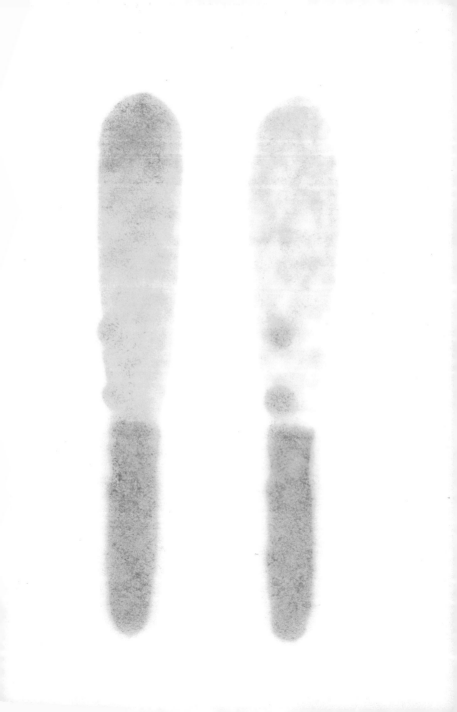

DATE DUE

GAYLORD   PRINTED IN U.S.A.